HUDSON & HALLS

HUDSON
& HALLS

THE FOOD
OF LOVE

JOANNE
DRAYTON

OTAGO

Squabbles are everyday but love is forever.

– DAVID HALLS, September 1992

Published by Otago University Press
Level 1, 398 Cumberland Street
Dunedin, New Zealand
university.press@otago.ac.nz
www.otago.ac.nz/press

First published 2018

Author's note
Every effort has been made to identify the photographers of images held in personal
collections. If you believe we have made an error, please contact the publisher with details
and an acknowledgement will be made in any reprint or future edition of this work.

ISBN 978-1-98-853126-7

Published with the assistance of Creative New Zealand

Editor: Jane Parkin
Design/layout: Fiona Moffat
Indexer: Diane Lowther
Author photo: Dudley Reed
Printed in China through Asia Pacific Offset

CONTENTS

Preface   8

1. Prologue: 1992   13

   Sweet Avocado Pie

2. David's Youth: 1936–59   23

   Stuffed Squid

3. Peter's Youth & a Visit to New Zealand: 1931–62   49

   Frosted Cheese Mould

4. Shoes, Ships & Stonewall: 1962–70   73

   Rolled, Stuffed Chicken Breasts

5. Julius Garfinkel & Quagg's: 1971–74   95

   Venetian Liver

6. *Speakeasy* & the Birth of *Hudson and Halls*: 1974–76   110

   Crisp Fried Fish with Lemon Sauce

7. *Hudson and Halls* & an Oyster and Fish Restaurant: 1976–79   129

   Crepe Cake

8. Cooks, Farmers & Entertainers: 1980–82   157

   Fruit Flans

9. Ratings, Rejections & the BBC: 1983–87   187

   Double Chocolate Cake

10. London & *Beginnings, Middles and Ends*: 1988–92   217

11. Denouement: 1993   245

    Christmas Pudding (Fr John and Stuart)

12. Postscript: 2001–17   255

    Acknowledgements   265

    Notes   268

    Select Bibliography   279

    Index   285

Preface

*H*udson & Halls: The food of love is more than just a love story, though a love story it certainly is. For New Zealanders, it is a tale of two men who changed the bedrock bad attitudes of a nation to that unspoken thing – homosexuality. Here were two gay chefs who lived together, who had loud domestic tantrums in a very public, on-camera kitchen. It is a story of globalisation, of international cuisine coming to a culinary outpost, of the beginning of the Pacific-rich, Asian-styled cooking phenomenon that would sweep the world and change western eating habits forever. It is about the reach of television in the 1970s, 1980s and 1990s and its power to reshape mass thinking; and about the rise of the celebrity chef – Graham Kerr, Des Britten, Alison Holst.

This book assesses Hudson and Halls' legacy, locating their contribution both locally and internationally. It brings alive the dizzy, hedonistic days of the 1980s, when dinner parties thrown by the dark, debonair Peter Hudson and blond-haired blue-eyed David Halls were legendary and their home the place to be seen for the cream of the Auckland social set.

But it is also a story of transformation. About English-born Halls, with a mother and a father in service, who escaped those humble beginnings in an unimaginable way; and about Hudson, whose partnership with Halls helped him transcend a privileged but troubled past in Australia. And most importantly of all, it is the intimate record of two ordinary lives that together, in the fury and frisson of the kitchen, became extra-ordinary.

On stage in front of a camera, in life and in death, the inseparable Hudson and Halls rewrote our recipes for life and love. Peter Hudson, a shipping officer from Melbourne, and David Halls, a working-class boy from Epping, met in New Zealand in 1962 and fell head over heels in love. Long before homosexuality was decriminalised, they introduced New Zealand television audiences to high-camp cooking. 'I am a star!' David Halls shouted to a friend as he skipped down an Auckland street in 1975, having heard they had been given a tiny afternoon slot in the magazine-style television show *Speakeasy*. Halls' raw, impulsive energy gave the programme heat; Hudson's mercurial wit its playful malevolence. Within a couple of years they were a household name, with an hour-long prime-time television show of their own.

They were archetypal figures at a time of intense change. Reluctant role-models for a 'don't ask, don't tell' generation of gay men and women who lived by omission, they were also the leaders of a culinary revolution that saw the overthrow of Aunt Daisy and Betty Crocker and the beginnings of international cuisine. At a time when people's pulses quickened over fish 'n' chips and a cream-filled sponge, Hudson and Halls introduced viewers to stuffed squid and sweet avocado pie. Their relaxed, accidental style, their bitching and bickering on screen, their spontaneous unchoreographed movements across the stage that left cameras and startled production crew exposed, broke taboos and melted formalities. They made an eclectic bunch of New Zealanders laugh and try something different, from middle-aged matrons to bush-shirted blokes. Hudson and Halls were pioneers of celebrity television as we know it today: the naughty, slightly risqué, not-quite-normal boys next door who rocketed to stardom on untrained talent and a dream.

They drank, they fought, they shouted at each other, and we watched on. In between burned baked Alaska, wildly boiling pots and frenetic capsicum-skinning demonstrations, we followed their spectacular rise to fame, their equally sudden dumping by Television New Zealand, and the start of their BBC series in 1987.

What remained unchanged was their abiding love for each other, which survived everything this fractiously flamboyant pair could throw at it – and at each other.

Sadly, today, there is very little left of the 300 programmes Hudson and Halls made during their 11 years on New Zealand television: just a handful of complete shows, some film excerpts shot in the late 1970s, a few interviews and some Telethon footage. The duo's sparse representation in our film and television archive is an indictment on our capacity to recognise what is great and value it. We are destroyers rather than hoarders of our past: Kiwis let go of their treasures too easily. The consequence of historical amnesia is a present that lacks wisdom and self-knowledge.

Fortunately, Peter Hudson and David Halls' story still exists in the fading memories of family and friends; in newspaper, magazine and *Listener* articles; in personal letters, notes, cards and photographs; in documentary footage; and finally in their three fabulous cookbooks. In these publications, released in 1977, 1985 and 1988, we find the essence of the duo's ideas about food and the evolution of those ideas over a decade of enormous change. They are important documents that both belong to and transcend their time.

*

Food and cookbooks are great records of who we are and where we have been. In the opening decades of the eighteenth century, Henrietta Wolfe compiled one of the world's earliest existing cookbooks. In it were recipes and remedies, handwritten in ink on unlined parchment. To turn the pages is to journey back in time. The kitchen this cookbook invites you to enter is one of cooking pots and boilers, open fires and spits; of hunted game and harvested herbs. The spelling is peculiar and the cooking conditions primitive, but embedded in every word and every line is a celebration of food, flavour and the quasi-religious ritual of cooking.

Many recipes are uncannily familiar – as if, like our genes, food travels with us through the generations, so that over three hundred years nothing much has changed. But other recipes belong entirely to their time. They are vile concoctions and combinations we now find repugnant.

'Doctor Salmon's famous Extract of Cows Dung to be made either in May, June or July' is one example. The ingredients alone will leave you gagging. 'Take a pound of new cows dung. Put to it 3 pints of water & about 1 Pint of Quick Lime. Infuse em together 24 hours, stirring it once in the middle of the time then let it drain thro a strainer & keep it for use.' It is good for 'cholick gout coughs Astmas Defluxions of Rhems Ptisick Consumption', and best of all it is guaranteed to 'revive ye spirits'.

Another recipe from a different book of the same period instructs the home medic to combine a peck of garden snails and a quart of green earthworms with herbs and three gallons of milk to create a wondrous recipe for consumption.

Fortunately, cow dung cures belong to their era, while other recipes and remedies, such as Henrietta Wolfe's Beef à la Mode or Lemon Pudding, have been packed in humanity's timeless suitcase and carried on. In the same way that going back to Mrs Wolfe's cookbook makes us appreciate how far we have come and what we have brought with us, so too does going back to the recipes of Hudson and Halls.

Hudson & Halls: The food of love begins at a time when you could be hanged for murder, when abortion was illegal, when women were expected to leave the workforce when they married – and were automatically paid less, when racism was the norm and homosexuality an abomination.

Sexism, racism and homophobia feel as repugnant to most of us now as consuming cow dung, snails and worms. *Hudson & Halls: The food of love* is the story of two men who were both of their time and ahead of it. Peter Hudson and David Halls lived together, loved each other, and died leaving a lasting legacy.

1. Prologue: 1992

Peter got to the phone slightly out of breath. 'Hang on a minute,' he called into the receiver. He fought to free himself from the entangling medical drip-line.

'I'm sorry you are on your own,' Janet Puttnam remembers saying. She had expected David to answer the phone. Peter dismissed her concern. He had sent David away for a day or two to give him a break but he wasn't on his own. 'There are lots of people looking in,' he said.[1] Peter sounded much the same as he always did, but Janet remembers the call: it was the last time she would speak to her brother David's partner.

Peter knew the cost of his care was high and unmercifully incremental for David. The sickroom was a gradual sinking into a quicksand in which everything eventually disappeared – health, happiness, then finally hope. Their Jermyn Street flat, the focus of so much optimism after they'd moved to London two years before, had become a home-hospice of tubes, liquid-filled plastic bags, needles and mind-numbing medication. The appointment times of home-helpers, nurses and doctors determined the pattern of their days.

Instinctively, Peter understood. It was easier for him to suffer the pain and the losses than it was for David to watch it happen to someone he loved. Peter had seen the suffering in David's eyes. That's why he had sent him away for a time to recuperate: to give him the mental space to get ready.

*

OPPOSITE: *In the 1978 television series Hudson and Halls prepared venison, trout, crayfish, avocado and oysters. Eight minutes of each programme were shot on location where the food was sourced – in Russell, Taupo, Rotorua, Gisborne and Eltham.*
COURTESY OF THE *NEW ZEALAND LISTENER*

The end had not always felt as inevitable as it did now. Their journey through illness had been marked with positive experiences, like befriending Edward McLeod during the early stages of his chemotherapy treatment in a London hospital. Blond, bronzed and utterly beguiling, Edward, who Peter called Emerald after the shipping tycoon Emerald Gernard, proved the perfect distraction when Peter and David's days still mixed optimism with despair.

Nothing seemed fair about either man's diagnosis of cancer, but the greater injustice had been handed to Emerald, who was not yet 30. With his smile and iridescent blue-green eyes, Emerald still glowed with youth. He captivated Peter, gave him a new focus. Emerald would be worth fighting for – and fight for him Peter did, even after it was clear that the conventional cures for Emerald's Aids-related leukemia had failed.

For Peter and David, life was a clock moving in slow motion, tick-tocking away the final moments of their remarkable partnership. Time slowed and experiences intensified. They lived all the setbacks together, along with each of the little victories that gradually got smaller. 'Peter home,' David wrote in his appointment diary on 25 August 1992, 'looking bloody good, a full sandwich with 2 slices of Mortadella – a chocolate and tea.'[2] This feat would once have gone unnoticed, but not now.

Finally, 'Peter is terminally ill,' David conceded. 'We don't know how long he has to live, but we are trying to make everything as good as we can for his remaining time.'[3] He watched Peter's life force slowly diminish. The appetite went and the lethargy intensified until Peter just stayed in bed. David wrote, 'I asked him last night to put his arms around me and he did and said "stay calm". Jesus dear, I have loved that irascible sod for almost 30 years and I'm going to miss him like hell.'[4]

In his desperation to make every last moment of Peter's consciousness count, David rang his old friend Jan Cormack – incessantly. 'Look, you've got to come, Jan, you've got to come,' she remembers him saying. Jan, who was playing in an international bridge tournament at Salsomaggiore in Italy, had planned to visit, but not at this exact moment. 'Look,' she said to him, 'I'm just about to play against the USA, and I don't think New Zealand would like it too much if [I took off].'[5] So David waited for Jan and watched Peter decline. And as soon as she arrived in London David snatched her up from the airport and sped her to their flat. She was his one last victory for Peter.

'Darling, darling, darling,' she remembers David saying as they approached the bed, 'Jan is here.' It's impossible to know what made Peter jolt slightly, as he emitted a tiny gasp. It could have been David's summons or Jan's voice. Something familiar brought him back for an instant, then he slipped away, but perhaps not so far away that he couldn't hear them. Without wavering, Jan sat down by his bed and spoke of the times they'd had together when David and Peter had come to stay at Piha, on the west coast of Auckland. She talked of the drama, the mayhem and the fun they used to have. That was where David wanted Peter's thoughts to travel right before his end.

*

On 12 September 1992 David wrote in his diary, 'My dearest beloved Peter died 1.35pm. I love him so much … p.s. On the eve of your birthday (62) this is such a trite thing to print – when I will never forget your kindness.'[6]

David was shell-shocked. Peter's cancer had taken over their lives and had been there in the background for five years. Now he was gone, and the business of dying had ended too. No more rushing to get the shopping done; no doctor's visits; no discussions about pain relief. Even the funeral required only David's numbed attention, which was all he had left to give.

Peter's funeral was held in a forgettable London crematorium. The service was private, as Peter had wanted. 'I think I sat next to Janet [David's sister],' Jan Cormack remembers; 'it was very quiet and very sedate.' David read the poem Peter himself had chosen, and afterwards their little group went to a pub in Battersea. 'David didn't want a lot of people.'[7]

A few days later David typed a letter to inform friends of Peter's death. On the bottom of the letter sent to close friends Carleen Spencer and her husband Jerry Podell in New York he scrawled a personal note: 'That you two should love as much as we did is the most wonderful thing on this earth. Squabbles are everyday but love is forever.' He also sent a copy of the poem read at the funeral, written in 1932 by American Mary Elizabeth Fry, and signed at the bottom by Peter himself.

> *Do not stand at my grave and weep*
> *I am not there; I do not sleep.*
> *I am a thousand winds that blow,*
> *I am the diamond glints on snow,*
> *I am the sun on ripened grain,*
> *I am the gentle autumn rain.*
> *When you awaken in the morning's hush*
> *I am the swift uplifting rush*
> *Of quiet birds in circled flight*

I am the soft stars that shine at night.
Do not stand on my grave and cry
I am not there; I did not die.

'This poem epitomises [Peter's] care and consideration to those of us he left behind,' David wrote, 'and reflects his thoughts, so that we may not grieve too much.'[8] He also recorded the time of Peter's death, '1.35pm', the way he had noted it in his appointment diary – as if time stopped then for him as well as for Peter.

But of course it hadn't. One last job awaited him. Peter had asked David to take care of Emerald in his last days, and David had promised that he would. Initially he did so out of a sense of obligation to Peter, but ultimately he did it for Emerald too.

*

A couple of weeks after the funeral, to lift their spirits and raise a glass to Peter himself, David organised a lunch at their favourite restaurant in Mayfair, Langan's Brasserie. This was to be a tribute to Peter's memory and to their relationship. Emerald was there, and Carleen and Jerry flew over from New York. David had obtained permission from the Langan's manager to scatter some of Peter's ashes in a planter box on the restaurant floor. When the last of the other diners had left, a matchboxful of ashes was ceremoniously spread over the soil around one of the lush green pot plants. 'I hope it's his tongue,' Carleen heard David say as he sprinkled the contents with all the care of an illuminator pouring out granules of gold to press into leaf.[9]

Emerald, meantime, was rapidly getting sicker. A decision was made quickly: David would pay for the tickets and take Emerald home to New Zealand to see his mother. It was an act of heedless generosity. Peter's long illness had been an expensive business, and David hadn't worked for months. Nor did he have the business acumen of Peter, the businessman-entrepreneur, who constantly calculated how they would replenish their finances even as money streamed through their fingers. Without him, David floated adrift, blown from one desperate spending spree to another. Nothing could satisfy David's need for Peter, but he would do something good for Emerald, and while in Auckland he would organise a memorial service for Peter.

*

One of those attending the service at St Mary's Church in Parnell was Richard Matthews, an old friend of the couple. Richard observed David's 'odd' behaviour.

To farewell and raise a glass to Peter, David organised a lunch at Langan's
Brasserie in Mayfair, where he deposited a tiny vial of Peter's ashes.
CARLEEN SPENCER, PRIVATE COLLECTION

He 'plucked' Billy Farnell, who played piano by ear, 'out of his seat and marched him over to the piano and instructed him to play "Moon River"', Peter's favourite song. The piano was locked and quite a ruction ensued before they could locate the key. Eventually Farnell sat down at the little upright piano and struggled valiantly to fill the cavernous space with sound. Coming out of the church after the service, David lost his temper and screamed at someone, and his pent-up grief and frustration boiled over again at the function after the service.[10]

At Langan's Brasserie, 1992.

CLOCKWISE FROM TOP LEFT:

John Fields, Carleen and David deposit Peter's ashes. JOHN FIELDS, PRIVATE COLLECTION

Edward McLeod (Emerald) and Carleen Spencer. CARLEEN SPENCER, PRIVATE COLLECTION

Edward, John Fields and David. CARLEEN SPENCER, PRIVATE COLLECTION

David's unpredictability made him seem out of control. He rang old friends Abby and Geoffrey Collins, inviting them to meet him for lunch at a restaurant in Parnell. Abby assumed it would be a casual 'catch-up', and brought along their young son and his friend. But David was 'a mess, a real mess', Abby remembers. 'He started drinking immediately, and in the end it was me and Geoffrey vying silently to get the boys out of there … [I] left Geoffrey with David … getting loud and angry … blaming everybody … So it was fairly traumatising.'[11] The most explosive moment came when Geoffrey asked, 'Well, David – you know – what are you going to do? Is there anything we can do to help?'

'Well how the *hell* do I know?' David shouted.[12]

Nothing could alleviate David's pain. All the old solutions, the friends he'd always run to when he and Peter had had a row, could not fix this. The only balm for his soul – Peter – was beyond reach, so he staggered on, blundering aggressively though social engagements and giving offence. The people who loved him the most, his friends, felt confused. 'I don't know what he thought he was going to come back to,' Abby remembers thinking, 'whether it was to "pick up where everyone left off" … [but] he was blaming New Zealand, blaming everybody here. It was just that he'd come back and people weren't falling all over him. They'd been gone a while and people get on with their own lives … and I think he expected everybody to drop everything and be there for him, because they had been there for so many people … They had been incredibly accommodating, incredibly gracious and welcoming and just lovely.'[13]

While David insulted and annoyed old friends and acquaintances, Emerald visited his mother; and at the end of their stay they returned to the UK together. David was adamant that this was where he wanted to be, though friends had encouraged him to think about shifting back to New Zealand. Emerald had to be considered and Auckland, David felt, offered nothing real to go back to. He had his family in Epping to think about, too. His sister Janet remembers the effort David always put into hosting her and her husband at his Jermyn Street flat. On one occasion he served up a magnificent and very English steak and kidney pie, which he knew they would love. It was the little things that tripped him up, David told Janet after Peter died. Like the memory of his gasp when he turned his morning shower from hot to cold before he stepped out. 'I really miss that shout of "Ahhhh! Ahhhh! It's cold!" … I really miss not hearing that any more.'[14] The silences in his day, the empty place in the room, the vacant seat in the car: these were the small things he stumbled over, so that he could not forget.

*

Loss is visceral and primitive, and, sadly, David was about to experience it again. He visited Emerald almost daily, reliving Peter's death one step removed, but not so removed that he wasn't immersed in it. '[Emerald] feels I am the closest to him who understands,' David wrote to friends.[15] It comforted him to know that Emerald's pain was under control, but still he had to witness the food that sat on the plate uneaten, the walk to the bathroom that became too much, and finally the slumber that ends everything. If Emerald's death seemed to many just another sad Aids statistic, for David it remained a symbol of sweet-natured youth ended. Within the space of a few months, he had lost a partner and a surrogate son.

Friends worried about David's state of mind. He felt concerned about it himself. Realising that he had reached his limit, he told his sister Janet he couldn't face Christmas on his own, and accepted an invitation to join Carleen and Jerry in New York. There he responded briefly to good company and new surroundings, though every night he sobbed inconsolably in his bedroom. The couple invited him back for another visit in the spring, but this time he brought his anger as well as his grief. 'He was really, really not very nice to people,' Carleen remembers. 'You know, to some of my friends, he was quite rude and he knew it. I came home from something and he was packing, and I said, "What are you doing, you're not supposed to be leaving yet." "No," he said. "No, I am really disgusted with myself, that I've been like I've been and I really think I should go back home", so he did.'[16]

At home other problems presented themselves. Pressing financial difficulties meant David needed to borrow money from friends. In the past, Geoffrey Collins remembers, when David and Peter found themselves broke, 'they hopped in their car and they'd go away for a few days, put it on a credit card and they'd always come up with ideas and come back and reinvent themselves.'[17] Now there was no Peter and no Bentley car. But an invitation from Carleen and Jerry to meet them in Paris (where Jerry travelled frequently for work) was another opportunity to get away.

Carleen and Jerry were staying at the George V, one of the city's most exclusive hotels. David had booked a cheaper room elsewhere. Carleen recalled what happened next. '"David, get in a taxi and come over here," I said, and he went, "What are you talking about? I can't afford the George V," and I said, "Honey, our room is bigger than our apartment in New York. I've already called housekeeping, they've brought another bed up. You're coming here." And we had like three or four of the funniest days laughing our heads off.'[18] It was almost as it had been before. The old David was back – loud, flamboyant and 'on stage'. They talked of him writing a cookbook for children and making guest appearances on UK television. Carleen, as well as other friends and family, including his mother Hilda, thought David had come through the worst of his grief.

Back in London Janet sometimes wanted to scoop him up and take him home, but of course she couldn't. He was an adult and he had to come to terms with things in his own way. Still, there was reason to hope that David's mourning period was over, and that he felt ready to push off from the side again and swim alone.

Sweet Avocado Pie

SERVES 8–10

We are all fairly familiar with avocados served with a seafood filling or mashed into guacamole or even with vinaigrette but we don't often use them as an end to a meal. This recipe is ideal when you can get avocados that are sometimes slightly damaged very cheaply, although you must not use any parts of the flesh that are discoloured. You may mash the avocado if you wish, but a food processor gives a much smoother result.

CRUMB CRUST

1½ cups finely crushed plain biscuit
    crumbs
¼ cup very finely chopped almonds
¼ cup castor sugar
¼ cup melted butter

Mix well together all the ingredients and press over the base and up the sides of a 9-inch loose-bottomed tin. Bake at Gas Mark 3 (325°F, 170°C) for 10 minutes. Remove from the oven and allow to cool.

AVOCADO FILLING

3 egg yolks, beaten
1 tin sweetened condensed milk,
    about 400 grams
2 large ripe avocados
½ cup lemon juice
1 teaspoon finely grated lemon rind
1 cup sour cream
1 teaspoon vanilla essence
1 tablespoon castor sugar

Combine the beaten egg yolks and condensed milk in a medium-sized saucepan and cook, stirring constantly over moderate heat until thickened. Leave to cool, stirring now and then. Process the avocados, together with the lemon juice and peel, until smooth. Now add the cooled milk and egg mixture and again process until combined. Pour into the cooled pie crust and chill for at least an hour. Mix well the sour cream, vanilla and sugar until the sugar has dissolved and smooth the mixture over the top of the avocado filling. Chill until set, at least 3 hours. The centre will be slightly soft when you cut it.

2. David's Youth: 1936–59

The new terror in the skies was the buzz bomb. Hilda Halls first heard the sound, like a lorry whining up a steep hill with its engine revving. Then suddenly silence, and relief. She and her young children, David and Ann, listened to that quiet violence, the pause before the big bang. In the hiatus, holding hands, they ran to the bomb shelter in their back yard. They were almost there when Hilda, like Lot's wife, looked back. In the dim-lit night sky she saw what looked like a plane dropping.

'Poor devil's on fire,' she said, watching it fall, unable to look away.[1] Flames curled from its rear. First the noise, then nothing, then the horrifying explosion that shattered everything Hilda believed about war.

Because this wasn't a plane at all, but a loathsome buzz bomb. The device that dropped near to where they lived in Gainsborough Road in Woodford was the first of a swarm of self-propelled flying bombs. During the next 80 days, through June, July and August of 1944, 10,000 Vengeance 1 (or V-1) buzz bombs would fall on London and nearby towns and cities. It was a terrible new plague. There would be some 20,000 casualties and 6000 fatalities, but the campaign was more about despair than death.[2] This was Hitler smacking one last blow against the civilian population of southeast England.

After the first air raids, Hilda's husband George took advantage of the free distribution of bomb shelters to poorer families, and buried an Anderson shelter in the back yard behind their flat. Measuring 138cm wide by 198cm long, these were made out of curved corrugated iron and sheet metal, and by law had to be dug at least 120cm into the ground. The 60cm or so that remained above the ground was required to be covered in at least 38cm of soil, to be planted in grass or camouflaging foliage.[3] In winter the shelter was cold, cramped and wet under foot. With some effort George had managed to squeeze in bunks for David and Ann; at capacity, the shelter accommodated six people.

On the evening of their first buzz-bomb attack, Hilda, seven-year-old David and five-year-old Ann were accompanied in the shelter by their Aunt Alice, who lived in the flat downstairs. Her husband, George Taylor, was their grandmother Nellie Halls' brother and an air-raid precautions warden, so he was usually on night patrol. George Halls, Hilda's husband, was often away with his work too.

*

George and Hilda first lived at 107 Prospect Road after they were married. Hilda had agreed to George's proposal of marriage on the condition that he provide her with a nice home. She was already pregnant with David when she issued this ultimatum, and knew from experience that a good home was crucial. George, a highly strung romantic, had threatened to throw himself under a train unless she consented to become his wife. With these non-negotiable positions established, they married at St Barnabas Church, Woodford, on 13 June 1936, and Hilda reluctantly left her work as nanny for a young boy at the 'grand house'. She was particular, and good at what she did, and this position had offered her a first glimpse of real comfort. This was where she learned what a nice home did for your soul. Her employers were sorry to see her go.

Everyone agreed that Hilda made a beautiful bride. She was attractive – slim, with an oval face and fine features, except for slightly pronounced front teeth, and thick, wavy, dark hair. In the wedding photographs her eyes meet the curiosity of the camera with knowing defiance. There was something robust about Hilda, not in stature but in spirit. George, tall and waif-like, appears more tentative. His aquiline face, full lips, close-clipped haircut and pensive expression made him handsome in an acquiescent kind of way.

His own father, George snr, was a casualty of World War One, his life blighted by shrapnel injuries to his head and chest. He survived on morphine and a war pension. His wife Nellie made the best of things, cleaning for 'ladies' houses' and doing odd jobs, but life was tough, and the couple did not have any more children. Hilda therefore was George's passion: the sibling he never had, the partner and the companion he needed. When they first met, George was employed as a labourer and groomsman on local farms; later he worked as a fitter and turner in London's new underground rail system.

Hilda and George Halls with their nine-month-old infant son David, 1937. JANET PUTTNAM, PRIVATE COLLECTION

Four months after his parents married, David George Halls arrived on 14 October 1936. Blond, blue-eyed and gorgeous, with a transfixing look like his mother's, he was the son to be proud of – the first child of his generation, and the cause of great celebration in the extended Halls family. His beginning was a mellow, much-cherished life of long, warm summer days before the winter of war.

In the period prior to the outbreak of conflict in August 1939, the family moved to a new flat in Gainsborough Road, slightly grander in scale and able to accommodate a new addition. Hilda and George's second child, Ann, was born in March of that year. Some two and a half years younger than David, Ann would be a war toddler who knew nothing of life without rationing, blackouts, the sound of sirens and the sight of ruination.

George was deemed unfit to serve and worked driving a lorry for a coal company. He and Hilda did what they could to make a happy home. Their own childhoods had been scarred by war and they wanted better for their children. George's father had sat every day by the kitchen fire with his delicate chest, almost blind from his head injury; Hilda's father, Henry Manley, suffered terrible nightmares after having been buried alive in combat. According to family accounts, Hilda's mother Annie had been notified that he was killed in action, and for a year she drew a widow's pension. It took that long for Henry to recover his wits and remember who he was.[4]

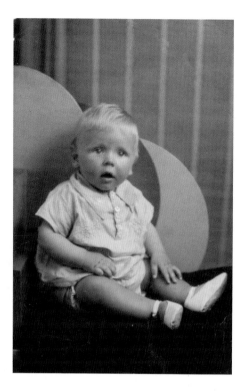

David Halls, 1937.
JANET PUTTNAM, PRIVATE COLLECTION

The Halls understood conflict intimately. War was the inter-generational glue that bound their extended family together. As parents, George and Hilda knew how to be resourceful, how to save money and how to make something out of nothing. Their new flat was an astute choice with its shared garden, indoor lavatory and black coal range that could be used for both cooking and heating. When rations of fuel got low and the gas and electric power were cut off, as they often were, they could huddle around the cosy coal range for food and warmth.

The front room was big enough for a three-piece suite, dining-room table, sideboard and four chairs with green seat covers, and a big open fireplace. Hilda, who kept a spotless house, used to stand in the upstairs window and admire the whiteness of her washing billowing on the clothesline like kites rising, fluttering and falling on the breeze. Very occasionally they had guests for a tea party and she would bring out her best jug and glasses set, green like the seat covers, with a craze-cracked glaze. It was difficult in wartime and on low-paying wages to accumulate possessions, but Hilda made something special of her home.

*

Up to June 1944 Woodford had been spared much of the bombing. The neighbourhood had survived the Blitz unscathed. The sound of dogfights in the night sky was terrifying, but when Hilda shepherded the children across the grass to the Anderson shelter that first evening of the V-1 buzz bombs, she felt reasonably sure their flight was merely a precaution.

This time, however, a bomb dropped close to their house, with catastrophic effect, damaging all the terraced houses nearby. The explosive impact was demonstrably different from anything they'd experienced before, because this was a new form of terror. The unmanned V-1 (V for *Vergeltungswaffe* or 'Vengeance Weapon'), proved to be a killing machine. Each missile, launched from bases in the French Pas-de-Calais and along the Dutch coast, contained a tonne of explosive and had a range of almost 250 kilometres. At their peak, more than a hundred buzz rockets landed in a day. After the V-1 attacks came the V-2s, which also delivered a ton of explosives but were capable of travelling at supersonic speed and made no sound.[5] According to one eyewitness account, 'They were less terrifying than the "Doodle Bugs" [or V-1 buzz bombs], but if you heard the explosion of a V-2 you were alive, if you didn't you were dead.'[6] Many of the bombs were intercepted and shot down by Allied planes, but the 20 per cent that got through were lethal.

It may have been the dawning awareness of this escalation of war that made Hilda choose the public bunker in Woodford Green rather than their Anderson backyard shelter the next time a major assault happened. She had noticed the bombing had become more intense, and that night had an uncanny feeling. She knew of cases where Anderson shelters had taken direct hits. In a garden in Tulse Hill, in south London, five or six people had died instantly when their Anderson was hit.[7] The shelters were really only protection against falling debris and flying glass. So the Hallses bedded down in the large concrete-reinforced bunker in Woodford Green. It held up to a thousand people, and was spacious enough to provide bunks and dormitory-style accommodation. People crowded in. The bombing continued through the night.

The next morning the family headed home. On Gainsborough Road they discovered their flat had been hit by a V-2 bomb. Rubble and shattered glass lay everywhere. The doors and windows had been blown out, the roof smashed in. The only bit of ceiling still intact was over Aunt Alice's kitchen. Much of what the Halls family owned was destroyed. Sifting through the rubble, Hilda found one of her bowls of precious eggs perfectly intact; outside, the chickens that had laid them lay dead. The house and its terraced neighbours were uninhabitable, and the family evacuated by Black Maria police van to Doncaster, 270 kilometres north. The Hallses were now refugees, homeless in their own country.

*

In Doncaster they were welcomed into the home of a mining family who proved both compassionate and accommodating. As poor as they were, they did their best to make the Hallses feel welcome; one of them even crocheted Ann a little lavender shoulder bag. At night Ann slept between her parents in their bed; David was in the next room on a camp stretcher which he shared with his cousin Brian, who had travelled with them.

For a while life in Doncaster seemed peaceful and more bountiful. Hilda noticed immediately that the people there were not subject to the same rationing restrictions as those in London. When she went into a shop to buy a block of cheese the shopkeeper gave her a whole pound without question. George, who was very partial to bread and cheese for his lunch, was delighted, but Hilda was angry. Food was not being fairly distributed.

Then the harassment began: the stares, the disgruntled mumbling, the pushing and the shoving. Not everyone was as sympathetic to the Hallses' plight as their hosts. The contempt of those desperate to hold on to the little they had boiled over one day when Hilda and five-year-old Ann were standing outside talking to the miner's wife. Rationing and austerity campaigns meant almost no one wore new clothes, but Hilda and George, who had an entrepreneurial flair and bought and sold items on the black market, had managed to treat their daughter to a new coat. When the assembled crowd of women and children began throwing stones and bricks at them, Ann started to cry. It was not about the deep cut on her head but about the fact that the blood that gushed out had run down onto her new overcoat. Through her tears and sobs of anguish she heard the mob chanting, 'Go back home, Londoners, go home.'[8] Woodford's proximity to London was a serious risk, yet clearly Doncaster was not a safe place to be either.

In the end, it was not crowd violence but a lack of money that drew them south again. George needed to look for work. His job had gone up in flames the night a V-1 hit the steeple of the Congregationalist church in Cranbrook Road, Woodford, just as George's boss, the coal merchant, was driving past in his lorry with his wife and young son. All three were killed when the steeple toppled and fell through the cabin of the vehicle. The couple's other children, all girls, had been left at home that evening. In the aftermath of this tragic event the orphaned girls were taken into care by an uncle. In the subsequent re-configuring of the coal merchant's business, George lost his job.

*

The Hallses arrived back in Woodford with nowhere to live. A visit to their flat on Gainsborough Road revealed that it was in ruins; even the remnants of Aunt Alice's kitchen roof had caved in. Their only option now was to look to family for help – and fortunately Nellie and George Halls snr were happy to take them in.

Although David believed he was more worldly-wise than his sister, the train trip from Woodford to their grandparents' place in Theydon Bois was a thrilling and slightly terrifying experience for both of them. The line had not yet been electrified, so steam trains still belched, hissed and chugged their way along its length. 'All aboard, all aboard!' the guard called out across the platform, and they were gone in a gush of steamy vapour. The flat, rolling countryside of Essex flashed past the window as the children sat in their seats with gas masks packed in cardboard boxes and slung across their shoulders on pieces of string. Theirs was not a childhood of innocence and fantasy, but of preparedness. In spite of this, the wonder of the journey was experienced intensely by both of them.

The rail network that had pushed through from London in 1865 had brought change to Theydon Bois. Grand houses, council houses and new businesses began to spring up in what would rapidly become a sleeper suburb 20 kilometres from London. When they reached the station, George took David and Ann by the hands, guiding them past the sights on the way to their new home. On one side of the station were coal yards and wagons, and on the other the workmen's tearoom, which looked like a little cottage with net curtains. Along the road they passed a builder's yard, petrol station with two pumps, and two pubs: the Railway Arms and the Bull Inn. Across the main road were the village green and a large pond, separated by a curving line of oak trees standing like sentinels along the avenue. The pond was alive with waterfowl: swans glided across the water in stately indifference, while the more democratic ducks quacked in raucous greeting.

The village seemed less affected by the war than Woodford, though two 'Retreats' in Coppice Row, close to the parish church of St Mary the Virgin, would later be bombed and four houses on the north side of the road destroyed. For the Halls family, and especially the children, it was a sanctuary. Nanny and Granddad Halls' Elm Tree Cottage, which they had visited for occasional holidays and at Christmas, remained a magical place for them. The last in its row, it backed onto Black Acre

Road, and Theydon Park Road curved around the front and side. The cottage had a small garden at the front, and what seemed like an enormous vegetable plot at the side that included a small orchard of fruit trees. The whole garden was bordered by a high privet hedge.

Stepping through the brown wooden front gate with the words Elm Tree Cottage etched into it was tantamount to entering Nanny Halls' world of warmth and welcome. She loved her grandchildren and cherished the time she had with them. The cottage itself was a simple two-up two-down. When you came in the door, the front room was on the left and the dining room on the right. Added at the back were a kitchen and flush toilet; outside was a coal shed. After the hardships David and Ann had endured in Woodford and Doncaster, it seemed like heaven.

George and Hilda slept in the smaller spare room with Ann between them, and David stayed downstairs on the settee. His sleeping arrangements were a cause of minor sibling resentment, as he had the front-room fire for heat at night and could never be sent to bed before the games of evening cards came to an end and the radio was turned off. It gave him a flicker of adult independence, and he loved it.

David's life had so far been dominated by the threat or the consequences of war. He had shifted with his parents; moving, meeting people then moving away again. He found his closest friends among his extended family. His cousin Brian, who was a similar age, was a particular friend and playmate, as was his other cousin, John. When Hilda took over the milk round at Theydon Bois because of manpower shortages towards the end of the war, David rode with Brian up on the float; they would help out until boredom took over and they disappeared off to play.

His father, however, had a less easy time of it. There were jobs labouring and clearing debris at bombsites, and repair and rebuilding work, but little of this was in Theydon Bois. Not long after the family had arrived, he had to relocate himself to support them.

*

In spite of the ever-increasing food shortages, which stole more from people's plates as the war progressed, Nanny Halls' home was frequently filled with the smell of cakes and freshly baked bread from Barnes bakery in the village. She made plum jam and preserved fruit from the garden in Kilner jars. William pears, Victoria plums; when the shop shelves were empty and other families went without, she needed only to go into her larder as a magician reaches into a hat to produce something special.

Love was communicated with food, and around eating there were certain customs. One of them was the way Nanny cut bread. A fresh loaf still hot and steaming from the baker's was a treat to be savoured. To avoid tearing the soft, moist bread she secured the loaf under her arm and buttered the exposed end, removing slim slices of perfectly buttered bread and distributing them among the eager family. Nanny liked to make a spectacle of food production.

Christmas was the highest of high feasts and the preparation of the Christmas pudding began months before short days and chill nights heralded the Advent season. The precious dried fruit and other ingredients were bought in stages as the household budget and rationing allowed. Cooking this rich dark emblem of family and food was a ritual.

David aged about 10, c. 1946.

HUDSON & HALLS: A LOVE STORY

Nanny Halls' recipes were passed down the generations from mother to daughter. Some were written down while others were passed by word of mouth, but all had their beginnings in memory. There was something powerful about this connection to the past, and at Christmas dinner the pedigree of the pudding was almost always discussed.

Nanny Halls would have had her own 'tribal' traditions around the pudding, Christmas cake and fruit mince pies, but these traditions were also influenced by the experience of working in one of the 'big houses' close by. While working-class men in the area were mostly farm labourers, the women predominantly worked in service to the grand country houses. In the opening decades of the twentieth century domestic service was still the most common occupation for single women in Britain and it remained so until after 1945.[9] During this period as many as one in three single women were domestic servants, and in Essex, close to the great city of London, this proportion would have been even higher.[10] Marriage made 'live-in' service more difficult for women; many of them shifted regularly from one employer

George and Nellie Halls, late 1940s.
JANET PUTTNAM, PRIVATE COLLECTION

to another and, in the process, learned how various households functioned. As a result there was a transfer of ideas and practices. The 'plain' cook who brought her own traditions encountered the cuisine of the grand manor, and vice versa; often both of them benefited.

Nanny Halls had been in service, but by the time she was caring for David and Ann the work she did was more casual. Her own day began early with the lighting of the dining-room fire. In the warmer months, Granddad Halls sometimes came downstairs to light it, but at the change of season and in the winter months the air was too cold for his chest. His wife then left to go to work for the extra pennies essential to top up their pension and help support the added family members now living with them. George Halls snr, war veteran and invalid, stayed in, tied to the warmth of the room like a man encased in an iron lung.

Nanny Halls cleaned for Mrs Abrams, the local vet's wife. Sometimes she took David and Ann with her when she worked. Mrs Abrams' house, with its spacious rooms and smart furniture, seemed like a palace to the children. The grounds were split level and magnificently landscaped. They were big enough for a child to get lost in, or at least to get lost in wonder at such plenty in the midst of their need.

Mrs Abrams had no children so she fussed over little Ann, who was allowed a mug of Horlicks, an unheard-of luxury, when her grandmother's work was finished. When the Horlicks jar was nearly empty, Mrs Abrams gave the last few spoonfuls to Nanny Halls to take home – a special night-time treat for the children when the only drinks available at home were cocoa and a coffee substitute made out of roasted grains, chicory or sometimes dandelion root. Both of these left a bitter, unpleasant taste.

Nanny Halls also cleaned and did odd jobs for two brothers who lived in a cottage near the Theydon Bois pond. George, one of the brothers, was very particular about his appearance and wore a dashing panama hat in summer, while his brother Horace looked more relaxed in his all-seasons cloth cap. They enjoyed having the children visit and welcomed them into their home, often playing cards with them around the kitchen fire. David and Ann both recalled these visits as some of the fondest memories of their childhood.

George and Horace's living arrangements and their model of companionship introduced David to a new sort of bond. There was no discussion of homosexuality in the Halls family; the subject was taboo. Whether the brothers' relationship was more or less than pure brotherhood is immaterial: their lives were evidence of a different sort of pairing.

David and Ann Halls, c. 1948.
HUDSON & HALLS: A LOVE STORY

Having settled in at Elm Tree Cottage, the children began school at the local primary, though only part time because of war restrictions. David attended classes in the morning and Ann in the afternoon. The other pupils, however, many of them from families who had lived in Theydon Bois for generations, had their own established groups of friends. David and Ann were interlopers, outsiders; for some of their classmates, Woodford might as well have been another country. The Halls children were teased, tormented, pinched and shoved. They learned that you either stood your ground or you were relentlessly bullied. Though David and Ann fought back, the classroom struggles they endured were not conducive to learning. Both children were bright, but school became, at best, a minor priority in their lives; at its worst, it had decidedly negative associations.

*

The end of the war came abruptly for many. Like a silent Vengeance bomb that no one saw coming, it hit in an explosion of intoxicated emotion. It seemed as if the missiles had only just stopped raining down when, on 8 May 1945, Victory in Europe day was declared. Winston Churchill stepped out onto the balcony at the Ministry of Health in Whitehall and looked down at the elated crowd below. At St

Paul's the bells rang out to proclaim the news they had waited nearly six years to hear. 'My dear friends, this is your hour,' Churchill began, once the clapping and the cheering had subsided:

> This is not victory of a party or of any class. It's a victory of the great British nation as a whole. We were the first, in this ancient island, to draw the sword against tyranny … The lights went out and the bombs came down. But every man, woman and child in the country had no thought of quitting the struggle. London can take it. So we came back after long months from the jaws of death, out of the mouth of hell, while all the world wondered. When shall the reputation and faith of this generation of English men and women fail?[11]

Churchill's words were full of poignancy. He was talking universally about the war, but also about people's individual struggles: this was the brilliance of his speech-making. In that instant, the heterogeneous crowd connected both in the celebration of victory over conflict and in the sense that they had survived a disaster the scale of which should never be repeated.

But when the crowd broke up and the realities of peace took hold, people had time to measure the cost to themselves, and to their families, property and prospects. The Hallses had little left: no home, no stable work and few possessions. The children were unsettled and their education had suffered. Britain had won the war, but many families must have wondered how they would survive the peace.

Hilda and George, then, probably couldn't believe their luck when they received a stunning piece of good news. Their applications for live-in positions as groundsman and groomsman, plus housekeeper and cook, had been accepted by Brian and Harriet French, who owned Theydon Hall on Abridge Road, less than a mile from the village of Theydon Bois.

The hall, a former manor house, had once been the centre of a vast estate that was broken up after World War One. The house retained its allure, at once restrained and dramatic. A long curving drive kept its magnificence a secret until the bend, where the jutting proportions of its elegant Georgian façade were revealed. The soft yellow with white trim, which would have been demure in another setting, was eye-catching in this countryside of browns and greens. There was also a playful incongruity in its air of urbanity. In fact the front part of the building, completed in the latter part of the seventeenth century, was modelled on the fashionable houses of well-to-do city dwellers. Theydon Hall, in this final incarnation, would not have looked out of place on a London street.

Theydon Hall in autumn colours. HUDSON & HALLS: A LOVE STORY

The main two-storey section, built in yellow brick, was flanked by single-storey wings. The round-headed doorway was completed with pilasters and a lead fanlight, and the frontage burst forward to form a two-storey bay.[12] Inside the house the magnificence continued, with the marble fireplaces, cornices and bookcases of the principal rooms decorated in the Adam style. On the ground floor there was a stately drawing room, a dining room, a study, a large kitchen, a cloakroom and service rooms. Upstairs were the main bedrooms and dressing rooms. The grounds, which were to be George Halls' domain, were park-like in their splendour and expanse. There was almost a hectare of landscaped gardens and manicured lawns, plus stables, outbuildings and the lodge, where the Hallses had their separate accommodation.

Hilda ran the kitchen. Her experience was as a 'plain cook', which simply meant a cook with no professional training. But even with this less-than-glorified title, she was still required 'to turn out three meals a day if needed, bake bread, scones and cake for tea, and cope with the family's entertaining'.[13] Being a 'plain cook' was not a small job in a big house, but Hilda was well prepared. In the 1900s the national curriculum in England increasingly emphasised girls acquiring 'the three Cs' –

cooking, cleaning and care of clothing. Some schools added a fourth C, which was childcare.[14] Hilda had these skills in abundance and was desperate to use them to help improve her family's prospects.

Things had changed quite markedly even in the 10 years or so since Hilda had been in domestic service. Virginia Woolf famously traced this evolution in the persona of the English cook and identified it as emblematic of a tectonic shift in human relations. In her 1924 essay 'Mr. Bennett and Mrs. Brown' she argued that 'in or about December 1910, human character changed':

> The Victorian cook lived like a leviathan in the lower depths, formidable, silent, obscure, inscrutable; the Georgian cook is a creature of sunshine and fresher air; in and out of the drawing-room, now to borrow the Daily Herald, now to ask advice about a hat ... All human relations have shifted – those between masters and servants, husbands and wives, parents and children.[15]

Had she lived to see the dawn of the post-World War Two era, Woolf would have noted even more change in the relationship between the majority of domestic staff and their employers.

The democratisation of war changed the rules of this ancient engagement. Six years of conflict diversified employment opportunities and lifted expectations. Many of those who fought or worked as seconded labour never returned to service, and the reduced number of people prepared to become domestic servants raised the cachet and bargaining power of those who did. Employment in the 'big house' was no longer perceived as a state of moral obligation and absolute dependency. 'Indeed,' argues critic and commentator Alison Light, 'turning dirty little girls into tidy maids was one of the great aims of Victorian rescue work. Nor was it negligible. Service was the great route to respectability, an insurance paid by the rich against the poor's rebellion. In training up future servants, the ladies of the house were saving the nation from the threat of "the mob".'[16] Two world wars, two decades apart, had changed everything. The territory had shifted from one of moral superiority and dictatorial power to one of negotiation and economic exchange. By 1945, staff in service were understood to have their own family commitments and not assumed to be available around the clock.

Brian and Harriet French belonged to the new group of more egalitarian postwar employers. This meant that while many of the negatives were removed, the benefits of working in a big house remained. In as much as service had ever been an opportunity for advancement and social mobility, it still was. Living-in as a domestic servant was the closest the working poor would get to 'seeing how the other half lived'. Hilda and George observed the way the French family lived, and so did their children. David was particularly impressed by the house and its opulence. This was a completely new level of aristocratic grandeur, and the remarkable thing was that he and his family were living in it. He was able to study, close-up, new codes of dressing, along with new manners and behaviour.[17] His and his sister's universe changed overnight. There was still school, of course: Theydon Bois primary school resumed normal teaching hours after the war ended, and David and Ann attended for the full school day. Holidays continued to be spent with Nanny and Granddad Halls at Elm Tree Cottage. But now there were new adventures to relish.

Harriet French was a magnanimous woman who reached out to Hilda's children and included them in the daily activities of her own two, Jonathan and Amanda, who were of a similar age. David and Ann became not just the children of staff but live-in playmates. But the French children's world views and expectations of where life would take them were different from anything the young Hallses had known, and David absorbed this difference like an adventurer exploring a new continent. He was often in the nursery, eating his meals there, or being taken on trips and given treats like a member of the family. His experiences at Theydon Hall instilled in him an aspirational dream that became the blueprint that shaped his future.

Nor would he forget that his entrée to this grand way of life was through food. Hilda's role facilitated his access to the family on the other side of the green baize door; his father's job outside did not have quite the same appeal. David understood the power of the kitchen; how central it was to people's wellbeing. The need to eat connected everyone.

The Hallses lived at Theydon Hall Lodge for four years, the longest period they had stayed anywhere since the children were born. Towards the end of their time there, Hilda and George began what could be described as a second family. While she was still working at the hall, Hilda gave birth to a second daughter, Janet, who was christened in the chapel near Theydon Hall. Janet was followed a year or so later by Tony. Although there were not so many years separating them, the two pairs of children were an epoch apart in terms of their formative experiences. The terror and disturbance that had defined David and Ann's childhoods were absent from Janet and Tony's sunny, stable beginnings. They might as well have belonged to different generations.

*

In spite of the interruptions to his education, David managed to get into Buckhurst Hill County High School, an academically oriented all-boys grammar that had opened in September 1938. He began there in 1948, at 12 years old, and left sometime during the academic year of 1951–52. He was placed in the bottom stream and not encouraged to excel. His sister Janet recalls, 'Mum allowed him to have quite a bit of time off school. It wasn't pushed on him. They weren't educated. They didn't see the importance of education then …'[18]

David made little impact on the school and later did not keep in touch with any of the friends he made while he was enrolled there. A photograph exists of him as a schoolboy, sitting in profile with a book in his hand, but this is not an accurate picture of the life he led. David was not one for long stints of concentration, and Janet recalls that he was a frequent truant: 'I can only remember him coming home from school once.'[19] Undoubtedly he attended more often than this, but it is clear that a formal academic education was not a priority. He was a hands-on, practical teenager in a school environment where sport and academic study ruled. He already had an eye for women's fashion, and was more interested in clothing design and cultural pursuits. He was working class; many of the other students were from the more well-to-do middle-class families, the sons of people who worked at the nearby RAF base at Chigwell. David was also homosexual, and becoming more agonised by the implications of this as he matured. School was not an easy fit, and he was far from the perfect student.

During David's time at Buckhurst Hill his parents ended their employment at Theydon Hall. There is no clear reason for their departure, but possibly circumstances conspired. The French family moved away from the property about this time, and it is likely that Hilda, coping with a very young child, was finding her job increasingly onerous. Working up at the hall was a serious commitment. Janet recalls, '[E]verything had to be done right, you know, like oatmeal porridge had to be real oatmeal done in a double saucepan … You cleaned the carpets with the tea leaves and things like that.'[20] Hilda suffered bouts of ill health and spent periods of time in hospital. In her absence, David became the family cook.[21]

So, the gorgeous gilded summer of Theydon Hall came to an end and the family was itinerant again. Once more Nanny Nellie and Granddad George Halls took them in. George and Hilda now had their hearts set on a council flat in a brand-new housing estate, yet to be built. The location was perfect, close to both the village green and the pond in Theydon Bois – just a brief, picturesque walk and you'd be at the train station with its newly electrified line to Epping and London.

In 1949 the electrification of London's Central Line was completed, with Epping at its terminus. This was a watershed in transport communication in the area. David could get quickly to and from high school in Buckhurst Hill, and later to Epping, where he took up his first job after leaving school. The market town of Epping was a much bigger centre than Theydon Bois. At its zenith at the end of the nineteenth century High Street could claim 27 public houses: many more than in most other towns of a similar size. The right to hold a market, which could only be conferred by a king or queen, gave the town its advantage; plus it was a transport hub. Since 1253 a weekly market had been held there, and just when the importance of this was fading, Epping Forest became a star attraction for the working classes.[22]

In 1878 Epping Forest was opened to the public in perpetuity. Queen Victoria, visiting the forest in 1882 for a public ceremony, recorded in her diary, '[T]he Park has been given to the poor of the East End as a sort of recreation ground.'[23] For decades after that day-trippers arrived via coach and steam train, then along the electrified Central Line, to spend their playtime in the park. 'The natural aspect of the forest is much stressed today, but a century ago a visit to the forest was very much thought of as a beano [party], with donkey rides, coconut shies, and a good meat tea.'[24]

Soon after David's parents finally settled into their new council flat at 12 Green Glade, Theydon Bois, David began his job at Epping's Co-op, a collective of retail outlets that sold everything from meat to men's clothes. The bustling town fed David's interest in food and fashion, but his social life still mainly revolved around family. He was especially close to his mother's sister Ethel, and he shared an interest in fashion photography with his cousin John. The two of them would go to Hilda and George's council flat, move furniture around and hang up white sheets in the front room to create a makeshift photographic studio. Capturing the natural light while avoiding glare from window reflections was a challenge and it took ages sometimes to get things just right. Their photography sessions were high-spirited fun. Ann, who was in her mid-to-late teens, was designated clotheshorse and catwalk model. David and John insisted she wore makeup, did her hair stylishly and changed outfits between photo shoots. 'In one photo she looks like Elizabeth Taylor,' Janet recalls. 'She was a lovely looking woman, my sister, like my mum, because she takes after my mum … John [became] a photographer in the end and worked in a camera shop.'[25]

There was often great hilarity in the Halls home. Hilda, who was close to her sister Ethel, used to giggle and rock back and forth with mirth at family gatherings. They knew what a good time was and how to enjoy themselves. Yet Janet remembers that both Hilda and Ethel had to work to help their mother, Nan Manley, who lived nearby. To 'earn a few more pennies' to survive, Nan Manley 'used to do a lot of buying and selling and she'd buy sheets and blankets, things like that, and they'd have to wash them,' remembers Janet, and 'do her housework for her.'[26] By then they had families of their own, yet Nan Manley's adult daughters were still expected to help out. This was the benefit of family in tough times.

Hilda mellowed over the years. When she was younger she would sometimes flare up in anger; with age she grew more tolerant. There was, however, one issue pivotal to David as he was entering adulthood that was not open for family discussion. Any revelation of his homosexuality, Janet believes, would have met with a violent response from both parents. 'She probably would have whopped him one,' Janet says of her mother. George was a simple, silent man with traditional ideas about sexuality. 'He wouldn't have liked it,' Janet says.[27] Perhaps Hilda and George suspected something, but there was no way this could be openly communicated.

Sex was not a comfortable subject for discussion anyway. The Hallses were working-class Edwardians – not puritanical, exactly, but well aware of conventional boundaries. Ironically, these rules were often more firmly entrenched among the lower classes. In 1907, when notorious literary 'sodomite' Lytton Strachey called across the room at a Bloomsbury tea party to his cousin Vanessa Bell (Virginia Woolf's sister), inquiring whether the spot on the front of her dress was semen, he knew it was shocking. Aware that his own way of life would horrify many, he continued to say outrageous things and live overtly as a homosexual because his class gave him the licence to do so.

David Halls enjoyed no such freedom. Love between men was illegal and, in his parents' minds, an abomination. Any encounters and liaisons would have been surreptitious and underground. Tightly knit communities in small villages talked.

David's flamboyant nature was beginning to define him. He laughed easily and was a natural performer. Humour was both a reflex and a technique. He had disappeared among the crowds of academically able schoolboys, but given the chance he could be a showman and take centre stage when he made people laugh. So he developed this talent – first to entertain, then to get ahead in his job.

*

David's workplace was in a row of antique buildings that slumped against each other like tired children on Epping's High Street. Its quaint eighteenth-century exterior, with its inelegant little dormer window and slate roof, belongs to the era

ANTICLOCKWISE FROM TOP LEFT:
David Halls at about 14 years old, c. 1950. JANET PUTTNAM, PRIVATE COLLECTION
David the dashing teen – about 16, c. 1952. HUDSON & HALLS: A LOVE STORY
Growing up fast – now 17 years old, c. 1953. HUDSON & HALLS: A LOVE STORY
David at 18, in 1954. JANET PUTTNAM, PRIVATE COLLECTION

of stagecoaches, multitudinous pubs and highway bandits. Within the evocative façade the interior space opened up to reveal a warehouse-sized floor area where the produce was sold.

The co-op, short for co-operative, was a Victorian gesture towards democratisation of pricing in which monopolies and exorbitant margins were eschewed. Ideally, local people owned the shop, the produce and a good slice of the profits. After World War Two, however, things changed in the co-op business. To compete with other giant retail outlets, co-ops shifted from local sourcing of food and consumer goods to centralised national and international purchasing. This was the practice when David was employed there. He became familiar with exotic fruits and vegetables and new imported produce. He handled food and sold food – and took his knowledge home when Hilda was sick in bed or in hospital, and cooked for the family.

David's interest in food went back to his earliest days, encouraged no doubt by Nanny Halls' hospitality and flair in the kitchen and his mother's years spent as a cook at Theydon Hall. Food had always fascinated him. As a 12-year-old he saved up his earnings from bagging spuds to buy *The English Good Housekeeping Cookbook* for 17 shillings and sixpence.[28] As an adolescent he took evening cooking classes.

David's confidence grew during his time at the co-op as he moved from handling food and produce to selling shoes. He was doing something that interested him, and was eager to get ahead. But he was also restless – keen to move on and to reinvent himself. If he stayed in Epping he would become set in the concrete of the postwar rebuild. He dreamed of travel to some distant exotic place, somewhere without class, without rationing: where he could be who he was without the judgement of his family. It wasn't that he didn't love them. He did, and he knew he had caring parents, but they wanted him to be something he was not.

It seems he attempted to join the navy around this time. As much as it was a strategy to see the world, it was probably also a deliberate attempt to try to meet homosexual men. Life at sea was traditionally lived away from women. Inevitably, men who loved men were attracted to this shuttered world of homosocial exclusivity. Unfortunately, David's medical tests revealed that he was colour blind, and his application was declined. In general, Janet remembers, 'his eyesight wasn't that good'. As an adult, 'He always did have glasses.'[29]

He left the co-op with a reference favourable enough to get him a job at Russell & Bromley's shoe store in Stratford. If Epping had been a step up in size and commercial enterprise, Stratford was a giant bound, and his position at Russell & Bromley a quantum leap. His particular interest was women's fashion shoes, but in his new role as store manager and sometime shoe designer he had to be careful with his colour choices and circumspect about revealing his colour blindness. Nonetheless, he was in his element.

David came to Russell & Bromley at an important time in the company's history. Its first shop had opened in Eastbourne in 1873, and by 1940 it owned 20 shoe stores throughout England. In 1947 Russell & Bromley opened a shop in Bond Street, London, selling some of the humbler stores to fund this new direction and changing its stock to suit a more exclusive clientele.[30]

Young and good looking, David had experience in fashion photography and was ideally placed to make the most of this magical period of transformation. Now he was making trips to London and purchasing new stock. His world was opening up.

He also became involved in amateur theatre – probably the Theatre Royal Stratford East, a large London community theatre. Since its opening in 1884 it had experienced the rush and retreat of waves of good fortune. In 1949 the tide receded once more and it closed, only to re-open in 1953 when it was used by theatre director Joan Littlewood as the home base of the Theatre Workshop Company.[31] '[David] did a few shows there. I can remember going to at least one [where] he was dressed as a soldier,' Janet recalls. 'He was into all that. There was a ballerina there, Jane, and he'd bring her home … We thought he might be going out with her. He always liked to be out there.'[32]

The theatre, another magnet for homosexual men, was an obvious place for him to seek out like-minded people. Flamboyant, liberal and egalitarian, it provided the perfect environment for David. The Theatre Royal Stratford East was the beginning of his love affair with the stage. The makeup, the lights, the props, the thrill of performing in front of an audience: it was all there as he walked out to deliver his lines. He loved it all, including the bright young things like Jane whom he met at parties afterwards.

But even this and his well-paid job at Russell & Bromley with its excellent prospects could not compensate for his lack of partnership. The companionship of another man could not happen in Theydon Bois, in Epping, or even in Stratford East. At home he would always be contained by his background, accent, education and, when everyone finally made the connections, by his sexuality. He would never be free of the pigeon-holing or the disapproval.

David was around 20 years old when he went to his father to ask him to sign the papers that would enable him to get a passport. George refused outright. He was

David is third from the right in the bottom row in this group photo, possibly of a theatre troupe he was involved in. JANET PUTTNAM, PRIVATE COLLECTION

angry. How could David even think of going as far away as Canada or New Zealand? The rest of the family were just as mystified. He had his younger sister and brother who looked up to him, and they had a special relationship. 'Having an older sister and brother was good,' remembers Janet. 'They used to buy us things Mum and Dad didn't or wouldn't have even thought of buying.'[33] He had cousins who were great pals, a job his father would never have dreamed of, and a social life to envy. George couldn't understand why his son wanted to go away. The issue was raw and they argued violently for a time. The outcome was that David promised to stay for his sister Ann's wedding and until he was 21, when by law he could sign the papers himself.

Ann's wedding was large, and so auspicious an occasion that the family borrowed an 8-millimetre movie camera to record the event. In film footage Ann, veiled and laced to the neck in her fine white wedding dress, stands on the steps of the church, looking radiant beside her new husband. Her life had started under the dark pall of war; now she was dazzling friends and family in the full glare of late postwar Britain. At the reception following the service, David stands out on the crowded dance floor, twisting and jiving with an enthusiasm that is almost ecstatic. Some of his jubilance was excitement: he too was beginning a new life. This home movie captures the last time he was embedded the way people are when they live close to family.

Janet was only 10 or 11 at her sister's wedding and Tony even younger. David would become a distant figure – not aloof, but far away. Janet doesn't remember him leaving, but recalls that he travelled to New Zealand by ship in 1959. 'It was time for me to make a break,' David would remember many years later. 'I went to Canada House and New Zealand House to plan my escape route. Canada at that time did not sound too exciting – but New Zealand sounded fantastic. All that open air appealed to me. So I sailed for Auckland on the Rangitani [sic].'[34]

David at his sister Ann's wedding, possibly sitting with his mother, c. 1958. HUDSON & HALLS: A LOVE STORY

In a stoic and enduring kind of way, his parents were heartbroken. George had done what he could to stop David from leaving. Now he must be resigned. On the one hand, he and Hilda had their steady life and their modest council flat in beautiful Theydon Bois; on the other, they had lost a son.

*

Two decades later David would tell newspaper journalists that he stepped off the *Rangitane* with just 'five quid' in his pocket. 'I paid my own fare (only doctors and dentists were getting paid to come here then).'[35] He was thinking his New Zealand sojourn might just be a year's leave from his job at Russell & Bromley. If things didn't go well, or if New Zealand wasn't the place for him, he would try Australia or perhaps even return home.

But as soon as he disembarked David picked up work as a shoe designer and marketer. This was a substantial advance on what he had been doing previously. That was the leap you could make travelling from England to the Antipodes, and it was the leap he desired. David was ambitious: his father was a labourer and his mother

Shortly before he left England for New Zealand in 1959.
JANET PUTTNAM, PRIVATE COLLECTION

a servant. He wanted to rise above them. Coming to New Zealand was about more than just the shaking off of the chains of the homophobia at home; it was a strategic act of social mobility.

His first position was with Clarke & Coventry, an Australian footwear company opening a store in New Zealand. David appealed to them as an excellent choice for the position of designer as he had 'trained as a shoe fitter and received a certificate on foot anatomy from the famed Cordwainers College in London'.[36] Cordwainers was a technical college that prepared students for the British footwear industry. Subjects in its syllabus included shoe design, construction and repair; the college also offered courses for those already engaged in the shoe industry. David, who had previous trade experience and could fairly claim to be Russell & Bromley's youngest manager, also had an eye for design. He expressed a desire to work on developing new ranges of shoes, and this together with his charismatic personality made him the perfect fit for the job.

Lois Neunz worked with David at Clarke & Coventry; she dispatched the orders of shoes that David and his manager developed. She remembers David as a 'camp guy' – unlike anyone she had encountered in her working life. 'I found him quite outrageously wonderful … quite artistic, and loud and vivacious … His personality just shone, and people who knew him just loved him … he was so funny.' When she first met him he was living with Colin Fenton, whom Lois remembers as a quiet man, about the same age as David, maybe a little older: short and almost Latin-looking, with very pale skin.

Colin had his own industrial sewing machine at home and did a lot of dressmaking, possibly also piecework for manufacturers. Lois recalls: 'In our off-duty hours David and Colin made me a ball gown for the governor-general's ball. I remember leaving it to them because I couldn't be bothered thinking what I wanted to wear. So they made this rather tight, very glistening dark … iridescent greeny-black dress. It was quite outrageous at the time for being so slender. Everyone was wearing those pink bouffant ones. When I got there I felt so out of place, but then I thought, no, I look spectacular. But I couldn't dance. I wanted to rip it up the back so that I could, but I didn't.' She describes the relationship between Colin and David as always a 'bit bumpy … I remember them parting. I think Colin … passed away quickly: I'm not sure how his life ended, but David was sad for quite a long time. I had a feeling that Colin had committed suicide, but I am not sure. I didn't ever ask about Colin any more.'[37]

What is known is that David was still feeling the loss of Colin when he was invited to a surprise party next door to his flat in St Stephens Avenue. And this is where he first met Peter Hudson.

Stuffed Squid

SERVES 4

We have all had it deep fried, haven't we? Well, if you have never tried it, do so, as it is really very good. One thing to remember is that squid either cooks for seconds or about an hour; in between those times you usually end up with a rubbery experience. We suggest that you buy already cleaned squid sacks measuring about 5–6 inches in length. As this is a fairly substantial beginning to a meal, a light middle course to follow is a good idea.

4 medium-sized squid sacks
fresh breadcrumbs dried in the oven
virgin olive oil

THE SAUCE
1 large onion, finely chopped
2 tablespoons olive oil
2 large bayleaves
1 clove garlic, crushed
good tablespoon plain flour
⅓ cup dry vermouth
⅓ cup water
a little salt and black pepper

THE STUFFING
1 large onion finely chopped
3 tablespoons olive oil
3 large tomatoes, skinned, seeded and
    chopped
2 thick slices of bread soaked in milk
    and squeezed dry
1 clove garlic, crushed
2 tablespoons finely chopped parsley
2 egg yolks
a little salt and black pepper

Start by making the sauce. Sauté the onion in the oil over moderate heat until soft, add the bayleaves, garlic and flour and stir to amalgamate. Now pour in the vermouth, water and a little salt and pepper. Stir together and when simmering, cover with a lid and simmer for 15 minutes. Remove from heat. When cool remove the bayleaves.

To make the stuffing, sauté the onion in a fairly large pan in the oil until soft, add the tomatoes and a little salt and pepper and continue to cook until the moisture has evaporated. Add the squeezed bread, garlic and parsley and mix well. Remove from the heat and mix in the beaten egg yolks. You may have to add a little water to turn this into a thick moist paste, but don't over moisten. Chill. Divide the mixture equally between the tubes; don't overfill because the mixture will expand. Secure both ends of the tubes with toothpicks to prevent the stuffing oozing out too much while being cooked. Lightly oil a baking dish just large enough to hold the squid in a single layer. Place them side by side in it and pour over the sauce. Sprinkle fairly thickly with the dried fresh breadcrumbs and drizzle over some oil. The crumbs must be thick enough to act as an insulation and protect the surface of the squid from drying out. Bake at Gas Mark 3 (325°F, 170°C) for about 50 minutes until the crumbs are golden and the squid are tender when you test them by inserting a skewer.

3. Peter's Youth & a Visit to New Zealand: 1931–62

Hire-car driver Reginald Papps watched in amazement as a car raced along Waverley Avenue at high speed.[1] This was unusual, especially nearing midnight in suburban Melbourne in 1926. The singularity of the incident left its imprint. Reginald would remember it in court: the image of a man driving rapidly along a lamp-lit street, rigid with concentration; two women sitting stiffly in the back of the vehicle; an overwhelming sense of urgency. Maybe it would have made less of an impression if 10 minutes later the very same vehicle had not shot past him again, travelling in the opposite direction. This time there was only one woman in the back seat. The missing woman, the car's speed and the lateness of the hour all struck him as peculiar.

Reginald Papps' disturbing recollection was part of an unfolding drama, the thread of which was picked up next by Daniel O'Sullivan, a linesman employed by the Melbourne Electric Supply Company.[2] He described how, driving after midnight along Chapstone Road in the suburb of Oakleigh, he made a macabre discovery. In the headlights of his car he saw the body of a woman propped in a seated position against a tree. She was fully clothed, as if she had been out shopping, with her handbag beside her. Daniel O'Sullivan knew from the position of the body, its chilling stillness and pallor, that the woman was dead. He notified the police immediately.

The first constable on the scene observed two things that made him suspicious. First, the shoes on the woman's feet were in pristine condition. There was no way her unsoiled footwear had carried her across the sandy, gritty ground to where she sat propped against the tree. In fact his colleagues would go further, deciding the woman had been dressed post-mortem and dumped for some unsuspecting passerby to discover. The other curious fact the constable recorded in his notebook was the presence of fresh car-tyre tracks in an area of sand 'ten feet from the tree and 18 inches from the tarred surface of the road'.[3] They showed that the car had turned completely around and retraced its tracks.

All the usual causes of death – drinking, drugs, domestic violence and misadventure – were quickly eliminated. The woman's handbag contained 'half a second-class return railway ticket from Glen Huntly to Melbourne' but no proof of her identity. Finally, a post-mortem conducted by government pathologist Dr C.H. Mollison revealed that Mrs Elizabeth Law, whose body was found mysteriously abandoned at the side of a lonely by-road in the early hours of 25 March 1926, had died of peritonitis following a septic abortion.[4]

On Friday 2 April, eight days into the police investigation of her death, Detective O'Keefe admitted to newspaper journalists across Australia that the case was deadlocked. The police were 'checkmated', he told them.[5] The next day, however, the police received a crucial new statement and there was a breakthrough. O'Keefe and his fellow detectives motored over to 3 Iona Avenue in Melbourne's exclusive suburb of Toorak. This was the address of nurse Mary Ethel Hudson, a known abortionist, and her husband Arthur. There was no one at home, so the officers left.

Later that day they returned to the property. The Hudsons' car had just pulled up. Arthur fled around the back of the house when he spotted the police, but Detective O'Keefe called after him, and it was clear that escape was impossible. Mary Ethel and Arthur stood in front of the detectives and 'shook and trembled all over'.[6] But when asked if they could go inside, Mary Ethel lied about not being able to find her key, then refused to go with them to the police station. At this point O'Keefe exploded: "'O yes you will; either in your own car or the police car.'"[7]

Mary Ethel stood speechless for a moment. She knew she must collect herself if she was to survive. Down at the station detectives questioned her for hours. She spent that night at home, but detectives were back on her doorstep before eight the next morning. This time she allowed them inside and was subjected to prolonged questioning. She denied everything until the evidence linking her to Elizabeth Law's death was clearly overwhelming. Mary Ethel broke down and wept. She desperately wanted to speak to her husband, Arthur. As soon as he entered the room, she said tearfully: "'Dot has made a statement against me.'"

Her husband replied, 'You have done nothing.'[8]

At 4.30pm on Sunday 4 April 1926 Mary Ethel Hudon was arrested and charged with the murder of Elizabeth Law. Two days later Dr Daniel Florance MacGillicuddy, who attended Mary Ethel's patients at 3 Iona Avenue, was also arrested and charged with murder. The pair were remanded pending an inquest to be held at the morgue by the city coroner. Bail was set for Mary Ethel at £600, and for Dr MacGillicuddy at £1000.[9]

News of the arrests swept across Australian tabloids like a bush fire accelerated by eucalyptus fumes. The dramatic way the body had been found, the arrest for murder of a prominent medical practitioner nearing retirement, along with the contentious issue of abortion,

Nurse and abortionist Mary Ethel Hudson, in about 1920. HUDSON & HALLS: A LOVE STORY

fuelled public interest to the point of frenzy. Attitudes to abortion and abortionists in the state of Victoria were mixed. The practice was illegal, but conviction rates were extremely low in comparison with the number of abortions conducted, and in 1907 the *Australian Medical Gazette* had argued that abortionists were 'looked upon as a public benefit rather than a common nuisance by juries'.[10]

For those seeking an abortion, the experiences of the rich and the poor were radically different. Most women could only afford the services of a back-street abortionist 'wielding a knitting needle, syringe or stick of slippery elm'. A subculture of corrupt businesses grew up around an illicit industry that included 'colluding chemists, taxi drivers, hotel keepers and hired touts'. More well-to-do women used illicit clinics and private hospitals such as the one run by Mary Ethel. The practice of abortion for both wealthy and working-class women occurred 'in the shadow of the law', and criminal prohibition drove those performing the procedure underground. The progressive outlawing of abortion in the latter part of the nineteenth century meant 'patients admitted [to hospital] following abortions trebled between 1910 and 1920. Between 1930 and 1933, 1069 women were treated at the Women's Hospital [in Melbourne] for septic abortions, 136 of whom died.'[11]

THE·NEWS OF THE·WEEK

...OLVING THE OAKLEIGH MYSTERY

Doctor and Nurse Charged with Murder

ALLEGED ABORTION.

Melbourne Trial Opened.

MELBOURNE, Tuesday.

The trial of Dr. Daniel Florence MacGillicuddy and Mrs. Mary Ethel Hudson on the charge of murdering Mrs. Elizabeth Law, whose body was found against a tree in Oakleigh, early on March 25, was opened to-day. The court was crowded.

The evidence was on similar lines to that at the inquest.

The Crown alleged that MacGillicuddy performed an illegal operation on the deceased at Mrs. Hudson's private hospital at Toorak.

The hearing was adjourned till tomorrow.

OAKLEIGH TRAGEDY

ACCUSED ON TRIAL

ARRAY OF BARRISTERS

MELBOURNE, Tuesday.

The graphic story of the finding of a body which some days later was identified as that of Mrs. Elizabeth Law, of ... fully clothed and propped up in a ... position against a tree near Chadstone road, Oakleigh ... was told in the Court before Mr. Justice Mann ...

MacGillicuddy and ... dson were charged ... Mrs. Law.

... barristers are eng... ndoe acted as Crow... A. Maxwell, the ... d with Mr. L. B. ... nd Mrs. Hudson ... H. Shelton and ... ur was taken up ...

... opening the Cro... s was a married ... r husband. It ... died from a... ... aw became a ... Hunter at Brig... Hunter gave h... ... ne, and she di... ... proved that ... ... venue, Toorak ... Hudson as ...

... that Mac... ... of the hou... ... aw and Hu... ... rnoon Mrs. ... ... maid rang ... ... Mrs. La... ... afternoon

---

THE OAKLEIGH TRAGEDY.

Arrests Made.

MELBOURNE, Sunday.

Unexpected developments occurred at the week-end in the police investigation into the death of Mrs. Elizabeth Law, whose body was found on the roadside in Chadstone road, Oakleigh, early on the morning of March 25.

Detective J. O'Keefe made an important advance in the investigations. Although it was felt on Friday that, failing certain information, a deadlock had been reached, a statement made to the detectives early on Saturday led to renewed activity. When the preliminary enquiries had been completed, suspicion attached to a house in Iona avenue, Toorak. From the appearance of the body the detectives were satisfied that death had occurred in a house, and that the body had been clothed after death.

When the identification of Mrs. Law was published last Monday morning, the police allege a man and a woman left their home at Toorak by motor car, and remained absent for several days. Although their presence was essential to the success of the investigations, no trace of them could be found. In addition, the detectives interviewed and questioned a second man and another woman. The second man, the detectives say, is a well-known medical practitioner. The detectives went to the house in Iona avenue, Toorak, and waited for some time. The sound of a motor car announced the return of the occupants of the house, and the man and woman were taken to the detective office. The police also seized the motor car, a well-known doctor, and another woman, who were also taken to the detective office and made a statement, in consequence of which the doctor was allowed to leave, and was told that his attendance would be required as a witness at the inquest.

A Charge of Murder.

Mary Ethel Hudson, nurse, a married ...

DEATH OF MRS. LAW

"MYSTERY" WITNESS

Doctor and Nurse on Trial

MELBOURNE, Today.

Interest was again keen today in the trial of Dr. Daniel Florance MacGillicuddy, of Heddle street, Richmond, and Mrs. Mary Ethel Hudson, of Iona avenue, Toorak, who are charged with having murdered Mrs. Elizabeth Law, aged 39 years.

The body of Mrs. Law, fully clothed, was found propped up in a sitting position against a tree in Chadstone road, Oakleigh, on March 25.

Mr. Justice Mann, counsel for the defence having ruled against the admissibility of certain evidence, a young woman (name not disclosed) stepped into the box and told her story in a low voice. She said about March 19 she went to the house of Dr. MacGillicuddy in Rich...

Nurse Mary Ethel Hudson and Dr Daniel Florance MacGillicuddy's exploits gave the Australian tabloids many sensational headlines.

DOCTOR AND NURSE SENT FOR TRIAL

Inquiry Into the Death of Mrs. Law

After the Coroner (Mr D. Berriman) had heard the evidence of many witnesses at the Morgue on April 22, he committed Dr. Daniel Florance MacGillicuddy and Nurse Mary Ethel Hudson for trial on a charge of having murdered Mrs Elizabeth Law. The trial will take place at the sittings of the Supreme Court on May 17.

Mr C. Book, of the Crown Solicitor's Office, assisted the Coroner. Mr G. A. Maxwell and Mr Leo Cussen (instructed by Mr N. H. Sonenberg) represented Dr. MacGillicuddy, and Mr P. J. Ridgeway appeared for Nurse Hudson.

The Government pathologist (Dr C. H. Mollison), who made the post-morten examination, said death was caused by an illegal operation, followed by peritonitis. In his opinion, the operation ... ... days before ...

We have lived at Bright six years. Two years after we arrived my father went away. I knew Mr Hunter, the news agent. He visited us often during the afternoons when we were at school and in the evenings. About March, 1924, mother went to Melbourne, and remained away three weeks. Again in March last Year she was away for two weeks. I do not know if she was ill. In June last year she went away again, and again at Christmas. She brought back with her two bottles of medicine (identified). I saw her about then talking to Mr Hunter outside our house. She went to Melbourne again in the New Year.

On March 2 I went to Mr Hunter, who gave me an envelope for mother. It was bulky. Two days later mother went to Melbourne, and I saw her off at the station. She had all the articles with her which I see here now.

(Witness was asked to identify several things, including a switch of hair.) I never saw my mother again, witness proceeded. A few days later I received a letter from her. In consequence I sent her 30/- to the Elizabeth street Post Office.

Mr Book here handed the witness a prescription which she identified as one found by her in her mother's drawer. It was stated "D. F. MacGillicuddy," and dated January 3, 1926.

Interview With Doctor

Thomas Hunter, manager of Bright, said: I had known Mrs Law for about six years. Her husband left Bright 18 months or two years after they first went there.

I had visited Mrs Law but not very frequently. I had been sorry for her being alone, with her children to look after, and had wanted to help her. I cannot remember what my relations with Mrs Law were in December 1923. Intimacy occurred later, beginning time to time till early in November, 1925.

MURDER CHARGE

WOMAN'S BODY FOUND ON ROAD

PROPPED AGAINST TREE

DOCTOR AND NURSE ON TRIAL

MELBOURNE, Tuesday.

A graphic story of the finding of the body of a dead woman, who some days later was identified as Mrs. Elizabeth Law, of Bright, fully clothed and propped up in a sitting position against a tree, in Chadstone-road, Oakleigh, was told in the Criminal Court today before Mr. Justice Mann and a jury.

DR. FLORANCE MACGILLICUDDY, Hadclv-street, Richmond, and Mrs. Mary Ethel Hudson, Jone-avenue, Toorak, were charged with having murdered Mrs Law.

A big array of barristers was engaged. Mr. H. G. McIndoe acted as Crown Prosecutor; Mr. G. A. Maxwell and Mr. L. B. Cussen appeared for MacGillicuddy, and Mrs. Watson was defended by Mr. H. Sheiton and Mr. R. Coleman.

Only detectives and people connected with the case were allowed in the body of the court. The gallery was crowded early, women being conspicuous in the front row. It took 40 minutes to empanel the jury. The Crown challenged 22, and MacGillicuddy stood aside 10. Miss Hudson challenged none.

Opening the case for the Crown, Mr McIndoe said that Mrs Law was a married woman living at Bright, apart from her husband. It was alleged that she died from an illegal operation and that the two accused, having engaged in the "shady" thought about her death.

Continuing, Mr. Macindoe said that two detectives visited Mrs Hudson's home and commenced themselves, Hudson and her husband trembled violently, and seemed very agitated. They had just returned home, when the detectives met them on the lawn. The detectives told Mrs Hudson that they wanted to talk with her inside the house, but she said she did not have the keys. When her husband was searched it was found that the keys of the house were inside.

When shown a photograph of Mrs Law, she said she had never seen the woman before. The police then locked her up, and later brought Dr. Mac... her up, and later brought Dr. Mar-gillicuddy to headquarters, and confronted him.

He denied that he had ever been inside Nurse Hudson's house at 5 Lonsavenue, but later admitted that he had driven there. He made this admission when a statement made by Nurse Campbell, an employee of Nurse Hudson's, was read to him. The detectives then asked him why he at first denied all knowledge of the house, and he replied that he wanted to avoid publicity. He said that Nurse Hudson had telephoned to him about 5 o'clock one day and asked him to attend a patient.

THE TOORAK MURDER

Charges Against Dr. Macgillicuddy And Nurse Hudson.

WITHDRAWN AFTER COMMITTAL BY CORONER

MELBOURNE 27-4-26—It is understood that the charge of murder against Dr. Daniel Macgillicuddy and Nurse Hudson have been withdrawn. Dr Pridas last they were committed for trial by the coroner.

The City Coroner (Mr. D. Berriman) found on Friday that Mrs. Elizabeth Law, whose body was discovered in Chadstone Road, Oakleigh, on March 25, died from peritonitis, the result of an illegal operation, which had been brought about by Mary Ethel Hudson and Daniel Florance Macgillicuddy, of a house in Lons-avenue, Toorak. He found them both guilty of wilful murder of Mrs Law, and committed them to stand their trial for her murder at the sittings of the Supreme Court on May 17. Mr Maxwell, M.H.S., and Mr E. J. Cussen represented Macgillicuddy, and Mr. P. J. Ridgeway appeared for Hudson. There were 16 witnesses.

William Dunlop Law, porter at Cranbrook railway station (aged 17 years), identified the body as that of his mother, aged 42 years, who had come to Australia six years previously from Scotland. His father and mother had been living apart for four years. On March 12 his mother told him that she had to undergo an operation.

... also under the names of Trown and Koast. Early this year I was employed by her as a cook in her private hospital in Lons., Toorak. The staff consisted of Miss Campbell and myself, and Dr Macgillicuddy was the doctor in attendance. On March 18 I saw Mrs Hudson and Mrs Law, whom I have identified from a photograph passing down a passage. Dr Macgillicuddy was in the bathroom, and two or three women had been there previously that morning. Later in the day Miss Campbell told me that Mrs. Law had a fit, and I then phoned to Dr. Macgillicuddy to come immediately. On the following day, Mrs Law's condition was worse. On the Friday, Miss Campbell told me that I could go away for the weekend. I did not see Mrs Hudson again.

Detective J. O'Keefe, said: "On April 5 Senior Detective Bell and I went to No. 5 Lons Avere, Toorak, and found both Mr and Mrs Hudson there. When we told them who we were, they shook and trembled all over. I said to Mrs Law, I came to your house after the illegal operation. Mrs Hudson said after having been shown a photograph of Mrs. Law, 'I have never seen that woman.' At 8 o'clock on the morning of the 6th of April I again questioned Mrs. Hudson for some time. She was charged with murder at half-past 4 o'clock in the afternoon. Detective McIntyre and I interviewed Dr. Macgillicuddy. He denied all knowledge of the matter, and when we asked for his books, he said that he did not keep any, as he was practically out of business, and took only a few patients to assist his son. He ...

Abortion when it hit the news was controversial. Fortunately for Nurse Hudson and Dr MacGillicuddy, their hearing date, Friday 23 April, was the day before Anzac weekend, a public holiday. Otherwise, the viewing gallery would have been packed. As it was, most of the country's main newspapers had a reporter present. Fourteen witnesses gave evidence, but the accused refused to say anything in their defence. When challenged by Coroner Berriman, MacGillicuddy declared: '"I do not propose to give any evidence in this court. My evidence may be given later in another court."'[12]

Mary Ethel pleaded not guilty.[13]

MacGillicuddy would indeed give his evidence in another court, as the coroner committed the pair to stand trial 'for the willful murder of Mary Elizabeth Dunlop Law, at the sittings of the Supreme Court'. Their trial date was ultimately set for 25 May 1926.

*

Dr MacGillicuddy and Nurse Hudson chose their legal teams with care. They were well prepared when the Supreme Court met to hear their case. MacGillicuddy's team was led by the notable blind barrister Mr G.A. Maxwell, assisted by Mr L.B. Cussen. Mary Ethel was defended by Messrs H. Shelton and E. Gorman. The chief prosecutor for the Crown was Mr H. Macindoe.[14] It took anything from 40 minutes to over an hour to empanel the jury, depending on which newspaper you read. The Crown challenged 22 jurors, MacGillicuddy's defence counsel challenged 13, and Mary Ethel's none.[15] Public interest was intense: there had been a rush for seats, and people still thronged the Supreme Court corridors after proceedings began in the hope that someone would vacate a seat. 'Women were conspicuous in the front row of the gallery, which was crowded early,' wrote the reporter for the News.[16]

One of the first important witnesses in the dock was Thomas Hunt, a newsagent living in Bright. He told the court that he became acquainted with Elizabeth Law after her husband deserted her four years earlier. Elizabeth, her husband and two children had moved to Australia from Scotland, and had lived in Bright for only 18 months before Mr Law took off. Hunt claimed he felt sorry for Elizabeth, and then later their connection became intimate. In February 1924 she came to him asking for money and a letter of introduction so she could travel to Melbourne for an abortion. This would happen three more times over the space of two years.[17]

On the first occasion Hunt went to Melbourne in person to see Dr MacGillicuddy at his Hoddle Street surgery.[18] There the doctor handed him a slip of paper on which he had written Nurse Hudson's Iona Avenue address. Thereafter Elizabeth would go to this address alone. Her last and fatal trip, nearly two years after her first, was a follow-up visit. An abortion conducted in December 1925 had not been successful. Her return to Melbourne at the beginning of March 1926 was to see what could be done about the failed abortion.

Another early witness was Elizabeth's 17-year-old son William Dunlop Law, 'a lad porter' at Craigieburn railway station. The young man confirmed his mother's trips to Melbourne and the periods of her absence from home. Next up was his sister Annie Isabel Law, who broke down in the dock and had to be given a seat when she was shown items of her mother's clothing. 'The dead woman's daughter … a schoolgirl of 14, made a poignant picture in the witness-box,' reported the *Weekly Times*. 'She was dressed entirely in black, and gave her evidence in almost a whisper.'[19] Annie Law spoke so quietly the crowd that usually rustled and fidgeted in the public gallery had to lean forward to hear. She confirmed the dates of her mother's absences, and that Hunt had been a regular visitor to their home while she was at school and in the evenings.

Subsequent witnesses included two of Mary Ethel's staff, who had worked for her both at her High Street maternity hospital in Northcote and at Kentley Lodge in Iona Avenue. Miss Irene Clayton Tatt, the cook for periods of time at both these addresses, told the court that Nurse Hudson, a registered midwife, had a number of aliases, including her maiden name, Melrose, Nurse Keast from a previous marriage in 1909 to Percy George Keast, and Nurse Brown.[20] When asked whether there were ever any live births at Iona Avenue she said no, but that babies were born at Nurse Hudson's High Street address in Northcote.[21]

Miss Tatt positively identified Elizabeth Law as one of the private patients who had arrived at Iona Avenue on 12 March. She had been given 'a small room at the end of the passage, where she had her meals'.[22] On 15 March Miss Tatt witnessed Nurse Hudson and Mrs Law going into the bathroom. Soon after, she heard Dr MacGillicuddy's voice coming from the same bathroom. That afternoon Mrs Law had a seizure and Miss Tatt was instructed to call Dr MacGillicuddy immediately.

Between 15 March and 24 March, Miss Tatt assisted Miss Dorothy Campbell, a registered nurse, in putting hot packs around Mrs Law's chest because they believed it was congested. Mrs Law 'hiccoughed' relentlessly for three or four days. When Miss Tatt came back from her afternoon off on Wednesday 24 March, Nurse Hudson suggested she and Miss Campbell take a tram ride. This they did, arriving back at 10.30pm.[23]

Miss Campbell stood in the witness box to confirm much of what Miss Tatt had said. Both women believed that Elizabeth Law had been picked up by friends and taken to hospital in their absence.

Detective O'Keefe's evidence was some of the most damning. His interviews with the defendants revealed a graveyard of unanswered questions and lies. From the moment Mary Ethel told O'Keefe she had misplaced her house key to the end of the trial, truth moved along a vague and slippery continuum.

When O'Keefe confronted her during initial police questioning with a photograph of Elizabeth Law, she denied ever having seen her. After this was proven to be a spectacular lie, Mary Ethel told the police the woman was there simply for bed rest; that she had been collected by friends and taken away for specialist care. Although Arthur Hudson's car was positively identified as the one tearing along Waverley Road and the tyres were a perfect match for the tracks left in the sandy dirt at the scene, she denied this also. It was not her husband at the wheel, she said to police, and she was not the woman supporting the dead Elizabeth Law in the back seat. No abortion had been conducted, she told the court; no woman had ever died in her care. Nothing illegal had happened at Iona Avenue in the month of March 1926. She was not guilty of committing any felony. She was adamant.

MacGillicuddy went through a similar process with Detective O'Keefe. He refused to admit meeting Elizabeth's lover, Thomas Hunt, in his surgery in February 1924; to ever having known Elizabeth Law; and to attending patients at 3 Iona Avenue. 'I have never aborted women,' he added.[24] In fact he had a letter supplied by friends guaranteeing that he was with them, and not in a bathroom where the alleged abortion happened on 15 March. The whole thing was a preposterous miscarriage of justice and he was innocent of Elizabeth Law's death. This he stated in the strongest possible terms.

In spite of the fact that Misses Tatt and Campbell both said he was in regular attendance at 3 Iona Avenue, sometimes daily when the numbers of women were high, MacGillicuddy's persistent denial of any wrongdoing was unfathomably persuasive. His word alone, however, was unlikely to have convinced the jury. The final climax was left to his brilliant blind barrister Maxwell, who, like a magician in the final throes of an enchanting magic act, whipped back the curtain to reveal a key witness. Maxwell told the court that when Elizabeth Law came to Melbourne in early March 1926, supposedly to correct an unsuccessful abortion, she had stayed at a boarding house in Prahran. The landlady, Mrs McGowan, he told the court, 'will tell you that on March 6, while she was in her house, Mrs Law burnt under the copper certain clothing'.[25] Mrs McGowan took the stand and explained further. The parcel of clothes burned under the copper was badly bloodied; she had offered Mrs Law a hot bath, but the woman had refused.

The defence counsel's argument in the end was that Mrs Law was already seriously ill when she was treated by Nurse Hudson and Dr MacGillicuddy. She had suffered either a self-inflicted abortion or a miscarriage. Either way, the accused were both innocent. The rest of the evidence, Maxwell told the jury, was unsubstantiated or circumstantial. Miss Tatt had heard what she believed was Dr MacGillicuddy's voice; she never saw him. No one could prove beyond reasonable doubt that he was in the bathroom or that an illegal abortion had occurred. Equally, there was no evidence to prove that Arthur's car was involved in the dispatching of the body, or that Mary Ethel had done anything more than nurse a woman who was already dying.

In his summing up, Mr Justice Mann told the jury that if they wanted to 'bring in a verdict of manslaughter', they could.[26] The jury duly adjourned to make their decision – and filed back just two hours later. 'Do you find the accused guilty or not guilty of the wilful murder of Mary Elizabeth Dunlop Law?' the registrar of the court asked the jury foreman. Twice he responded: 'Not guilty.'

A shout went up from the crowd. Any dissension was drowned by rapturous applause. 'As Dr MacGillicuddy left the court scores of hands were outstretched toward him. Cheers were given for Mrs Hudson by a crowd of more than 100 spectators.'[27] Family, friends and supporters rushed to congratulate them. They had been acquitted, and now walked free.

*

If there was any lesson for Mary Ethel to learn from this experience, it was that truth is a dangerous thing. Detective O'Keefe had repeatedly urged her to confess – or to betray the doctor to save herself. 'Why not clear yourself at this stage?' he demanded.[28] But she never wavered, even after nearly 22 hours of questioning.

Mary Ethel was a steely character whose nerves were tempered by harsh experience. Elizabeth Law was not the first woman to have died as the result of an abortion in her care. Minor prosecutions and near misses with the law dotted the murky path of her career. As far back as November 1920, Mary Ethel and MacGillicuddy were linked to the death of 32-year-old Jean Kelly following a septic abortion. According to evidence given in court, Mrs Kelly became ill and was visited by Mary Ethel (known then by her married name of Keast) and taken to her private hospital in High Street, Northcote. Mrs Kelly was seen by Dr MacGillicuddy, but when her condition deteriorated she was taken to Uxbridge House, another private hospital, where she died.

Both Keast and MacGillicuddy denied any direct involvement in her death, saying that 'her condition was caused by pills which she had taken'. The coroner's findings suggested otherwise. Rather, her 'death was due to septicemia', the 'result of a certain operation, performed by some person or persons unknown. It was serious, he said, that an otherwise healthy woman should have died under such conditions.'[29] The most likely suspects to have conducted this fatal abortion were Nurse Keast and Dr MacGillicuddy.

But pregnancy was dangerous for women anyway. There were no guarantees. People accepted the fact that mothers died when giving birth just as they did when trying to abort a foetus. There were women sitting in the courtroom when the 'not guilty' verdict was read out whose lives had been transformed by Nurse Hudson. In some cases, she was all that had stood between them and ruin.

Iona Avenue in Toorak was a privileged address. Its location was no accident. Upper-class women needed the attentions of Mary Ethel as much as solo mothers like Elizabeth Law. The difference was that for the rich people of Toorak, the service was local. And they paid well.

The lure of money meant Mary Ethel kept taking risks. Abortion was profitable, as was the business of adopting out babies born at her private hospital in Northcote. Elizabeth Law paid her at least £20 a visit. During the trial Detective O'Keefe told the court that Nurse Hudson had two bankbooks in her handbag, and that she had drawn sums of £50 on 17 March, 24 March and 26 March. 'For one week between January 18 and January 25 the payments to credit amounted to £350.'[30] To put Mary Ethel's cashflow in context, the average weekly wage was £5/1/6 for adult males, and £2/14/2 for adult females.[31] While the murder trial may have changed some of her practices, it did not prompt any profound soul searching or change of career. She was immersed in the business of abortion and baby farming, and the money was too good to give up.

There had been earlier lessons she had chosen not to learn from. In 1915 Mary Ethel Hudson, again known as Nurse Keast, had been involved in what the newspapers called a 'Babies to Order' scandal and 'baby bonus fraud'. The story began when a baby girl born in Keast's private hospital in Fitzroy Street was handed over to 24-year-old Mrs Hines who, unable to bear children, 'passed off the child to her husband as her own'. Nurse Keast registered the baby and Mrs Hines collected the £5 baby bonus available to all new mothers in Australia from 1912 to assist with

Mary Ethel Hudson's involvement in a sensational 'babies to order'
hoax further tarnished an already questionable reputation.

childrearing. Some time later, Mrs Hines appealed to Nurse Keast for a second child, this time a boy. The child was already three weeks old when Mrs Hines' husband registered the birth and collected the baby bonus on his wife's behalf. 'I never gave Nurse Keast any money for getting the child or for my supposed confinement,' Mrs Hines stated in court in 1915, 'but I believe my husband paid her three guineas [for midwifery services].' The hoax was discovered when another nurse, greedy for her share of the baby bonus, wrote to Mr Hines, exposing the scheme.[32]

This did not stop Mary Ethel's baby business. On 9 January, 22 March and 6 April 1932 she put advertisements in *The Age* newspaper, as she habitually did when organising the adoption of a baby. When the identity of the child's parents had to be concealed, Mary Ethel and Arthur could be given as the parents on the birth certificate. It was an easy deception. Mary Ethel often registered the birth, and there were few checks. She had influence with the medical profession and undoubtedly in the offices of the public service, and Arthur was a willing participant in his wife's subterfuges. She was often paid for this service by the child's birth mother, and paid again by the adoptive parents. It was a lucrative business.

The January advertisement read: 'Wanted, kind person to Adopt healthy baby boy, 2 weeks old; also Boy, 4 months. Nurse Keast, 683 High-st., Northcote'. In March, Mary Ethel was looking for a 'R.C. [Roman Catholic] Family, to adopt bright, healthy baby Boy, 7 months old. Nurse Keast. Kentley Lodge, Iona-av'; and in April: 'Nurse Keast Kentley Lodge Iona-av., Toorak. – Wanted M.C. [married couple] to adopt healthy baby boy, 11 days old; also R.C. family for 7 months.'[33]

It is very possible that Peter Hudson was one of the babies referred to in these or earlier advertisements. Certainly, there is among them a close enough fit for his supposed birth date of 8 November 1931. The registering of a baby's birth was often

A typical house on Iona Avenue in the wealthy Melbourne suburb of Toorak, where Peter lived in his early years. AUTHOR'S PRIVATE COLLECTION

delayed, and any date could be given: everything depended on the honesty of the person supplying the information. Peter John Hudson's birth certificate gives Kentley Lodge, 3 Iona Avenue, as the place of birth, and Mary Ethel and Arthur Harold as his parents.[34] Mary Ethel was 44 years old, and unlikely to have been his mother.

It is probable that he was either the child of one of the mothers in Mary Ethel's care or the son of Bridget, Mary Ethel's unmarried daughter from a previous relationship. Bridget, known as Biddy, was 21 years old when Peter was born.[35] But the latter theory begs the question: why would the daughter of an abortionist persist with an unwanted

Bridget Melrose or Keast, generally known as Biddy Hudson, in about 1945. Peter's mother, sister, or neither? HUDSON & HALLS: A LOVE STORY

pregnancy? But sure ground was in short supply in Mary Ethel's life, so Peter probably never knew the true identity of his mother and father. His cousin, Brenda Righetti, believes his parentage is impossible to ascertain: 'The fact of the matter is,' she states, 'we [his family] don't know anything more … and Peter, bless his little soul, didn't know, either. It was a secret. He was just a little adopted boy.'[36] A little adopted boy who, in all this melodrama of make-believe, would struggle to work out where he fitted in.

*

Peter Hudson grew up in a counterfeit world of veneered formality that barely concealed a raft of clandestine activities. For the first years of his life he was brought up to believe that Mary Ethel was his mother. 'The main person in Peter's life was Aunty Ethel,' Brenda Righetti remembers. 'She was … a very kind and loving lady, and a very capable person … She mothered him, without a doubt.'[37] Later, Peter was told his real mother was Biddy – a possibility strengthened by the fact that of all the babies Mary Ethel had available for adoption, she kept only Peter. On the other hand, she could have done this on a whim, or as appeasement for some of the damage she had done over the years.

For the first 10 years of his life, Peter lived at Kentley Lodge with Mary Ethel, Arthur and Biddy. The building there was like a boarding house, the closest thing to a private clinic Mary Ethel could arrange. Then, on 2 July 1940, Mary Ethel died suddenly and without a will. Arthur Hudson was granted probate of her estate. He acquired the money and property, and Biddy took over the running of the maternity, adoption and abortion business. Suddenly, the semblance of security life had offered Peter was swept away. On 16 November 1940 a notice was placed in the newspaper to advertise the sale of the contents of Mary Ethel's house.[38] Another advertisement placed in January 1941 gave notice of a demolition sale of bricks, fittings and other items at 3 Iona Avenue.

Thus far Peter had been raised in a world dominated by women. Mary Ethel was the entrepreneur, the visionary; she had the business acumen and the nursing registration. Arthur, an advertising agent, played a passive but supportive role. Later, Peter would rarely mention him. He told close friends he never knew his father. His childhood was one of strangers coming and going, of unspoken dramas, and of births and deaths. Instability and shifting realities left him with few anchors. Perhaps the one abiding imperative came from within, and that was the overwhelming need to connect, to bond with someone who would love him unconditionally.

*

There were many challenges for Peter to contend with growing up. The knowing stares, for instance, the whispers behind hands: a feeling always of being watched and talked about. Peter knew he was part of a difficult dynasty with a secret. Their association with abortion was stigmatising in the wider community: the link to Elizabeth Law's murder case made them infamous. Although they lived, in Peter's early years, along leafy, salubrious Iona Avenue with its established homes and money, they were regarded by many as pariahs. Their life was not truly genteel, and living where they did came at a cost.

Biddy proved to be every bit as domineering as her mother. Although she inherited money and the control of Mary Ethel's empire, she was not generous to Peter as her mother had been. She counted her pennies and was mean about things like food. Peter remembered his life as a roster of nurses and governesses until he was 'herded' off to board at 'Geelong Grammar' school. The gist of this is probably true, but unless he went to the exclusive private boys' school under a fictitious name, Peter never attended Geelong Grammar. This may have been where he wished he'd gone, because it assisted him in cultivating 'an image of a respectable, well put

Peter in about 1937. HUDSON & HALLS: A LOVE STORY

together young man', but it is certainly not the school he attended.[39] Fabrications were second nature to the Hudsons. When you did illicit things as part of your profession, you automatically covered your tracks. After a while, fact and fabrication became indistinguishable: if they weren't, you got caught out.

Brenda Righetti remembers Peter as a solitary boy who liked indoor activities and rarely ventured onto the cricket ground or the 'footy field'. He liked drawing and art and was attracted to beautiful things: antiques, fashion houses and exclusive designer labels. He was always smartly dressed. Peter understood how clothes worked to define or disguise you in the world.

In his adult life Peter would invent a number of different childhood stories for friends, associates and the media. The underlying theme was affluence. To a reporter from the *Christchurch Star*, he explained that he was born in 'Melbourne and brought up on outback farms'.[40] Generally, however, he held on to the idea of Iona Avenue as if he always lived there in leafy luxury. Sometimes it was with his elderly parents. 'Peter comes from a marvellous mother', remembers Ross Palmer. 'Somewhere there is a wonderful painting of her. She was a very autocratic, Melburnian person …

He didn't talk much about his father.'[41] To his friend Abby Collins, Peter was more candid. He mentioned Biddy and told Abby he was illegitimate. 'The only story I ever got,' she remembers, 'was that his mum worked in Elizabeth House in Elizabeth Bay, and he grew up there surrounded by antiques and fabulousness and wonderfulness and their house was full of … beautiful paintings, silver. They just loved all of that stuff.'[42]

He told Abby's husband Geoffrey that 'his family owned Rose Bay in Sydney'. Geoffrey recalls: 'There was this huge angry portrait of his mother [at Peter and David's house at 7 London Street in Auckland]. He hated his mother, but he kept her portrait on the wall and always swore at her as he walked past her. You know, "You bitch", or something like this every time he walked past.'[43]

In 1990 Peter told *Sunday* magazine that he was the child of older parents, and that his family were directly descended from Alexander Macleay, one-time governor of New South Wales. 'The Macleays and another family introduced merino sheep to Australia so it follows that the Hudsons were not short of a dollar,' the impressed journalist wrote.[44]

David Halls would remember Biddy, but no older parents. He explained to the *Auckland Star* in 1985 that Peter 'is the proud possessor of two recipe diaries which belonged to his mum Biddy, now deceased and buried in Melbourne'. Biddy, recalled David, was a messy cook: 'Pots and pans everywhere, peas in one, something in another, but it didn't matter because she could afford someone to come in next day and clean up … She kind of figured that anything as ordinary as an egg coming out of a chicken should be free. One evening, while I was staying with her, I crept into the kitchen and broke three eggs into a pan and as quick as that she yelled from her room, "I heard you. Three eggs!"'[45]

For all their diversity, there is likely an element of truth in all these stories. They suggest Peter's discomfort with his past, and his urge to manipulate it into a multitude of shifting shapes to satisfy the listener. He could be anything for anyone.

*

After leaving school at 17, Peter got a job at the stylish Georges department store on Collins Street, Melbourne. It was the perfect beginning for an artistic young man with an acquired taste for elegance. Begun in 1883 by William and Alfred George, the store had as its motto *Quod facimus valde facimus* (What we do, we do well). Georges did everything it could to fulfil this promise. It was the first store to install lifts, and it had a bargain basement. 'There was a ladies' lounge, an elegant Regency

Georges department store, Melbourne, where Peter got a job on leaving school.
HUDSON & HALLS: A LOVE STORY

Room café, fashion parades, wonderful window displays and ... on the top floor there was a Cyclotorium where ladies could learn to ride and buy a bicycle. Georges was a gracious and sophisticated place to shop and it became a Melbourne institution.'[46]

Peter's job there was in window dressing, interior design and soft furnishing. Georges was a snobbish store, or at least its clientele were. They were generally successful and affluent. Peter handled the accounts of some of the wealthiest people in Melbourne.

Growing up as an only child, he had watched his family, a world of adults, behaving oddly. This was the survival mechanism of the neglected child: to observe what worked to gain people's attention and what did not. As he grew older Peter added an interior monologue, his own witty thoughts, to critique the absurdities. He was intelligent; he could see the irony and the hypocrisy inherent in the actions of others, and found them humorous. When he pointed these out with what would become his characteristically dry, sometime devilishly sardonic wit, others

65

responded. He quickly recognised the power of making people laugh. This made him popular, and good with everyone, especially wealthy clients. He became one of the rising stars at Georges: a valued staff member. And he was well paid. By 19 years old he'd bought his own 'lime green Fiat 500'.[47]

Peter's relation John Corbett was never sure exactly who gave Peter the cash to go to London. He had a feeling that Biddy supplied some of the money for his ticket, but that Georges might also have contributed.[48] In any case, in the early 1950s Peter left his job and headed for the UK.

Britain was still emerging from the deprivations of war and rationing, but even dreary London of the 1950s made Melbourne look provincial. Peter was swept away by the sophistication of Savile Row and Jermyn Street, the centre of men's upmarket tailoring. Away from Australia, he felt he could recreate himself. He had no past, just a future. But the euphoria didn't last. He soon found that his shop worker's wages did not keep him in the way he wanted. Mary Ethel's empire, even in its second iteration under Biddy, generated an affluence that was impossible to recreate in London on a shop wage. He loved the city, but it was a tough place without influence or connection, and life there would always be a compromise. When the buzz, the nightlife and the shopping began to lose sway to the difficulties and the cost of living, he took the boat home.

The sea voyage back to Melbourne may have provided him with the idea of finding work with the P&O shipping company. Long sea journeys suited single men with few family ties, and numbered among them were numerous homosexuals. For example, 'the stewards' quarters on the *Rangitane*, which travelled between the Antipodes and Britain' – and on which David Halls travelled to New Zealand – 'and the *Wanganella* and *Monowai* between Auckland and Sydney [were] venues for many a queer party during the middle decades of the [twentieth] century'.[49] This homosexual subculture of the sea spilled over onto the waterfront and streets surrounding the wharves.

Peter knew he was homosexual from a young age. His early experimentation very likely happened at school, but as a young man he would certainly have gone in search of liaisons that satisfied his need to connect. Psychologically and sexually he was driven to bond with other men, and his employment at Georges and with the P&O line guaranteed he would meet other homosexual men.

But Melbourne was no Mecca for men who loved men. Staunchly staid and provincial compared to London, Paris and Berlin, it exhibited an unrelentingly parochial attitude to homosexuality. The introduction of six o' clock closing, in 1916, was the kiss of death for city nightlife. The only positive for homosexual men was that the police and the courts were not aggressively hunting them down. This was no small thing, as the penalty for 'acts of sodomy, attempted sodomy' or 'indecent assault upon a male person' could be as great as 10 years in prison with hard labour.[50]

A more benign attitude to homosexuality in the inter-war years was replaced in the 1950s and 60s by an aggressively punitive approach. Homosexuals were tricked and trapped by zealous vice squads who used '"pretty police" as *agents provocateurs* to lure homosexual men' as well as 'using beats and drill holes in the walls of flats to gather evidence'.[51] Life as a gay man in Melbourne was unavoidably clandestine. There was simply no choice. All legitimacy was denied, and those looking for same-sex liaisons were forced underground.

There were a number of covert places for men to meet, including the Fitzroy, Carlton and Flagstaff Gardens and, south of the Yarra River, the Alexandra, Botanic and Snowden Gardens.[52] But men also met men in public bars and cafés; hotels and boarding houses; in parks and public toilets; in railway and bus stations; and in taxis and cars: almost anywhere a legitimate encounter could lead to an illicit liaison. Others connected through church organisations, universities, theatre groups, clubs, and business and social organisations.

The first detectable dawning light of liberation did not come from a political movement, but from the proliferation of a new kind of urban dwelling. 'Flats allowed middle-class homosexuals the opportunity to move out of family homes and boarding houses and establish private lives for themselves; to entertain friends and lovers without having to explain themselves to landladies or parents and without the fear of their movements and visitors being noted by suspicious third parties.'[53] The world of flatting and flatmates and their wider circle of friends opened up new possibilities for parties and get-togethers.

Peter flatted in Melbourne but his great passion was to travel. His job as a shipping agent immersed him in the domain of grand tours and luxury liners. But it wasn't just the urge to travel that fed his desire to move. It was also his need to shift away from the familiar and from those familiar to him. Writing about homosexual men in self-imposed exile, William J. Mann describes 'square pegs born into families of round holes, yearning from a very young age to escape their communities of origin, often rejecting career paths chosen by their parents and leaving home to redefine themselves elsewhere'.[54]

To be transported was also to be transformed. Without the strictures of the past, with its set routines and soured attitudes, a life could be re-made. By 1962 Peter, now in his third decade, felt the yearning for movement once more. He had lived in

Peter Hudson and possibly Biddy, c. 1960. HUDSON & HALLS: A LOVE STORY

London and this had proved to be prohibitively expensive. Back in Melbourne he had a comfortable job with career prospects in the shipping office, but this was not enough. If anything, he was longing for a development in his personal life. So, he remembers, he decided 'to have a look at New Zealand'.[55] It was a chance to get away from home to encounter something new.

*

Homosexuality was as shunned in New Zealand as it was in Australia. It had troubled lawmakers since the earliest days of colonial settlement. Coastal whaling colonies, the remote shantytowns of gold prospectors and coal miners, forestry encampments, stockmen's huts and labourers' and road-workers' cottages: all were regarded as seething sites of sin and debauchery. Fuelled by alcohol distilled by distance and isolation, these frontiers of homosocial encampment were seen by colonial administrators to be in moral peril. The arrival of boatloads of single women from the UK in the mid-nineteenth century redressed some of the gender imbalance but did not stop sodomy. Legal intervention was deemed a necessary next step.

In 1867 the law relating to the Offences Against the Person Act surpassed the parameters of its English origins by setting a punishment of between 10 years and life for 'buggery'. This was legal jargon for a collection of offences that included bestiality. Laws relating to homosexuality were further augmented in 1893, when more specific detail was added. Prior to this only two sexual acts could result in incarceration: forcible assault and sodomy. Lawmakers now stepped into men's bedrooms, into boarding houses, and into private, public, surreptitious and salacious spaces to spell out exactly what was permitted. All homosexual activity was now defined as an assault against the person whether it was consensual or not.

Oscar Wilde's trial in London in 1903 stirred New Zealand media into a frenzy of outrage. Writer of gay history Chris Brickell sees the impact of the trial as substantial. 'The Wilde scandal became well known here. The local newspaper coverage … which included the *New Zealand Herald, Auckland Star, New Zealand Times* and various other newspapers denounced the "vile", "bestial" and "unprintable" practices Wilde was said to have engaged in with male prostitutes.'[56] But as well as being salutary, Wilde's story was a signalling. Worldwide coverage made it a watershed in the dissemination of ideas about homosexuality. For some men and women, it was enough that they had a name; for others it now became a topic open for conversation and a cause for affirmation.

If religious dogma enshrined by law and enforced by punishments such as hard labour, flogging and incarceration dominated the nineteenth century, then doctors in white coats with their psychoanalysis, electroconvulsive therapy and aversion therapy dominated the twentieth century.[57] While this new brutality seemed benign, its reach was far more pervasive. Suddenly, as well as what happened in the bedroom, what happened in the mind could be regarded as sick. Homoerotic thoughts and passionate friendships could no longer claim their platonic innocence, but became symptoms of a bigger medical problem. In 1952 homosexuality was officially classified as a psychiatric illness in the internationally disseminated and respected *Diagnostic and Statistical Manual of Mental Disorders*. The doctor was now the publicly sanctioned replacement for the jailer.[58]

But not completely, because convictions and imprisonment continued with more malicious intent as police entrapment became an accepted practice. Known offenders and sites of same-sex encounters became the target of deliberate stings as homosexual men were set up by police decoys to break the law. On one hand, there was an effort to find a 'cure' for homosexuality; on the other, there was an increasingly systematic and draconian approach to identifying and punishing offenders. Even this was not enough for the zealots. In parliament, Justice Minister John Finlay had despaired of anyone finding a cure for homosexuality. 'The miserable sexual pervert has no more chance of being reformed than the greatest lunatic has of being cured of his aberration,' he said in 1910. His solution was to lock them away in a 'criminal asylum'.[59]

This vitriol would resurface in the mid-1950s, when evidence of sickness and laxity in New Zealand's postwar society, and particularly among a new kind of teenager, was documented in the Report of the Special Committee on Moral Delinquency in Children and Adolescents (the Mazengarb Report) of 1954. Sex gangs who roamed the streets of Petone and the Hutt Valley, according to the report, were conducting orgies in private homes while parents were away. Delinquent homosexual activity was a plague fostered by popular culture: music, films and pulp fiction.[60] This relationship of cause and effect was explored comprehensively in American psychiatrist Frederic Wertham's tirade against comics, entitled 'Seduction of the Innocent', also published in 1954. Comic super-heroes were not super-heroes at all but flying members of a seditious sexual subcult. Batman and Robin were a homosexual duo. The vase of flowers, the particular way they fussed over details of housekeeping, were give-aways. The other super-subversive passing as a normal citizen was Wonder Woman, whose day job was being a lesbian. You could tell this by her strength of character and unfeminine ambition to save the world.

If Justice Minister John Finlay was a lone voice in the desert, then more than three decades later Mazengarb and Wertham were his self-righteous chorus, and their case would be proven that very year by a same-sex teenage crush that ended in the ultimate depravity, murder. The relationship was immediately labelled lesbian and linked to evil, reinforcing the idea that not just sexual but social contact could be suspect.

On 22 June 1954, 16-year-old Pauline Parker and her friend Juliet Hulme, 15, took Pauline's mother up to Victoria Park on Christchurch's Port Hills and beat her to death with a brick in a stocking. The girls believed that Honorah Parker was the only obstacle to their leaving the country together to pursue writing and filmmaking careers. Juliet's English-born parents were planning to divorce and return home to the UK. Juliet was to be left with an aunt in South Africa. To prevent this separation, Pauline hatched a plot to murder her mother, who had become increasingly disturbed by the intensity of the girls' relationship.

If Oscar Wilde's trial had been a watershed for homosexual men, then the Parker–Hulme murder had the same impact for women. The girls' trial was reported worldwide, disseminating ideas about lesbianism that had not been discussed in public before. Queen Victoria's blind-spot towards lesbians had made them legally and to a large extent socially invisible, but the outrage generated by the Parker–

Hulme trial turned the inquisitorial spotlight on all women's relationships. In the outpouring of contempt for the girls, the connection was made between romantic, passionate, intense and even platonic female relationships and murder. For years after Pauline Parker and Juliet Hulme were released from prison, newspapers, magazines and books continued to feature the case as one with a cautionary link to homosexuality.[61]

*

The particular purpose of Peter Hudson's trip to Auckland in 1962 was to catch up with his friend Noel Combine, a steward for the P&O line. Peter flew over from Melbourne and Noel drove out to Auckland airport to pick him up. When they arrived at Noel's home in St Stephens Avenue the place was in darkness. But as soon as they walked into the lounge there was a flood of lights, and the crowd who had been hiding in the darkness leapt out from behind furniture and curtains, and out of doorways, and shouted, 'HOORAY!' 'HELLO!' at the tops of their voices. Peter was surprised and delighted. According to Noel Combine, his smile went from ear to ear.[62]

Moments later Peter looked across the room and saw David, 26 years old, with his blaze of golden hair and dazzling smile, standing at the mantelpiece. It was a life-changing moment of mutual attraction. Peter – tall, slender and dark haired with a Roman nose – was 31. The chemistry between them was instant and exclusive. For them, amid a crowd of people, there was no one else in the room. Even as an onlooker, Noel Combine saw the power of that first meeting and, with hindsight, its significance. From that point on Peter and David were in each other's thrall.

'David's and my back doors were opposite each other and I didn't see much of Peter for the rest of the three weeks. The nights were David and Peter's,' Noel remembers. This new passion so inhaled the oxygen of their days together they could barely breathe, and in an instant their time together was gone. 'It could have been a three-week fling [but it seemed] they'd fallen madly in love.'[63] When it was time for Peter to go back to Melbourne, it was David, not Noel, who took him to the airport. They continued writing to each other, and Peter made it clear that he planned to come back to New Zealand.

Frosted Cheese Mould

SERVES 6–8

This can either be used as a first course or, with the addition of frosted grapes, melon balls and orange segments, served instead of the traditional cheese and fruit course after a meal. It also makes a satisfying light lunch.

1 cup milk
1½ tablespoons gelatine
700 grams cottage cheese
1 wedge Blue Vein cheese, crumbled
2 tablespoons lime juice
½ cup salted cashew nuts, toasted and
   broken
6 drops green food colouring
1 cup cream, whipped

Pour milk into a large saucepan, sprinkle gelatine over and allow to soften. Place over low heat and stir until gelatine has dissolved. Remove from heat and let cool.

Beat cottage and Blue Vein cheeses together until well blended, stir into gelatine mixture. Add lime juice, nuts and food colouring, mix well. Fold in whipped cream.

Turn into a lightly oiled six cup ring mould and chill for four to six hours. Unmould on to a serving dish. Fill centre with melon balls, orange segments, frosted grapes, and some sprigs of mint.

***To frost grapes, lightly beat some egg whites, brush on to grapes and dust with sugar. Lay on waxed paper and leave to dry.

4. Shoes, Ships & Stonewall: 1962–70

Peter and David arrived: two terrifying peacocks in a blaze of uncompromising colour.

'I met them in Peter Jenkins' law office,' remembers Michael Williams, 'in what used to be the AMP building on the corner of Queen and Victoria Street East in Auckland.' It was 1963, and Williams was working as a clerk while completing the third year of his law degree. Peter Jenkins had what many considered to be 'the best one-man practice in the country'. His reputation for generosity and for having a somewhat outrageous character, as well as his consummate professionalism, attracted big-name clients. These included the bandsman Harry Miller and other high-profile entertainers and notable personalities.

When David and Peter arrived in Jenkins' office, exotic and unedited, alarm bells sounded. Michael Williams had been given several pieces of legal work to do for them and now he was properly disturbed. They had asked him over for drinks. 'As a 19-year-old fairly uncompromising heterosexual male and boxing for the university … I remember being extremely diffident about it,' he recalls. So he went to his boss and explained: '"Look, I'm a bit dodgy about these two."' Because, he remembers, 'The word gay wasn't even used in Auckland in those days. It was "homosexual" or "poofs", and these two were "poofs" on any red-blooded scale of reckoning.'

The benign Peter Jenkins, who obviously wanted to facilitate this introduction, offered a solution. '"Don't worry about those guys. It's on my way home. Why don't you come with me one night after work and we'll both drop in together and have a drink." … Sounds so twee what happened now,' Michael admits, 'but we became good friends.'[1]

*

When Peter Hudson had first arrived back in New Zealand he stayed in David's flat in St Stephens Avenue. Then they bought a cottage together at 103 Brighton Road, Parnell, and quickly infused it with their flair for outdoor grandeur as well as interior design. Initially they stapled fabric to the wall instead of wallpaper to get the effect they were looking for. Their lounge was like a Matisse painting in which the rich swirling patterns of burgundy-coloured wall coverings were carried through in an identical curtain fabric so that everything merged with optical intensity. In New Zealand in the 1960s this was a daring concept. The house was 'piss elegant', recalls Murdoch McLennan, who was a frequent visitor at Brighton Road, but it was tiny. The space 'was configured in such a way that they actually lived in one room. The rest of the house functioned: kitchen, dining room and all that sort of thing … but their bedroom was tiny and they had two small separate beds in that room and that was it.'[2]

Outside, their ostentatious style continued with classical architectural forms and Greek statuary down the path to a pool – an echo of Theydon Hall with its driveway lined by classical Greek sculptures. Brighton Road was the small-scale manor house of David's dreams. The pool was their own flashy addition to make sense of a narrow back yard abutting a precipice that swept down into a gully. For years Peter and David were referred to as the 'gully girls', perched as they were on the edge of this urban chasm. After parties they would often lob empty wine and spirit bottles from the pool area into the distant pit. 'Whoever bought that section down the back … they would have to have been digging for days to get through the bottles,' Murdoch recalls. But it was 'the cutest swimming pool, I think, in all of Auckland, or that I've ever seen in Auckland. It was tiny … nobody would ever get in the pool because there was so much broken glass around. I think a couple of bathing beauties might have dived in but no one would ever have touched the bottom of it … because of the shards of glass.'[3]

Peter and David's cottage became a place that was transfigurative for them, and freeing from the humdrum conformity of early 1960s Auckland for others. Six o'clock pub closing was still in place. There were after-pub parties, which meant drinking could continue in clubs and private homes, but for most New Zealanders the consumption of alcohol ended with the call for 'last drinks'. Eating out was rare and reserved for the weekends. 'There were few restaurants apart from hotel dining rooms,' writes Richard Matthews, a friend of Peter and David's. 'The latter served nursery food, mostly mushroom soup, a little bit of fish and roast of the day … Later came the period of deep fried, crumbed, frozen scallops immersed in hot fat.

If shaken, you could hear the shrunken scallop rattling in its case. This delicacy was usually followed by trifle or ice-cream sundae with a pink wafer on top. Other dining experiences were fish and chip shops and pie carts where you could dine on a pie with khaki peas and mashed potatoes.'[4]

Brighton Road was the perfect place to entertain, and Peter and David had the culinary flair to pull it off. The occasion began for most people with drinks, but if you became a friend the parties could get larger and more elaborate. Michael Williams remembers: 'We did a lot of socialising and they were wonderful hosts, of course, and you'd kill not just for their cooking but for their wonderful company. They were bloody funny and interesting guys.'[5] Thanks to their hospitality, guests forgot the drudgery of their day jobs and were transformed. Brighton Road was transgressive, and just being there helped party-goers loosen up, especially when revelries were mixed with large amounts of alcohol. In this atmosphere of tolerance, Peter and David's sexuality became to a large extent irrelevant. They didn't discuss it; they didn't make an issue of it. 'That's what made their house so, you know, vibrant,' recalls Murdoch McLennan. 'You'd start off the evening and things would be all posh as anything: "Oh darling, lovely to see you." This was all done with rather plummy voices, followed by air kisses. "Kiss. Kiss. Kiss." Then two hours into it and you'd swear there were 60 people in [the room].' Some events ended in near riot. 'These sophisticated people, they knew it was so naughty. [Peter and David's] lawyers were very highly respected people outside, but you'd go around there and … Peter Jenkins … [and his colleagues], frightfully Remuera until they were with Peter and David.'[6]

But the heavy drinking that went with these evenings of food and entertainment created stresses between David and Peter that occasionally ended in fights. After Michael and his wife Kate moved into a flat around the corner, they were among a number of friends who sometimes found themselves lending a sympathetic ear to one or other of them. 'I can remember occasionally they … had a tiff and they'd come down on the Saturday morning and sit on the end of our bed and we'd do a bit of an arbitration. One would say, "This cunt did this or that last night and I'm really pissed off about it …"'[7]

Possessiveness was the cause of many of their rows. They were territorial and protective when one of them appeared to wander. There were many temptations among the attractive young crowd of people, both straight and gay, that they invited into their home. Flirtation became a frequent cause of conflict between them. 'Johnny Ray the singer was in town,' recalls Michael Williams. 'He was an American singer … and gay, and he used to cry all the time … when he was singing. Anyway, through the network, Johnny Ray had been given the contact [details] of Peter and David in Auckland and there was a bit of a party there one night … There was a very attractive man in the Johnny Ray entourage that David had been flirting with a bit … and I'll never forget … [Peter was annoyed and grumbling] and the following day David was pretty sort of casual about the whole thing and finally he … utters the immortal line: "I don't know what he's bitching about. He turned out to be a closet heterosexual."[8]

But attraction and envy went both ways. Sometimes it was Peter causing difficulties. 'They were fiendishly jealous of one another,' remembers Murdoch McLennan. 'Peter would fall madly in love with somebody, but as far as I know nothing took place. There [was this Kiwi] guy living in England called John Fields who … was one of their very, very closest friends. Wonderful guy … And I know that especially Peter was madly in love with him, but I'm positive nothing went on. No hanky-panky.' There were other close friends as well, like Richard Lewisham of the Lewisham food awards (which celebrated excellence particularly in fine dining in Auckland), who was 'constantly there at their place'. He was 'very smart-looking and a really nice person as well'.[9]

*

Peter and David saw their home as a stage set for the fun, laughter and the fury that not infrequently erupted between them. It was important, therefore, that Brighton Road be exactly the way they intended it to be. So when some interior decor didn't turn out the way they wanted, they refused to pay. The case then went to court. 'God, you can imagine they were in a royal bloody tizz about giving evidence,' recalls Michael Williams, who was now a qualified lawyer and representing them. 'The pre-match hosing down I had to give them to make sure we didn't have a drama queen performance in the witness box was a considerable piece of work … I remember it was about Sanderson's wallpaper and they had been promised it would be Sanderson's and it wasn't.' As it turned out, David proved a model witness and they ended up winning their case. 'He controlled himself, behaved himself, and did everything according to the book.'[10]

In some respects this was not completely surprising. Although he was capable of spectacular hissy fits and could be carried away by the drama of a situation, David was also single-minded and driven. He had worked under pressure in his job and survived difficult moments under the spotlight of scrutiny since he'd arrived in New Zealand in 1959.

In the late 1950s and early 1960s the shoe industry was changing. The era of austerity was passing, and the baby boomers were gestating or on their way to adulthood. For women, sensible wartime shoes made way for the stiletto of gender- polarising peace. Shoe design now shackled women in an ultra-feminine look. The agenda was to get middle-class females out of the workplace, into the marital bed, then the kitchen, and out to cocktail parties as glamorous escorts to their breadwinner-husbands. The savagely fashionable shoe was in concept not unlike Japanese foot binding. But this was just one side of the polarity. Historian and commentator Robert Corber has described this period as a 'post-war crisis of masculinity', which led to a period of 'stark male–female behavior in the 1950s … [when] life as a consumer-driven, breadwinning suburban husband and father replaced the independent entrepreneur'. The choices were even less rewarding for women, 'who could either be happy homemakers or dried-up old maids – or the evil, twisted dykes of [the 1950 movie] *Caged*'.[11]

The slim, sleek, low-backed stiletto shoes that David designed were very much in keeping with the leading fashions of the time. The difference was that David and his boss at Clarke & Coventry designed shoes for the New Zealand woman's foot. Lois Neunz remembers the firm's salesmen would come back from the country towns and 'would chew our ears a bit because none of the [imported] shoes would fit their clients' feet'. David expanded the lasts and made shoes that were bigger and broader, yet still fashionable. He would draw the shoe from the sides, then by looking down on it from above. 'They would shape up the top line, and how high they wanted it to come on the foot, and what sort of heel they wanted and how high.'

New Zealand designers were limited by what could be made in local factories. Clarke & Coventry had three main designs. Lois remembers: 'The Suzettes were the highest ones and then there was the Pappagallo, which [had] a small elegant heel, and … another casual range … a soft elegant brogue.' The Pappagallo was modelled on an Italian shoe, and the Suzette was the most popular. 'The shoes were pointy and cut quite high because the top line shouldn't show the crevice between the front and second toe.'[12]

The advantage for Clarke & Coventry was that when David designed shoes he understood the process from inception to manufacture and sales. After an initial stint with Clarke & Coventry, he then worked for the shoe manufacturer Trenwith Brothers, ultimately returning to his previous employer on more favourable terms and remaining there until 1971.

David's job as a designer and sales representative meant he moved around the country facilitating fashion events. Carleen Spencer's first vivid memory of David is of working with him at Kirkcaldie & Stains on Lambton Quay in Wellington. This was New Zealand's marked-down equivalent of Harrods in London and Saks Fifth Avenue, New York. Its stock was exclusive, its staff imperious and the clientele frequently well-to-do because it was Wellington's most upmarket department store. 'Kirkcaldie & Stains [was] my favourite, favourite store,' recalls Carleen, and David's company had scored an exclusive showing.

Carleen, who was 23 or 24 years old and already a close friend of David's, was modelling the shoes as a special favour for him. She had begun her working life as a 'telegram delivery girl on a bicycle' in Auckland, but now had regular work with a modelling agency. She was big-eyed, elegantly proportioned and beautiful, and her personality made a lasting impression because of its rare combination of genuine warmth and glamour. Carleen and David had fun setting up the display: they always did. On this occasion, Carleen recalls, 'We [were getting] all the shoes lined up and all of a sudden, [when] we were halfway through, David says, "Well, thank you very much ladies and gentlemen that'll be all for now," and I said, "What are you talking about, we've got all these other shoes to do," and he said, "Nah, let's go to lunch!"'

Carleen was one of a number of women who had very close, life-long relationships with Peter and David. She remembers their meeting as something special: '[It was one of those] times in your life when you meet people that you are totally comfortable to say anything you want to say to them and they will say anything they want to say to you. If they're angry they'll tell you and if you're angry you'll tell them. But all through everything it was very caring. Peter was already in the picture, working for a shipping company … They were my little escape to. I would run around to their little house in Parnell, it was so cute. I got married in 1958 [then separated a decade later], and then left New Zealand [for London] in about 1969.'[13] But through letters, phone calls and visits, the close friendship with Peter and David remained.

When David was away on his frequent business trips, Peter felt utterly alone. But it wasn't just work that divided them. The rows were ongoing skirmishes in a war of domination. Both men were strong willed, and they both wanted to lead. Quite often Peter was annoyed by David's over-the-top reactions and arrogant public outbursts, especially in restaurants. David had the greater class consciousness. Peter on the other hand was more egalitarian; his view was that unless an atrocity had been committed the more stylish thing was not to make a fuss.

The eruptions between them weren't always alcohol driven but just points of incompatibility that rubbed, and they continued to share these flare-ups with any of their friends who would listen. 'The things they would say about each other, and especially if you were with one of them by yourself!' remembers Murdoch McLennan. 'They would be, "Oh he's this and he's that and it's all over between us, it's definitely all over."' Then, if they had one of their rows, or if David was away on business, there would be Peter sitting by himself in the front of Caballe, one of the gastronomically interesting restaurants in Auckland, with an entire bottle of expensive red wine and eating something amazing: 'They were very famous for doing things with tripe and liver.'[14] The meal and the wine were comfort food to console him in David's absence.

Peter was witty and acerbic at times, and had a fiery temper. As friend Ross Palmer recalls, 'You lit the blue paper and stood clear.'[15] Occasionally he could be cruel, but this was usually just in the moment to show off: whatever venom was released was soon gone.

Peter came from an idiosyncratic kind of privilege and didn't have David's urge to get ahead in his employment, but he loved style and spending money. His job as P&O's PAPR (Personal Assistant, Public Relations) was important to him not just because it maintained their lavish way of life, but because he was fastidious about detail. He was particular about the way he looked at work and about the service he delivered to customers. Ross Palmer recalls: 'I met him … because my grandfather [who was a naval commodore] and all his friends travelled a lot and Peter was that gracious hospitality man who looked after people … He had the most wonderful

Peter and David's lifelong friend Carleen Spencer, who began her working life as a 'telegram delivery girl on a bicycle' in Auckland, and quickly gained regular work with a modelling agency. At 23 or 24 years old Carleen Spencer was modelling shoes for David at upmarket stores such as Kirkcaldie & Stains in Wellington. HUDSON & HALLS: A LOVE STORY

speaking voice and he could have been English, but he had a Melburnian speaking voice.' He had 'enormous style' in his dealings with people. 'You can imagine with the older couples ... he was just wonderful with them.'[16]

His endless efficiency may have been the thing that made him move on. When he finally got sick of satisfying every whim of a stream of privileged passengers, he left shipping in the mid-1960s to run a tiny art supplies shop selling John Papas-style paintings in Parnell. Originally a butcher's shop, its floor was covered in black and white tiles and it still had the butcher's rail running around the front window. Parnell was a very different place in the 1960s. Before its gentrification, the now upmarket shopping and dining district was a sleepy residential suburb of rundown houses with an occasional store dotted among them. Peter's art supplies business did not flourish. Towards the end he was not even managing to pay the rent, which was £4 a week. So when an offer was made to purchase the shop, Peter was eager to sell. 'For the fixtures and fittings, I think I paid them £10,' remembers John Mains, 'which was not a lot even in those days.'[17] Peter and David struggled financially, and it was some time before they recovered. Ultimately, the pair would formulate a new plan – for something much bigger and better for both of them.

*

New Zealand was a strangely divided place in the 1950s and 1960s, and Peter and David were oblivious buckers of the trend. While the United Kingdom still separated itself by class, and the United States over the schisms of race and colour, New Zealand polarised the sexes. Robert Corber's 'post-war crisis of masculinity' was probably most poignantly felt on the rugby field, in the public house and in the rural back paddocks of the macho New Zealand. In 1956 a visiting German professor said in an interview that he thought there was more homosexuality in New Zealand than in his own country, and according to historian Chris Brickell he attributed this to segregation of the sexes. 'Nowhere in his travels had he found such segregation. So much of our New Zealand culture is exclusively male; this is particularly illustrated in our drinking habits and sport. The concept of the "man's man" had its most extreme development in this country.'[18]

To a large extent the sexes in New Zealand had been divided from the earliest days of colonisation and European settlement. This divide, which became entrenched, gave homosexual men like Peter and David the perfect opportunity to pass as bachelor-males who banded together as a matter of economic expediency. But they were not interested in the practice of homosocial segregation. They found their friends among straight, single, married or homosexual men and women without distinction. What mattered was simply that you were friends.

There was an active homosexual subculture in New Zealand, but this was not Peter and David's exclusive or even probably first choice for socialising. In Auckland, you could meet like-minded men and women at the Ca d'Oro in Custom Street, 'the Shakespeare, on the corner of Albert and Wyndham streets … the Star, on the corner of Albert and Wolfe streets, and the Occidental in Vulcan Lane'. Many of these places had a public front door but also a private entrance. 'The underworld right down to the clubs were hidden underneath buildings with little windows that opened up to make sure you weren't the police … at six o'clock the city just died. It was rather beautiful. There was a calm in the evening … apart from the gay pubs and clubs.'[19]

This secret world was strictly underground because the stigma attached to homosexuality was more firmly established now there was language around it and a label attached. The post-World War Two medicalisation of homosexuality meant a range of destructive 'treatments' became commonplace, and the pressure to try them intense. Sometimes they were adopted as a result of self-loathing and personal choice and other times they were the 'compassionate' option offered by authorities instead of a fine or imprisonment. The sleep-inducing drug Pentothal and shock treatment were both used, along with aversion therapy, during which the patient was shown repulsive images and made to feel nauseous while having homoerotic thoughts. The outcome of this Pavlovian strategy was to establish a strong link between homosexual thoughts and physical revulsion. Arrests also increased for 'cottaging', a coded term used by gay men, especially in the UK, to describe anonymous sexual encounters with other men in public toilets.

While the persecution of same-sex love continued with more persistence than ever, Peter and David navigated their silent way through this minefield of consequence and punishment. They lived together but said nothing, and there was no affectionate contact between them in public. 'I never observed any physical intimacy – any sort of a pat on the back, or a peck on the cheek, or anything like that,' remembers Murdoch McLennan.[20] But no one who visited them at home could have doubted the fact that they were lovers.

Peter and David were used to the relative tolerance of their social circle, so it would have been a shock when the murder of Charles Aberhart hit the headlines in New Zealand in 1964. Aberhart, a drapery store manager from Blenheim, had travelled down to Christchurch to holiday with a friend. He had recently been jailed for three months for an act of sexual 'assault' involving a willing male partner. This meant he had a criminal record and was on a police register of offenders. The evenings were long and hot, and it was the height of a sizzling summer. Soon after arriving in Christchurch on 23 January, Aberhart drove along Armagh Street to the entrance of the expansive Hagley Park. He went into the grounds and visited the men's toilets near Little Lake Victoria – a well-known cottaging site.

On that same evening, a band of six bored and ill-intentioned 15- to 17-year-olds left their homes determined to beat up a homosexual. One of the youngest of the group was bait. He approached several men before he got into conversation with Charles Aberhart, who made it clear that he was interested in sexual connection. The situation immediately escalated with the arrival of the rest of the gang. Aberhart was suddenly surrounded. He tried to mollify the mob by offering to buy them a cup of coffee. When this attempt to defuse the situation failed, he called for help from a man walking a dog. This man, who was later a witness in court, walked past the fracas without offering any assistance. He believed Aberhart was up to no good in the toilets and could look after himself.

Only a couple of the teenagers were directly involved in the beating, but Charles Aberhart died at the scene. When the case came to trial on 5 May 1964, it was evident from Aberhart's injuries that he had been restrained and beaten. According to the autopsy report, he had bruises to the face, a broken nose and a small fracture at the base of the skull. The issue that allowed 'reasonable' or 'unreasonable' doubt to enter the equation, depending on the side taken, was that there was a medical complication. Charles Aberhart was born with an unusually thin skull around the eye sockets, and blows that might not have been fatal to someone else were sufficient to kill him. He died of a massive brain haemorrhage.

An all-male jury found the six youths not guilty of manslaughter and they were released without conviction. This was exactly 10 years after the Parker–Hulme murder, but unlike in that case, there was no cautionary note sounded for young people here. The perpetrators' youth was rightfully taken into consideration, but the underlying message was that you could go out intentionally looking to beat up a homosexual man, and if you inadvertently killed him you could walk free.

This should have been a disturbing subtext, but few voices were raised in consternation. One of those who did speak out was journalist Monte Holcroft, writing for the *New Zealand Listener*. His point was that 'an alleged homosexuality has been felt to be an offence which mitigates a crime. And the crime itself came out of an unhealthy concern about sexual deviation.'[21] A precedent had been set. Not only did medical practitioners and police have a right to take 'an unhealthy concern about sexual deviation', but the civic population were permitted to do so as well.

In this context, it is not surprising that young gay men and women began to become politicised. The term 'gay', which had been used in relation to homosexual men for nearly a hundred years in the US, began to be used more widely, joining 'drag queen', 'queer', 'camp' and 'bull dyke' (also not new words) as part of the language of liberation. Words like 'homophobic' were accepted as describing the ill-treatment of homosexual men and women, and used to identify prejudice and discrimination. Expressions such as 'in the closet', 'coming out' and 'straight as opposed to gay' became more commonly used.[22] Language facilitated the politicisation that would ultimately result in action, first in the US.

*

The Stonewall Inn on Christopher Street in Greenwich Village, New York, catered for some of the most marginalised members of the gay community. On the evening of 28 June 1969, after an early-morning raid of the inn by the New York Police Department, its patrons decided to resist police harassment and brutality by demonstrating. For four nights gay men and adolescents confronted the police in an attempt to stand their ground and stop the routine raiding and closing down of gay clubs. During the ferment, the front line of the crowd formed 'a Rockettes-style kickline that blended defiance with camp humour. "We are the Stonewall girls / We wear our hair in curls / We wear no underwear / We show our pubic hair", they sang.[23] Police lines were broken in places by the sheer number of men responding to this call for mass civil disobedience. When the turmoil calmed down, the world had changed.

A group of gay men had asserted their strength against the authorities. 'Stonewall', as the incident came to be known, was a victory because it demonstrated the tremendous power minority groups could exert if they acted together. Theirs was the cohesion of an angry mob who had been persecuted to the point where they felt they had nothing left to lose. The force of feeling and the numbers were there: the next step was to channel this power politically.

The pre-conditions for organised protest were of course already in existence. In 1966 the New York Mattachine (a gay society established in 1950) organised a 'sip-in' at Julius, another gay bar in Greenwich Village. That year, too, there was a riot at Crompton's Cafeteria in San Francisco when a police sting to arrest drag queens and transvestites incited violent retaliation. In 1967, after a raid on the Black

Cat nightclub in Los Angeles, more than two hundred people stood up to police in protest against the systematic persecution of gay people and clubs. Stonewall marked the end of these isolated gestures and skirmishes. 'Within months … radical gay liberation groups and newsletters sprang up in cities and on college campuses across America and then across all of northern Europe as well, and ultimately around the world.'[24]

Stonewall connected and politicised gay men. Lesbians, bi-sexual and transgender women soon joined them to create a confluence of energy fired by both the gay liberation and women's liberation movements. A small flame tossed in parched grass was now a furnace. The heat and the momentum were unstoppable.

For many young gay people the battle lines were set, and society had to change. But revolt was felt much more widely, and touched on many more aspects of society than just same-sex relationships. In their introduction to *You Say You Want a Revolution? Records and Rebels 1966–1970*, Victoria Broakes and Geoffrey Marsh write:

> *In the United Kingdom in 1965 society was in many ways unrecognisable. Homosexuality was illegal; police entrapment was common; abortion was illegal; you could be hanged for murder; a woman had to be married to get the pill; divorce was uncommon and rarely granted; racial discrimination was commonplace; women could be paid less than men for the same work; theatre performances were subject to official censorship … yet by 1970 much of this had changed in most Western countries.*[25]

Systemic change was needed. It was about the right to self-determination of the individual. For the generation of young people who were driving the rebellion, the state and its structured forms of outmoded morality were seen as an unwelcome intervention in people's lives. Student riots all over the world, and especially in France in 1968, called for a social and political revolution. Value judgements were questioned and power structures overturned. The struggle for women's rights, black civil rights and gay liberation overlapped on one unifying agenda item – the need to revolutionise the world. 'By the end of the decade, so-called "second wave feminists" had moved from challenging the straitjacket of wifely domesticity to questioning the entire patriarchal order.'[26] Things were evolving rapidly and every 'establishment' value was under scrutiny.

The conflict in Vietnam was another contentious issue that galvanised communities worldwide. Anti-war protesters came especially from increasingly affluent student groups and their university campuses, but people from all walks of life could become activists for peace. Pacifist militants merged with psychedelic hippie counter-culture groups to form a collective resistance. In San Francisco in 1967, 'tens of thousands … gathered in Golden Gate Park for what they called a "Human-Be-In" where they listened to Timothy Leary exhort them to *"Turn on! Tune in! Drop out!"*'.[27] This was a call to be wild: to take drugs, resist convention and defy the Establishment. The use of recreational drugs set the younger generation apart, particularly from their parents and from the authorities.[28] Marijuana was illegal in both Britain and the US in the 1960s, yet lysergic acid diethylamide (LSD) was not regulated until 1966. This strong psychedelic drug was the untamed horse used by baby boomers to buck the system. Some drug experiences were mind-expanding while others trampled the fragile or unfortunate tripper underfoot.

Marijuana lasted longer than LSD as the recreational drug of choice: the length and intensity of an LSD trip made it unsustainable long term. Marijuana became the emblem of counter-culture and especially of hippies, who displayed their difference not only by their drug habits but also by their dress. The kaftan was synonymous with long hair and communalism. Other hippie clothing included 'vintage granny dresses, cowboy hats and boots, and American Indian-inspired beads and headbands, embossed leather accessories, embroidered jeans, fringes and feathers'.[29] Anti-war sentiments, eastern mysticism, drugs and youth culture combined to give baby boomers the sense that not only could they change the world, but one day they would own it.

*

The ferment that seethed overseas was slower to reach New Zealand. But there was already a generation of young people desperate for counter-culture connection. Perhaps the most disenfranchised groups were young gay men and women who were isolated by their upbringing and looking for a lifeline. 'Growing up gay was a lonely business,' writes commentator David Herkt. 'For every Kiwi gay child or adolescent, it was an adventure into the unknown. There were no role models or exemplars, and few explicit stories. Desires, when followed, led into uncharted territory. Words would have to be discovered – and not all of them would be pleasant. It was an unspoken and vastly coded country.'[30] By the late 1960s there was a language ready to illuminate what Herkt refers to as 'the great New Zealand dark', but it would be a few more years before these words would become the battle cry of liberation.

In New Zealand there was a vast difference between the experiences of urban gay people and those living in the provinces. Increasing urbanisation during the 1960s and 1970s meant that more and more gay men and women were living in closer proximity in the cities, and this increased consciousness and cohesiveness. Conversely, leaving the main centres was like changing countries. Richard Matthews remembers spending a night at the Gretna Hotel in Taihape. 'We checked in and were shown to our cell-like rooms upstairs with a long walk to the communal bathroom. We headed to the public bar for pre-dinner drinks. The bar was full of farming labourers in heavy checked shirts and boots. The patrons looked suspiciously at the two poncy Aucklanders and we felt distinctly out of place sipping our pink gins amongst the jugs of beer.'[31] Mainstream notions of masculinity were turgid and prescriptive, and anyone who didn't fit the pattern might as well have materialised from Mars.

Discrimination, however, was not universal, and in line with Peter and David's own experience, there were pockets of tolerance and sophistication. In certain professions and social circles, gay people, especially gay men, were accepted as part of the social world. They were often regarded as fitting escorts for married and older single women. Ross Palmer knew of 'married women who absolutely adored the gays'. He remembers: 'They were so welcoming and loved having them for dinner with their married friends … Married women were very accepting and they [would] very, very, very unobtrusively … have quite a few of us for dinner … who knew their husbands. We'd play golf with their husbands and suddenly and in no spoken words we'd all be having dinner together and it was marvellous because their husbands realised that there was another side to life apart from their boring professionalism.'[32]

Some gay adolescents grew up with parents who accepted their sexual orientation, but this was almost never openly discussed. Most gay lives were kept hidden. There might have been acknowledgement and tolerance behind the expression 'He's covered the field', but this was not what the next generation would be calling for – they wanted *visibility*.

For many of Peter and David's contemporaries, visibility was anathema. They had been conditioned by years of awkward silence or open hostility to keep quiet and to pass as much as possible as heterosexuals. This was not Peter and David's style. They were not ashamed of being gay. They belonged to a transitional generation: not one of veterans of war or baby boomers, but one containing elements of both. They had what social commentator Barry Miles describes as 'a new flamboyant personal style [that] was a reaction to the cold, war-hardened, emotionally repressed male embodied by the returning soldier. Young men were almost purposefully effeminate in their satins and frills, in their revealed vulnerability and innocence.'[33] But like the generation before them, Peter and David were not anti-Establishment. In spite of their extroverted flamboyance, they would not talk about being gay or discuss sexual matters in public. They were also smart enough to realise that being politically rather than privately gay might hinder their progress in parochial New Zealand. Instinctively, they adopted the 'don't ask, don't tell' approach and continued being outrageously gay without talking about it.

One of the great and perhaps most humorous gestures Peter and David made at the beginning of the 1970s was for Jan Cormack, another of their close female friends. They had met Jan and her husband Gavin, or Gabby, when the couple were living around the corner in St Stephens Avenue. Jan remembers that after she had given birth to her first child, Danielle, 'Gabby brought me home, and down the driveway [David and Peter] were sitting there with a candelabra with all the candles lit up … They had it all there … set up for dinner out on the lawn to welcome home the new baby.' David and Peter later became godparents to Jan and Gabby's second child. 'When Jamie was born [in 1973],' says Jan, 'I phoned from the theatre and told them, "You've got a lovely bouncy baby boy." So they came into National Women's the next day, once again with a candelabra, the champagne, the caviar, the tablecloth, and everything, and we had a lovely time until I managed to throw up.'[34]

Peter and David loved having a godchild and they participated actively in Jamie's life. Things got off to a rather rough start when Jamie vomited all over David's best suit in the middle of his christening, but they took real pleasure in watching their young godson and his sister grow up. When Jamie was at school at Little King's, a teacher asked all the children in the class to write a story about their godparents. Jamie wrote about his godfathers Hudson and Halls, by this time on television and a household name, and the disbelieving teacher tackled him about it. This couldn't possibly be true; perhaps Jamie should rewrite his story. 'So I made the mistake of telling them,' remembers Jan, and as living proof Peter and David 'went straight around to the teacher at King's and said: "Excuse me!" … They were furious.'[35]

The duo lived their life in constant motion. They moved quickly and often impetuously, and they took their right to live together and love each other without asking. And when unjustly challenged, they took no prisoners.

*

Peter and David had a fondness for filling their house with beautiful young men. Two of these, both with connections to the antiques business in Auckland, which overlapped with Peter's art supply shop and retail interests in Parnell, were partners Richard Matthews and Murdoch McLennan. Richard was the son of wealthy businessman and entrepreneur Russell Matthews and his well-to-do wife Mary. Richard was a savvy businessman himself, with a wry sense of humour and a talent for playing the piano, while Murdoch, aside from being decidedly good company, was gorgeous in a modish androgynous kind of way. 'My family never had a problem with my sexuality apart from some confusion when they first met Murdoch,' writes Richard in his memoir. 'I took him to stay [at my family home] at Tupare at his angelic best and with the long hair of the seventies he looked like a young Indian Squaw. Mary thought he was a girl at first and Russell called him "she" for several days. He was wearing an ostentatious garnet ring, the shape of half an egg, and at dinner my father, rather rudely, couldn't take his eyes off it.'[36]

During a gap year-or-so in the UK, Murdoch had worked as a fashion model. Describing a party they both attended while in London, Richard Matthews writes:

> *Inside were a gaggle of gays, all older men whose wit flew round the room like a tennis ball in a tennis match, leaving Murdoch and me looking purely attractive and very dull. Dinner was served, cooked by the Queen Mother's former cook, Jonathan, who, according to Howard, liked to dress up in women's clothes, in his own time of course. Howard was a friend of Rock Hudson and organised for me to stay with him on my way back to New Zealand, before I decided to go by ship ... Howard took us out to shows and lunches and dinners but I never felt I could equal the wit of the smart set, and we drifted apart at the end of my stay in London. We were there to be decorative bait.*[37]

Peter and David's own parties at Brighton Road, though not as 'high camp' as those frequented by the 'gaggle of gays' in London, became more ambitious and better planned. The food and drink was more elaborate, too. The dinners were now themed and much anticipated by their guests. But there was no knowing how the evening would end when David and Peter had been drinking and were in an argumentative mood. 'Look, the ingredients were always fantastic,' remembers Murdoch. 'You'd go there and the smell would be divine, but you often didn't get it, because it would erupt in this incredible fight and World War Three would start and you just didn't get the dinner.'[38] Guests often left so ravenously hungry they would end up having to go home and make a sandwich, or stop at the White Lady to buy a hamburger. 'You'd usually get the entrée and it would be smart, but that was sometimes it.'[39]

Initially there was a degree of shock and horror around the table at such public displays of animosity, but after a while friends became desensitised. 'It was very funny because … these fights would brew and … the rest of the people at the party would sort of just go on as if nothing was happening and then all of a sudden there would be this declaration and *WHAM* something would be airborne. Whether it was David's briefcase or an ornament or something.'[40] The projectile phase of the dinner party had begun. When their rage was blue, items were flung without any thought for the consequences. Richard Matthews remembers, 'The silversmith was always having to take dents out of the cream jugs and teapots.'[41]

On the cusp of the new decade, the 1970s, Peter and David decided to host an exclusive dinner party. In part it was a gesture of thanks to two wealthy factory owners who gave them piecework. 'David and Peter were often on the bones of their bums,' Murdoch remembers, and they were desperate to make money any way they could. The factory owners would provide them with boxes for assembly, and Peter and David would call on all their friends to help them out. 'We used to go around there with a bottle of wine and help them get all these packages, and they would send off the boxes and get a couple of bob and that kept them going for a while,' remembers Jan Cormack.[42]

Peter and David's box-making benefactors, Suzi Kitt and partner Trevor, arrived at the party in their Rolls Royce and were 'pretty posh', Murdoch recalls. He remembers them as 'a very, very strange couple', the man being substantially younger than the woman, though they were both attractive and made a striking pair. The theme for the evening was David's choice: it was to be a kaftan party. This was a very up-to-the-minute thing to do, as kaftans were not only all the rage in the burgeoning hippie culture but had also been appropriated as haute couture. As street styles were picked up by fashion designers and reconstituted as chic, magazines like *Vogue* and *Harper's Bazaar* published photographs of 'jet-set' hostesses staging elegant dinner parties in alluring new kaftans.

David stood at the door and handed everyone a kaftan to change into before gathering to drink cocktails. Murdoch recalls that dinner was late in coming, as usual, 'so we were completely smashed' by the time it began to arrive. Then a marijuana joint appeared. This was the new recreational drug of the privileged elite and it arrived at the party along with the Rolls Royce almost as a matter of course.

Murdoch and Richard, and David, had tentatively experimented with 'dope', but Peter had never smoked anything but tobacco and was adamant he was not about to start smoking marijuana. As the joint circulated around the table and David and the dinner guests got higher, the pressure for Peter to participate mounted. 'He basically refused,' remembers Murdoch, 'and said, "No, no, no. It's crap and I don't want anything to do with it."' But the guests, who were now both generously drunk and stoned, would not hear of him missing out. They became more and more insistent. But still Peter held firm. Smoking marijuana was something he had promised himself he would never do.

Then, 'Finally he was seduced … and he was a heavy smoker [of cigarettes] so he took a huge big swig of a joint, and he said, "I told you it was absolute crap. It's absolute nonsense," and then he … snorted back a lot more. "No effect whatsoever. None whatsoever: just a load of shit. Why are you wasting all your money?" … Then he just fell silent.'

The party, its guests doubly intoxicated by wine and dope, carried on oblivious. They giggled away at the smallest provocation and laughed and chatted until suddenly there was 'this voice at the end of the table that boomed out: "*What* have you done to me!"'

With his thunderous utterance, Peter leapt up from the table and took off, leaving the room at top speed, running through the house, out the front door and along Brighton Road. It was late at night and pitch black apart from the occasional streetlight. By chance, just as Peter began running down the middle of the road, flailing his arms in the air and screaming, Murdoch remembers, 'a bloody police car' appeared. 'So here's this … tall, elegant, very shickered man standing in the middle of Brighton Road in a kaftan, waving down a policeman.'

Panic struck the party guests when they saw through the window the police car pull up outside.

'Christ, we're going to be caught here with this thing,' Murdoch and Richard said to each other, and ran into Peter and David's tiny bedroom. There they struggled 'to get out of our kaftans so we would present as "sober upright little individuals". We leapt into a wardrobe,' Murdoch remembers, 'and we're quite largish people, so we just started giggling more … two young guys trying to get out of kaftans in one wardrobe.' The harder they struggled the more they thought about how crazy it must look, the more they laughed. Finally, they were laughing so hard they could barely move.

Peter at Carleen and Jerry's Chelsea apartment in New York, towards the end of the 1970s. CARLEEN SPENCER, PRIVATE COLLECTION

David was the only person sane enough to save the situation. Disrobed of his kaftan and dressed elegantly again, he went to the door. Peter was standing behind the policeman on the doorstep, screaming over his shoulder: '"They're all dope fiends. It's a den of iniquity!"' and the policeman was completely bemused. 'David said, "Ah, no, he'll be all right. It's fine. He's just had a little too much to drink, officer." And of course the whole place *stank* to high heaven of marijuana. The police people were just desperately trying to turn a blind eye to the whole thing, which effectively they did.'

Unfortunately Peter was so overwhelmed, the party ended there. 'Oh my God, the beautiful dinner, I don't know where it went,' says Murdoch, regretfully. But they were very fortunate. These were the early days of marijuana smoking in New Zealand, and everyone was relieved that the police hadn't searched the place and charged people with possession in order to set an example and send a message to 1970s revellers. Was it tolerance? Or the fact that the police were more interested in 'getting rid of this lunatic' than making an arrest? The guests weren't sure. 'But we did get a shock,' Murdoch admits. Peter treated drugs with enormous caution after this. As far as anyone remembers, he never touched them again.[43]

Perhaps the most ironic thing about Peter and David's brush with the law was that wearing kaftans was 'fancy dress' for them, not an expression of counter-cultural rebellion, and smoking marijuana was not a common occurrence, even for David. They belonged to an older generation of substance abusers who began drinking rum and Coke early in the day in the same way other people kicked off their morning with a cup of tea or coffee. 'I think it was Peter … who gave me the trick to stop the room from spinning,' recalls Abby Collins. 'He said, "You lie in bed and you put one foot on the ground and it stops … the world from spinning."'[44] Though Peter and David usually managed their alcohol consumption enough to function fairly effectively, their world was often spinning. Booze always had the potential to take them right over the edge.

One night at 3am a close friend of theirs, restaurateur Bob Sell, received a phone call from Peter. The garbled message was 'a dramatic goodbye. He was on his way out, he said, meaning he was going to kill himself.' The implication was that he had 'taken an overdose of pills'. Bob Sell was tempted not to take the call seriously. It was the early hours of the morning and Peter sounded so 'pie-eyed', it might be just a drunken hoax. But Bob's partner told him he would never forgive himself if he didn't go around, so, half asleep, Bob jumped into his car and drove the short distance to Peter and David's house on Brighton Road.

He was shocked by what he found. 'David was flaked out fast asleep on the bed. Peter was lying unconscious on the floor, surrounded by spilled pills and tablets and what seemed like dozens of bottles still unopened.'[45] He rang the emergency services and an ambulance was dispatched immediately. Bob and a huge sole-charge ambulance driver lifted Peter onto a stretcher and he was sped off to hospital where his stomach was pumped. 'Neither of them talked to me for the next two years,' Bob Sell recalls. 'Perhaps it was embarrassment.'[46]

Peter and David's public image remained unsullied. They knew the importance of appearances, and the image they cut in Auckland made people turn and look. They were both incredibly stylish and exorbitantly well dressed. 'David was always a sight to behold on Queen Street, you know: tall and that shock of hair; and usually a beautiful homburg hat, lovely; beautifully tailored coat; immaculate shoes.' Peter made his own splash in the style of the shipping magnate. 'Peter was always more of the blazer, reefer jacket … Very, very well … dressed, beautiful shirts. He was a very elegant man,' remembers Murdoch McLennan.[47]

But the couple were looking for a new public image. They were still folding boxes and doing piecework, but they wanted to move into the world of business as *entrepreneurs*. Neither of them was good at working for someone else. Their hot tempers and tendency to say exactly the first thing that came into their minds did not make them ideal employees. They were also imaginative and experimenters. Peter and David wanted to try things out, to have autonomy, but the micromanaging and restrictions were endless when you worked for someone else. They were bored and wanted a new challenge. Peter was keen but had no particular skills, and the only thing that David knew was shoes. So that was the beginning of Julius Garfinkel.

Rolled, Stuffed Chicken Breasts

SERVES 6

These are best made the day before so that the mushroom mixture releases its flavour into the chicken.

3 large mushrooms, chopped
3 tablespoons butter
2 tablespoons plain flour
½ cup cream
dash cayenne pepper
¼ teaspoon salt
150 grams tasty cheddar cheese, grated
6 whole chicken breasts, boned
flour for dusting
2 eggs, lightly beaten
1 cup fine breadcrumbs

Cook mushrooms in butter for five minutes. Blend in flour, and add cream. Season with cayenne and salt, stir, and cook mixture until very thick. Stir in grated cheese over low heat until melted. Chill at least one hour then divide into six equal 'sausage' shapes.

Remove skin from chicken breasts, and place boned side up between clear plastic wrap. Overlap where split, and pound with a rolling pin from the centre outwards until about a quarter inch thick.

Take out of plastic wrap, sprinkle with a little salt, and place a mushroom and cheese 'sausage' on each piece of chicken. Roll up as for Swiss roll, tucking in the ends first and sealing in the mixture completely.

Dust each roll with flour, dip in beaten eggs then in breadcrumbs, cover and chill thoroughly in fridge for at least two hours, or overnight. About an hour before serving, heat a good quantity of flavourless oil in a pan, and fry chicken rolls for about five minutes until golden. Be careful not to break them.

Transfer to a baking dish, and bake at 150°C for 30 to 45 minutes. When cut, all the filling trapped inside is released and makes a delicious sauce.

5. Julius Garfinkel & Quagg's: 1971–74

The Māori name for Auckland is Tāmaki Makau-rau, or the isthmus of a thousand lovers. This narrow strip of land between two shimmering harbours has been the meeting place of British and Australian travellers since the beginning of European settlement. In 1769 Captain James Cook sailed around New Zealand, linking it politically to New South Wales by claiming both places for the British Crown by right of discovery. Cook's trans-Tasman proclamations, and the fact that New Zealand was subsequently administered from New South Wales, meant many of Auckland's first settlers came from Australia. These were itinerant immigrants moving to a more temperate climate to make a living. Two years after the sovereign signing of the Treaty of Waitangi with Māori in 1840, shiploads of British joined Australian settlers coming to colonise this lush, semi-tropical isthmus.

The fabled thousand suitors of Māori mythology were joined by many more, and Auckland grew verdant like the red-flowering pōhutukawa trees fringing its azure-blue bays. People came to Auckland to make money. In the beginning the city glutted on gold from the nearby Coromandel Peninsula, and when the cycle of boom-and-bust finished, there were rich hinterlands to exploit. Growth was sustained by gum digging, kauri logging, livestock farming, market gardening and merchandising.

The very first retail outlets in Auckland were a straggle of shanty shops and warehouses that ran down a steep valley to the sea. This became Queen Street, the main thoroughfare of the central business district and its waterfront. By 1900 Auckland had the biggest population of any centre in New Zealand. Business diversified. A rapacious middle class wanted to buy more goods, more exclusively.

The idea of an elegant gallery of shops with a leisured display of luxury goods began in Paris with closed-in walkways like the Passage du Caire, built at the end of the eighteenth century, and the Passage des Panoramas, opened in 1800. London followed Paris's lead with its Burlington Arcade, opened in 1819. The arcade had a glass roof and 72 magnificently carved mahogany shopfronts.

Auckland's grand answer to exclusive shopping was the Strand Arcade, running between Queen and Elliot streets and linking the busy foot traffic of both footpaths. Finished a year before Queen Victoria's death in 1900, the building was a spectacle of Italianate fabulousness, transporting untravelled New Zealanders to exotic places like Paris and London. The magnificent glass-covered roof that ran the full length of the building gave it a lofty sense of soaring, light-filled space. The upper floors were linked by ornate bridges that crisscrossed the void. Bay windows, black wrought-iron balconies, ornate parapets and decorative plasterwork announced its luxury.

The Strand Arcade became the hub for prosperous shoppers. On the ground floor was restaurant space, as well as 19 small shops. The front of each shop was an enormous plate-glass window with a wood-framed glass door facing into the arcade.

*

David and Peter had come to Auckland for love and for money, just as many British and Australian adventurers had before them. Now, nine years after they first met and made their home in the city, they were ready to take on the challenge of running a business together.

The Strand Arcade came almost instantly to mind when they were considering options for their women's shoe shop. David's old English employers, Russell & Bromley, had decided in the 1950s to aim for a more exclusive market by changing their stock and style of shops, and David was keen to attract a similarly elite clientele. He would use his contacts and knowledge of the shoe trade to ensure he could offer the most up-to-date products possible.

Around the time he and Peter began planning the new business, David made a trip back to England. His sister Janet remembers: 'He had to come over to see the fashion in London … what shoes were selling … the designs here. I used to get a meat skewer and put a hole in every one' — so that they were damaged stock and he could avoid import duties when he took them back to New Zealand.[1] For David, this and other shoe-scouting trips combined business with the pleasure of spending time with his parents, George and Hilda, and his brother and sisters.

But it appears that although Peter accompanied David on these early trips to England, he was not taken home to Epping or Theydon Bois to meet the family. David had two lives half a world apart, and this no doubt suited his desire to be discreet. But still there were the difficult questions when he went home. Had he met a nice girl yet, and when was he going to settle down and bring her to meet them? While his siblings married and had families of their own, David remained a bachelor, and as time passed this seemed increasingly strange to his parents. As Chris Brickell asserts, marriage was traditionally 'about more than individuals' sexual desires. Many believed that matrimony signified responsibility and adult status … [while] bachelorhood represented "selfish and bad citizenship".'[2] For David, his maturity was not defined by marriage but by the creative and business challenges he took on. But this was something he could not discuss with his family.

Julius Garfinkel was a leap into something new. This would be David and Peter's shoe shop and they could run it exactly the way they wanted to. The duo said they named it Garfinkel after the previous leaseholder. Adding a flash first name, 'Julius', to the funky-sounding Garfinkel could have been a nose-in-the-air gesture to posh, or it may have been a reference to Julius, the oldest gay bar in New York. Just two years before the naming of the shop it had, like Stonewall Inn, been a site of gay rebellion. Peter and David were international travellers. They would have known about both bars and the uprisings associated with them. David later explained the reason for his choice of Garfinkel, adding the throwaway line: 'It sounded a nice name to ring a till with.'[3] Another conceivable source for the name was Julius Garfinckel (spelt with a c), the great New York department store owner and philanthropist, who remained single and was possibly gay himself.

Julius Garfinkel, in the newly renovated Strand Arcade, began ringing its cash register in 1971, the City of Auckland's centennial year. The shop was simply fitted out in a chic, brown wood-and-brass theme. The stock, elegantly displayed, was mainly women's fashion shoes, but there were also accessories such as handbags. David recalled, 'The most expensive items were boots – about $30 – which was quite dear in those days.'[4]

Sharply designed and stridently coloured, the shoes in the window of Julius Garfinkel bedazzled the passing customer. In spite of his mild colour-blindness, David had an astute and subtle eye when it came to purchasing stock. Shoe aficionado Neville Burke remembers David especially for his understanding of colour.

In the 1970s almost every shoe was height enhancing. The most impressive were the quintessential platform shoes, which had extraordinarily thick soles and wedge, cut-out or chunky square heels. The drama was in the height, especially when worn with hip-hugging bell-bottomed trousers. Also in vogue were comfortable clogs with a shaped wooden sole and a leather upper, and reasonably priced Go-go boots. The Go-go boot with its square platform heel and shiny, skin-tight vinyl upper had shot to fame in the 1960s when worn to head-swivelling effect with the decade's classic miniskirt or hot-pants, but they were not widely available until mass production began in the 1970s. The most popular colours were black and white, though they came in a rainbow range of pink, lime-green, baby-blue, yellow, orange, red, mauve and silver. The hippie-inspired, hand-stitched American Indian moccasin with tasselled trim, beadwork or silver buckle was another exotic new line.

The psychedelic colour revolution of the late 1960s was still influencing fashion footwear when self-confessed 'shoeaholic' Sue McBride 'couldn't resist visiting' Julius Garfinkel. She remembers: 'The drawcard was the colour. I bought a pair of sandals that were bright turquoise. Wooden soles … I remember the wood had been stained or dyed with a matching strip of leather for the upper. The shoes were a gorgeous colour but didn't get brownie points for comfort so they didn't last long! I was served by the H[udson] and H[alls] that didn't have glasses or grey hair.'[5]

This was David and Peter in their prime. In their forties, they were vital and dynamic, still holding on to the blossom of youth. David, especially, continued to turn heads on Queen Street in his immaculate pin-striped suit. Julius Garfinkel was the duo personified: funky, flamboyant and camp, with an affectation of poshness that lasted as long as some of their shoes. Neil Burke recalls going into Julius Garfinkel one day to browse. 'Keep your thieving effing hands off the footwear,' came a disembodied voice from out the back.[6] He looked around to see David laughing with all the gusto of a gurgling drain. David loved a laugh; and he loved the drama of his little stage, of being his own boss, and staying ahead of the game by travelling and keeping an eye on overseas trends. He got pleasure out of beautiful things, out of ordering new stock and spending money they didn't have. His jump on the local knowledge gave Julius Garfinkel its edge.

The other edge was Peter's sharp wit while serving customers. He could be polite and attentive to a point, then, when the sardonic, slightly cynical side of his nature could no longer be contained, he would lob an incendiary device into the proceedings. Some of his one-liners remained unexploded, others made people laugh uproariously, and a few sent people flying for the door, even if no insult was intended. John Fields recalls taking his sister to buy a pair of shoes at Julius Garfinkel.

"'She's tried on everything in the shop,'" John remembers Peter telling him in a tone of high-camp exasperation. 'He could be very abrupt with customers if they weren't buying.'[7]

While Julius Garfinkel was doing well, ructions continued between Peter and David at the Strand Arcade. Usually David, but sometimes Peter would rush into the shop next door, waving his arms in the air over some new row that had erupted. The sympathetic shopkeeper listened compassionately to David or Peter's story of hardship and abuse, believing that this was the serious and singular event that would end their partnership. Concerned, she would hurry into Julius Garfinkel the next day to talk to one or other of them, only to find that everything had been forgotten and forgiven and that they

Women's fashion footwear in the 1970s did not always put comfort to the fore, as featured on the cover of the New Zealand Listener *in 1976.*

were mystified by her anxiety. This happened repeatedly. The fights occurred during work time, at home and at parties, but none of them was relationship-ending. Close friends and colleagues eventually became immune. 'They would fight like hell at times,' Carleen Spencer recalls, 'but the whole thing was forgotten by eight o'clock the next morning. They were very, very caring people.'[8]

*

Just a stroll along the road from the Strand Arcade was a burgeoning subculture of gay-aligned bars, clubs, haunts and pick-up places. The Ca d'Oro coffee bar was still operating down the bottom of Queen Street near the wharves. 'The West Wind coffee house [also] in Queen Street and the Tap Room bar on Elliot Street were popular during the mid-1970s.'[9] Queer nightspots were also brewing and about to burst onto the scene. 'Lew Pryme's Backstage nightclub opened in Greys Avenue in 1976, and Mojo's – on Queen Street opposite the Town Hall – had drag shows similar to those of Carmen's Balcony' in Wellington.[10]

But it was also fun to go out with a group of friends to the theatre, to listen to music, or to have a meal. Ross Palmer recalls, 'I used to meet them at La Boheme restaurant because we were all millionaires on £8 4s a week. A great friendship started … they were also associated with the antique business. Especially Peter. He had a lot of friends … who I knew.'[11]

Peter loved antiques, but it was the world of food and fine-dining restaurants that pulled him and David in a new direction, thanks in part to the influence of Bob and Jean Sell. They ran 'La Boheme, Hungry Horse, Hungry Leopard and Your Father's Moustache and the lovely [Fisherman's Wharf] Restaurant under the harbour bridge which is still standing,' remembers Ross Palmer. 'It was an incredible era. It was all fairly new, and Bob and Jean Sell lived down the road and we used to go there for dinner and go to Peter and David's, and they were marvellous cooks from the start.'[12]

To this point food and entertaining had been a vehicle of Peter and David's friendship: a way of hosting a social occasion, of sharing and showing their talent in the kitchen and being in charge. Bob and Jean Sell inspired them to think differently, to begin to see food as an opportunity and a money-making proposition.

The other prompt was meeting two Americans who were shocked and puzzled by the poor standard of ice-cream in a dairy-rich farming country like New Zealand. 'They had an American friend called Dick, and he and his wife came out to New Zealand and they decided to [help Peter and David] set up … an ice-cream parlour, [very upmarket like] Quaglino's in London … I think Dick helped fund it,' remembers Robby Agnew, one of the young shop workers they hired.[13] There were no ice-cream parlours in Auckland and nothing exactly like it in the rest of the country.[14]

This entrepreneurial and forward-thinking approach to fast food was well timed. The 1970s was the decade when big American chains such as McDonald's and Pizza Hut established themselves in New Zealand. In August 1971 the first Kentucky Fried Chicken outlet opened in Auckland's Royal Oak. The home-grown Georgie Pie, owned by Progressive Enterprises, was franchised throughout the country. It looked like Peter and David's ice-cream idea might take off.

New Zealanders tend to think of ice-cream as their own invention, but not so, according to Sydney Greenbie, a contributor to *Recipes from Many Races*, published in New Zealand in the late 1940s: 'Ice Cream is an American concoction, and is seldom seen at its best outside the States. For good ice cream is a rather expensive and thriftless combination of cream and eggs, flavoured with sugar and any one of a score of bland flavours. War time rationing has been the ruin of ice cream.' Mrs Greenbie felt American servicemen's lack of discernment was evident in their meal-

Jan Cormack and Di Toohill with David in the back yard at 103 Brighton Road, Parnell. JAN CORMACK, PRIVATE COLLECTION

time behaviour. Her concern was that the fashion 'of adding a blob of ice cream to any and every dessert' might catch on and melt Kiwis' resistance to self-indulgent pleasure. 'American servicemen were young and hungry, and were intent on making new and war rationed food palatable,' Mrs Greenbie continued. 'They did not have the stabilising influence of more discriminating tastes and social criticism such as puts some limitation, even in the States, on the use of ice cream. So it is well for the New Zealander to examine this new custom and try to arrive at some standard himself.'[15]

Ice-cream manufacture in New Zealand improved in quantum leaps after Mrs Greenbie's cautionary comments, which goes some way to explaining why Quagg's ice-cream parlour was an immediate sensation. Driven initially by Dick and then by Peter's enterprise, it opened to some fanfare just along from Julius Garfinkel in the Strand Arcade. The interior was immaculate, down to the last detail. The colour scheme was chrome and black with dashes of red. Jan Cormack was in her thirties, and remembers that she and a friend dressed up as young Pippi Longstockings to publicise the store's range of ice-cream. Her hair was pulled up into child-like pigtails and freckles were painted on her face. It was just a little bit crazy, the way all David and Peter's ventures tended to be.

The ice-cream parlour sold 'multiple flavours … and things like sundaes', recalls Robby Agnew. 'We made liquid chocolate to pour over everything, and banana splits … David was always laughing, and Peter would queen around the place … he would come in and I can remember him fussing and moving things, and everything had to be just so … They were just terrific fun … Dick adored them and would roar with laughter every time he was with them … They didn't manage the shop or roll an ice-cream or anything. They'd just swan in and tootle around and make sure everything looked fabulous.'[16]

Quagg's ice-cream parlour was so successful they opened a second shop. This was a mistake. 'It was in Customs Street opposite … the Queen's Arcade near the hotel, and there was no foot traffic, and nobody came … it was unbelievably boring,' Robbie Agnew remembers. Peter's dream had been to open a chain of ice-cream parlours throughout the country, but the failure and eventual closure of this second shop put an end to the project.

Change was in the air. The shoe business was an all-consuming commitment and a tie. Already the Strand Arcade was losing its capacity to pull people into the city centre. Auckland was sprawling and at the heart of this expansion was the suburban mall. Local rather than centrally located exclusive shopping was the way of the future. St Luke's shopping centre in Mt Albert opened in 1971, and a hundred thousand people visited the mall on opening day.[17] The convenience of shopping centres, the difficulty of finding parking in the central city and the sheer volume of competition made the Strand Arcade seem anachronistic. Quagg's ice-cream parlour was similarly affected. While many New Zealanders adopted the American practice of adding a 'blob of ice cream to any and every dessert', they were less discerning about its quality than they would later become. The demand for boutique ice-cream was still some way off.

Peter and David's businesses had lost momentum, and the couple's energy and drive were going to waste. The question was where in New Zealand would their potential take them next?

*

In 1972, a year after Julius Garfinkel opened, a group of queer activists – mostly students and intellectuals – met by the fountain in Albert Park, Auckland, to protest at discrimination against gay people. Campus life in the 1970s fostered liberal ideas about all aspects of oppression. Issues of race and colour, class, gender, pacifism, environmentalism and sexual orientation were all hotly debated. For gay youth brought up in 'un-asking' and 'un-telling' isolation, this was a breakthrough into the light. Suddenly they were part of a movement, a groundswell they hoped would challenge the prevailing homophobia. 'News of Stonewall had broken, and activists in Wellington, Hamilton and Christchurch set up Gay Liberation groups in the second half of 1972,' writes Chris Brickell[18] These collectives were as much about solidarity as they were vehicles for protest and the propagation of new ideas about lives lived on the 'other' side of New Zealand's stark polarisation of straight and gay communities.

Homosexuality was still listed in the *Diagnostic and Statistical Manual of Mental Disorders*, and would be for another year, when activists in New Zealand penned the Gay Liberation Manifesto. This was a direct response to the oppression that occurred in all aspects of life and was supported by the pillars of society: the government, the church and that bugle of law and order, the media.

The group in Albert Park had its counterpart in other cities: small bands of placard-waving protesters also gathered in Cathedral Square in Christchurch and Parliament Grounds in Wellington to challenge the Establishment and change ideas. It was the faltering beginning of a movement that would gain momentum alongside the women's liberation movement and the Māori land rights movement. The 1970s in New Zealand was a time of counter-culture rebellion, filtered by distance from epicentres in London and New York, but with its own urgent intensity.

The ferment of ideas, however, was already evident in literature and other cultural influences. English writer Radclyffe Hall's *The Well of Loneliness* (1928), which tracked the usual tragic or unrequited end to same-sex love, was on bookshelves in New Zealand, along with Virginia Woolf's *Orlando* (1928) and *Olivia* (1949) by Olivia (in fact by André Gide's translator and Virginia Woolf's cousin, Dorothy Bussy). Gide's own novels gave gay men a sense that their lives were resonant in literature. But the younger generation looked to a lead from the US, and it was the writings of Christopher Isherwood that captured imaginations. *The World in the Evening* and *A Single Man*, from 1954 and 1964 respectively, were influential, as was Gore Vidal's *The City and the Pillar* (1949). These books were thin beams of light penetrating the miasma of ignorance and constructive silence around same-sex love and relationships.

In film, the radiance was dimmer. Homophobia in Hollywood during the Cold War years of the 1950s had resulted in a radical shut-down of gay careers and stories. Homosexuals, like communists, were hounded by McCarthyism. By the 1950s, as John Loughery points out, 'Three decades of thought about Reds and three decades of thought about sexual dissidents had at last dovetailed ... Both groups were antifamily, antireligious, scornful of bourgeois morality, devious, manipulative, cynical, loyal only to one another and their cause, abhorrent to God, eager to convert the young and remake America.[19] This meant the gay talent that could have contributed to movie-making in the US was lost. Films coming out of Hollywood were also strictly censored for their suitability for a mainstream audience. If there was any homosexual subtext at all it was usually to reinforce all the negative stereotypes about same-sex love. Film communicated prejudice in an oversimplified and often grotesque shorthand.

From Britain came another 'type' of popular-culture homosexual. Roles for men who dressed as women (especially while women were not allowed on stage), and for the effeminate or comic 'camp' male, had a centuries-old history in British theatre. Audiences understood these identities as intrinsic to the theatrical world and did not necessarily see them as having a coded homosexual subtext.

The icon of camp homosexuality was English actor Kenneth Williams, who played a variety of effete characters in the *Carry On* movies produced between 1958 and 1992. These low-budget British comedies were wildly popular in New Zealand. Of the 31 movies made, Kenneth Williams appeared in 26, including *Carry on Cruising*, *Carry on Up the Khyber* and *Carry on Camping*. His falsetto voice delivered hilarious lines that played on the ambiguities of his sexuality. He was a funny but also sad caricature of the homosexual English male, often dressed in Bombay bloomers and cloth-covered safari hat, military-style uniform or dapper English business suit. His high-pitched tones were also heard on New Zealand radio, where the BBC's *Round the Horne* was scheduled late in the evening. 'Williams played one of the characters in the regular Julian and Sandy skits, in which the characters communicated in the camp *lingua franca*, Polari, a gay slang dating from the 18th century.'[20]

Kenneth Williams was like an unmarried uncle. He was both effeminate and asexual. Although his humour was bawdy and his histrionics akin to pantomime, his sexuality had no agency. He was a comic eunuch. The role he played was impotent except in its capacity to make people laugh. Audiences giggled with and at him. But behind this benign trope was a much more complex reality. As long as the camp man was only ever a foil for the arc of heterosexual love or lust, he and the audience could keep laughing.

For many young gay men in the 1970s this was an uncomfortable cliché. Instead of seeing themselves reflected back in this sometimes bizarre character, they were repulsed by it. The grating falsetto and lewd innuendo pushed some men further back into the closet. This younger generation wanted characters they could relate to – role models, even. There was a desperate longing for an honest, open telling of gay experience that filled the between-the-lines text with words and meaning.

Nonetheless, Kenneth Williams and his lineage of camp character actors offered an older generation of gay men at least the scraps of identity. They understood the Polari coding and innuendo in a personal way. Belonging to a secret subculture could be a thrill. Private bars, discreet clubs: they were part of a covert movement, and this carried real dangers. The secrecy and the resistance to convention and authority created solidarity. Many older gay men would mourn the loss of this camaraderie and look back nostalgically on the era before homosexual law reform as golden days in the war against homophobia.

When 'camp' actors did finally come out of the closet and declare themselves gay, the media often turned against them. English actor Christopher Biggins remembers that 'in the 1970s and early 1980s, some parts of the press still hinted at some awful link between homosexuality and paedophilia.'[21] Even superstar Elton John did not come out publicly in the 1970s.

*

Elton John and his manager, John Reid, first met Peter and David through friends in the music business, Dolly and Ken East. Jan Cormack explains: 'Dolly East was the public relations person for Cliff Richard and so that's how they got to meet Elton John and John Laws …who we went to stay with in Oberon in Australia. [Laws] was one of the big DJs over there … and so we had a few dinner parties with Elton John at their house and played lots of charades and things.'[22]

Jan, her husband Gavin and Peter and David travelled together, meeting up with Elton John in various parts of the world. 'We went [to the UK] and stayed with him. His mum was living on Henley-on-Thames. We went to Elton John's birthday. We [also] went to Dolly and Ken's in St Ives in Australia and then out to stay with John Laws at Oberon. He had a farm out there and he invited all the local farmers, which was not a good idea because they were all down one end and all the city slickers [were] down the far end and we're all sitting there staring at each other; and then my ex-husband Gabby got Peter up for a dance and that sort of broke the ice.'[23]

Dolly East was English and 'a riot', recalls Ross Palmer. Ken was the managing director of EMI, Elton John's recording company. '[Ken and Dolly] always stayed with Peter and David in their place in Brighton Road and that's how Elton and John Reid came to be in [that] house … [It was] a social thing.'[24]

David, Gabby (Gavin) Cormack and Peter in the late 1970s.
JAN CORMACK, PRIVATE COLLECTION

Ken and Dolly moved with work between England, Australia and New Zealand. The 1970s was a wild time in the music business and they had to keep up with a rapidly expanding and ever-changing industry. The beginning of the decade saw the break-up of the Beatles and its members moving on to solo careers and albums. Hard rock saw the rise of Alice Cooper, Deep Purple, Led Zeppelin, Black Sabbath and Kiss, who came to the fore mid-decade. Psychedelic rock celebrated the music, then mourned the deaths, of Jimi Hendrix, Jim Morrison and Janis Joplin. Soft rock was dominated by chart-topping performers such as James Taylor, Billy Joel, America and Chicago. Carole King's *Tapestry* was among the biggest-selling albums of the decade, but it was Elton John who was one of the greatest solo stars of the 1970s. He and David Bowie were part of the glam rock phenomenon that emerged out of the UK early in the decade. Glam rock was all about spectacle. The outrageous costumes, flamboyant platform shoes, over-the-top glasses, extravagant hairstyles, drag-queen makeup and androgynous sexuality were part of an act designed to thrill and shock audiences. On tour Elton John carried with him 'an eye-watering $200,000 worth of personal baggage, in elaborate trunks that folded out into a series of traveling wardrobes filled with costumes and shoes and hats and glasses'.[25] When he toured Japan, Australia and New Zealand in 1974, 'he planned to unveil two new outfits … The first was a tight black Lurex zip-up suit strung with dozens of small red, orange, blue and green balls, while others sprouted from his shoulders on piano wire. The second involved a voluminous arrangement of outsized feathers … that made him look like a psychedelic peacock.'[26]

'Elton John was a superstar, but he wasn't as … up there … as he was later on,' recalls Jan Cormack.[27] Still, his glamour-studded stardom lit Peter and David's sky – until one fateful day, when everything fell to earth and the friendship was extinguished. The drama began on 27 February at a pre-concert event at the Rose Garden in Auckland, put on by Festival Records, Elton John's Antipodean recording label. He and manager John Reid were welcomed with an ominously spine-chilling haka. Free drink flowed in the cream-coloured colonial pavilion until supplies ran low. First they ran out of beer, then John Reid requested a whisky and was told it was not being served. When events manager Kevin Williams tried to pacify him with a glass of champagne, Reid exploded: 'You're an incompetent!' he shouted as he threw the contents of the glass in Kevin Williams' face.[28]

The atmosphere became instantly toxic. John Reid's blatant bad behaviour rankled. The drinking had been heavy and tempers became progressively frayed. Judith Baragwanath, a writer for the *Sunday News*, remonstrated with Reid. 'How could you do that to anyone … you rotten little bastard,' she demanded. Witnesses heard the words 'you little poof', but there was an irate crowd and it was never proven who said them.[29] Without thinking, Reid hit Judith Baragwanath in the face, leaving her with a black eye. Alcohol undoubtedly played a part, and possibly drugs such as cocaine, but the gay slight was the trigger, and John Reid lost control.

The event shut down immediately. John Reid grabbed Elton John and they were gone. If the evening had stopped there, things may have ended differently, but events escalated at an after party for a concert by American pop sensation David Cassidy, who was also performing in the city. John Reid, already highly charged, believed he overheard David Wheeler, a reporter for the *Sunday News*, mumbling under his breath that he and Elton were 'marked men'. Reid decided it was time for them to leave. Instead, the infuriated Elton went over to Wheeler and grabbed him by the collar. '"You've threatened my manager,"' he spat.

Wheeler was adamant in his defence. '"I don't know what you are talking about,"' he protested.[30]

Again, John Reid snapped, hitting the journalist in the face. Then the assault escalated. While David Wheeler was on the floor, he was kicked in a minor free-for-all. Musician, manager and minders left the party early, and this time somewhat more speedily.

Carleen, David, Peter and a young family friend after a day at Fire Island, Bay Shore, New York, in the mid-1970s. CARLEEN SPENCER, PRIVATE COLLECTION

Peter relaxing in Carleen and Jerry's apartment in New York in the late 1970s. CARLEEN SPENCER, PRIVATE COLLECTION

The next morning a carload of police arrived at their hotel and both John Reid and Elton John were arrested for assault. This was a disaster. Elton was due to perform for a crowd of 36,000 at Western Springs Stadium that night. Reid was charged with two counts of assault and was let out on $AU5000 bail only after lawyers proved that he was essential to the show.[31] Elton John was charged with assault and also granted bail. While the concert was a huge success, this did not change the fact that they were both facing a court case the next day.

For his court appearance Elton John dressed down in a grey suit, and got off relatively lightly. He pleaded guilty to assault and received a $50 fine. John Reid wasn't so fortunate. Peter and David's lawyer, Michael Williams, was Reid's junior counsel, led by Roger Maclaren, and Lloyd Brown QC represented Elton John. 'Reid ran into a horrible piece of work of a magistrate in Auckland … who took the approach that John had so much money that a fine wouldn't hurt him,' Williams remembers.[32] In an attempt to mitigate his punishment, Reid 'promised to pay civil damages to both victims', but this did not convince the magistrate that he was sufficiently contrite. David Wheeler had 'chipped and cracked teeth and bruising', and this was Reid's second offence on the same day. The magistrate said that he had shown 'an ill-mannered, arrogant indifference to people'.[33] Reid 'ended up with a month in the slammer in Mount Eden and Elton [went] on with the tour', recalls Michael Williams.[34]

While John Reid was incarcerated, Peter and David took him hampers of food to make prison life more palatable. On the day of his release there was a massive party at their house in Brighton Road. 'I was there when they had the party to welcome him out of jail,' remembers Carleen Spencer. 'It was like breakfast, lunch and dinner. They [went] to pick him up out of jail, and Elton John was supposed to jump out of this cardboard birthday cake but he couldn't make it from Sydney. So there was just this huge party that went on and on.'[35]

It was 1974, and this was the party to end all parties, but drugs and drinking were taking a serious toll on Elton John and his entourage. They'd played a part in John Reid's conviction, and after Australia and New Zealand, Elton was 'wiped out. There was no way he could face the European tour due to begin in April, so all of its dates were cancelled.'[36] After the New Zealand fiasco, Elton John, John Reid, and Peter and David lost touch. The impact of this might have been more devastating had David and Peter not been swept away by a new venture.

Venetian Liver

SERVES 4–6

The art with liver – which, incidentally, is very good for you – is to cook it very quickly, and not too much. It should be sliced very finely, not in great chunks that become tough and leathery and lack moisture. This recipe is delicate and most enjoyable.

2–3 tablespoons olive oil
4 tablespoons butter
750 grams onions, finely sliced
1 rasher of bacon, chopped
1 kilogram calf's liver
salt and pepper
6 sprigs parsley, finely chopped

Slice liver very thinly. Heat oil and butter in a frying pan, add finely sliced onion and sauté very gently until soft, but not brown. Add bacon and liver, stir well. Fry for about five minutes over a high heat until brown, tossing and stirring all the time.

Always keep liver moving, particularly when over a high heat, as it stops it sticking and also keeps all the ingredients alive and evenly cooked. Add salt and plenty of pepper, dust with the chopped parsley and serve at once. Either pour over rice or serve with wedges of toast. Do not overcook, the meat must be pink and succulent.

*** If you have any leftover liver, make this paté. Chop the liver and put through a blender or a mincer. Place in a bowl and add the same weight of softened butter, and a good sprinkle of mixed herbs (fresh herbs would make this out of this world). Add about one tablespoon brandy and one tablespoon madeira. Mix very, very well.

Butter several bowls, or whatever dish you wish to store this in, pour in, and chill in the refrigerator for at least two days. Serve with dry toast and thinly sliced gherkins – or make sandwiches of the same thing – beaut!

For a dinner you can dolly this up with side dishes of sieved egg yolks, finely chopped egg whites, and of course the finely sliced gherkins!

6. *Speakeasy & the Birth of Hudson and Halls: 1974–75*

Television and David Halls both arrived in New Zealand the same year: 1959.

The first television equipment berthed at the Auckland dock in January and was lifted off the freighter *Canberra Star* and transported to the 1YA radio station in Shortland Street. The transmitters were installed and the first experimental signals were sent out on 23 February 1959. It was a quiet beginning to something that would become big news.

Television was risky. People would have to dig deep into their pockets to find the £100 needed to pay for a receiver. It was also hard. New Zealand's length, wild windy weather and mountainous terrain made installation enormously difficult. But everything overseas suggested that television was a medium that would be bigger and more globally connecting than radio.

On 1 June 1960 the first formal television signals were sent out to receivers in Auckland. There was no local television programming, no local production staff and no budget to pay for the service.[1] Initial transmission time was two hours a night, two days a week, and the first imported show was *The Adventures of Robin Hood*. The programme was a quintessential choice. Its roots were English, and the otherness of Sherwood Forest and Robin Hood a familiar myth. But it was also about men trying to create a more egalitarian society by breaking old rules. New Zealanders lapped up its clichés and episodic happy endings.

In October 1960 transmission was extended in Auckland to five nights a week. The rest of the country twitched in the darkness, waiting to be plugged in. On 1 June the following year transmission began in Christchurch, and a month later Wellington was hooked up.

Food was first on the menu of homemade programmes. Graham Kerr, initially working in his capacity as a chef with the Royal New Zealand Air Force, was one of television's first stars. Good-looking and flawlessly presented, in 1960 he stood over a primitive spirit burner and told viewers, in his immaculate English accent, how to whisk up the perfect omelette.

A man in the kitchen glamourised a domain that was drudgery for many women. His dapper presentation and professionalism were compelling viewing. The kitchen was now a stage and the cook its star.

When transmission began in Wellington, Graham Kerr's show *Entertaining with Kerr* moved to the capital. During an early rehearsal a backing curtain caught fire, causing a small sensation. Kerr, however, was a heartthrob: he could have cooked the whole backdrop and served it à la carte and many women would have been happy. As programme production became more advanced, Kerr's recipes became more sophisticated. His cookbook recipes also became more refined. *Selected Recipes* (1963) listed 'Crepes Antonin Careme (or how to make an old boiler go a very long way)' while *The Graham Kerr Cookbook* (1973) featured 'Toheroa (Giant Green Clam from New Zealand – the Rarest Food Item in the World)' and Venison Pot Roast with Cream Sauce.

For a number of months audiences watched Graham Kerr uninterrupted, but when the commercial arm of television became operative, first in Auckland, then in the other centres, viewers had to watch his programmes sliced up between advertising breaks. The broadcasting authority was besieged by letters of complaint. But the government-owned model could not be funded by television licensing alone. In 1962 the Broadcasting Act established the New Zealand Broadcasting Corporation to administer public radio and television as a state-owned corporation.[2]

Local programme production began to diversify. This time the target was the baby-boomer audience. Dinah Lee and 19-year-old Ray Columbus became the faces of the music programme *Time Out for Talent*. Imported programmes included *I Love Lucy* and *Perry Mason*. By 1962, when transmission began in Dunedin, Graham Kerr's cooking programme had moved from spirit burner to *cordon bleu*. International programme purchases included *The Flintstones*, *National Velvet*, *Rawhide* and *Dr Kildare*. By the beginning of 1963, television was reaching one-eighth of the population. Eighty thousand licences had been issued to an audience of approximately 300,000 viewers.[3]

Television was a way of life by the mid-1960s. People arranged lounge furniture to face the television set. Dinner moved from the dining-room table to the knee

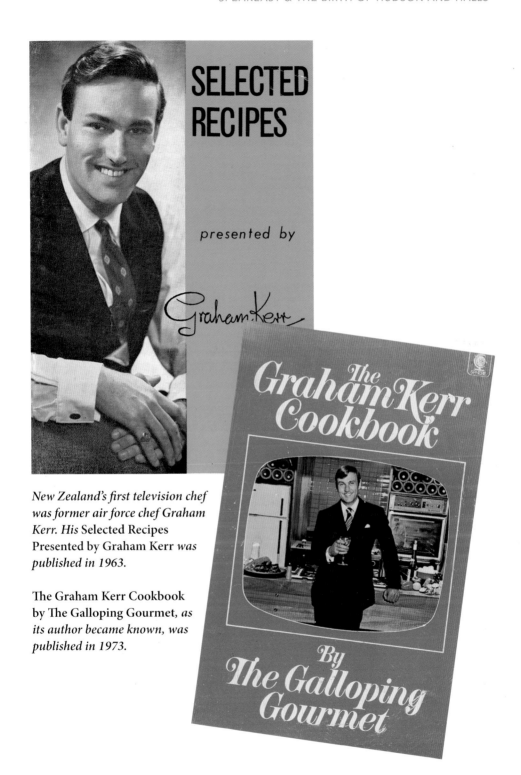

New Zealand's first television chef was former air force chef Graham Kerr. His Selected Recipes Presented by Graham Kerr *was published in 1963.*

The Graham Kerr Cookbook by The Galloping Gourmet, *as its author became known, was published in 1973.*

so families could sit entranced in front of the box while they ate. In 1967, when pub closing shifted to 10pm from 6pm, there was barely a ripple because alcohol consumption had already moved from the public house to the private home to accommodate the watching of television. Programmes were discussed in children's playcentres and kindergartens, in schools and clubs, at university, and at work during tea breaks. New Zealanders were mesmerised by the moving images at the heart of the home that could transport them everywhere and nowhere at the same time.

In 1965 New Zealanders were in the trenches of 'The Great War – the biggest television documentary of its kind ever undertaken' by the BBC.[4] In horror, in 1968, they watched the assassinations of Robert Kennedy and Martin Luther King, but also a local awarding-winning documentary of the sinking of the inter-island ferry *Wahine* during a massive storm in April of that year. When astronaut Neil Armstrong walked on the moon in 1969, 'film transmitted from the moon's surface [was] relayed by satellite to Australia to be recorded and specially flown to New Zealand where it was transmitted around the country'.[5]

By the end of the 1960s the majority of television programmes were still coming from overseas. In terms of local production, drama was very expensive, so light entertainment dominated, especially music shows. The spine of television production still belonged to the UK and the US. Viewers were a captive audience, but programming was also strong with *Get Smart*, *The Avengers*, *The Man from U.N.C.L.E.*, *The Fugitive* and *Bewitched*. These were the honeymoon years, vibrant and stable, when television was the wooer and the viewer its prize.

The halcyon days of television were over by the beginning of the 1970s, however, and the infatuation would never be unconditional again. Viewers wanted choice; politicians wanted power; and television bosses wanted profit. By 1970, transmission engineers had established the facilities to make New Zealand into a single network, and in 1973 colour transmission began – eight years after it was introduced in the US, five years after it began in the UK.

Suddenly, the blood of the battlefield was red and real; the vivid colours of Vietnam were being delivered directly to people's lounges. The bombing. Civilians fleeing. The deaths – not just statistics but graphically bloodied corpses. The battlefield had moved into the living room, and the relationship of the viewer to the news story shifted from voyeur to witness with this new layer of realism. In 1974 the American series *M*A*S*H* began its long run on New Zealand television, interrogating the issues of war in a more subtle and sophisticated way. On the flattened tableau of the screen, real war news mixed with fictional war, and audiences – and television – lost their innocence.

With the cost of a colour television set still high, many New Zealanders either put themselves in debt or hired a set to watch the 1974 Commonwealth Games in Christchurch. Broadcast coverage of the event was the biggest undertaking in NZBC history.[6] Ironically, the year before New Zealand hosted the games and film footage was beamed around the world, Britain had joined the European Economic Community, shutting the door on its old economic alliance with New Zealand.

The brave new world was a frightening prospect for New Zealanders. As Britain turned to face Europe while New Zealand floated away into the distance, economic self-sufficiency was the crucial issue. The country would have to find its own way in the global economy.

Outward-looking still, with many of its programmes coming from the UK and the US, the imperatives for New Zealand television were commercialisation and greater choice. Picking up on these energies from abroad, the NZBC felt the pressure to diversify. But more channels and more choice had to be paid for. One solution was a second, privately funded channel to compete with state-owned commercial television. At the last minute, this option was broadsided by the Labour government's preference for a more controlled evolution towards private enterprise.

When the new purpose-built television studio opened in 1975 at Avalon, near Wellington, the model of one government organisation controlling two television channels was put in place. Television One and South Pacific Television would be both complementary and competitive. In the division of existing resources, Television One would keep the staff and almost all the hardware, and South Pacific Television, with its much smaller budget, was left to recruit new staff, buy programme stocks and establish studios. This was a brutal beginning. But some television personnel recognised the opportunities and moved over to South Pacific Television. This was the first time in nearly 15 years that scope for new work, new ideas and new people had opened up. The field of possibility had never been as promising since technicians had installed the first transmitters in the Shortland Street studios in Auckland in 1959.

*

Peter and David were avid television viewers, and they had followed Graham Kerr from his earliest days on screen. His food and his approach fascinated them.

Graham Kerr had grown up in the food industry. His father was a hotel manager and Graham had been a hotel manager himself before moving to New Zealand. The food he presented on television was based on English hotel and restaurant cooking.

'It must have seemed as if Kerr and his food had dropped in from another planet,' writes New Zealand food historian David Veart. 'His recipes took home cookery to another level with the use of herbs and wine, and lectures on what he took to be some of the barbarities of New Zealand food traditions.'[7] Ultimately, in 1975, his show would move to the United States where his face, name and born-again healthy cooking style became familiar to households across the nation. His future would be international, but Graham Kerr's reputation and career were made in New Zealand.

The next chef propelled into the limelight of early television celebrity was Des Britten. Unlike Graham Kerr, he was a local boy. Born in Otane in Hawke's Bay, he had made his name as a radio broadcaster before moving into television. His talent in the kitchen was well known, as in 1967 he had established The Coachman, one of Wellington's most successful restaurants, which he ran for nearly 30 years.

His *Thyme for Cookery* and *Bon Appetit* television shows were immensely popular in the 1970s. Des Britten's lively presentation of simple food ideas was highly appealing to New Zealand audiences. His logic was that good-quality food has its own elemental flavours that need enhancement rather than major intervention. His rule was to keep things simple and fresh, and let the inherent flavours stand for themselves. *Thyme for Cookery* was accompanied in 1973 by a generously illustrated cookbook that laid out his philosophy as well as his recipes.

Once again, here was a man in the kitchen telling a mostly female audience how to cook. This was significant. In the strictly gendered division of labour, the kitchen had long been given over almost exclusively to women. If they felt chained to the kitchen sink, then many men felt excluded from it. The 1970s saw the beginning of a shift in sex roles fostered by the feminist movement, the changing nature of the family unit and new work patterns. And as soon as men were visibly involved in cooking, the status of the kitchen and the masculine taboos around food preparation altered. In 1975, women and men in 800,000 homes could watch men become celebrities by preparing food.

This seismic shift in the bedrock would be followed by significant aftershocks. The geography of the standard heterosexual home was changing. The kitchen for baby-boomer males was no longer feminised and off limits. Peter Hudson and David Halls' recipe for television celebrity was about to complicate the picture even further. They were gay men in a domestic kitchen, using the cut-and-thrust banter of their private relationship to sell themselves as food presenters. If they made it on to television, they would be an event in themselves.

*

The precedent for celebrity cooking stardom had been well and truly set when Peter and David were considering their options and began wondering vaguely whether their food and humour had a place on television.

In 1973 they were travelling abroad and out of their usual routine. Flying high on the buzz of a 'giant party in Miami' with its inevitable guest list of stars, they stopped over in Sydney and cooked a meal for friends. The evening 'consisted mainly of taking the tops off bottles', David would recall.[8]

'You two dopey so-and-sos should be on television,' one of the dinner guests told them.[9]

That was the epiphany: the moment when their talents, personalities and lives together coalesced in a way forward. It was a dream, and it was one that they would work on when they got home.

Thanks to their contacts in the entertainment world, Peter and David knew how to go about breaking into television. They made a demonstration tape of a cooking show format they thought might work on New Zealand television, and sent it to NZBC producers in 1973. But there was little or no interest – until programmers began searching for new local content for the South Pacific Television channel due to begin in 1975.

At a party, Peter and David met Marcia Russell, one the presenters for the new channel's *Speakeasy* show, a magazine-styled afternoon programme. She and co-host Jeremy Payne were looking for variation; for something that was cheap, entertaining and resolved. The format had to be instantly workable, and there was no time to waste. Marcia Russell invited them to do a live demonstration.

The pressure was on, especially for David. The ambition to become a star belonged to him more than Peter. He wanted the limelight; he saw the opportunity to use cooking as a vehicle; and he had more of himself invested in the outcome. Peter followed David because the idea resonated for him as well, and because he was in a partnership. He was no introvert, but his instincts when sober were to be private and to gravitate towards exclusive groups and close friends. But both men were risk takers, and who knew where it might end.

The audition for the *Speakeasy* staff and producer went unbelievably well. David and Peter were determined to set the standard high and prove beyond a doubt that they would be an asset to the show. The banter and the Beef Wellington were a winning combination. In a small kitchen, on set, they conjured an impressive dish as if by magic, and they made people laugh. Right from the beginning they were funny. They were natural, unscripted and unpredictable.

David and Carleen at a birthday party he and Peter threw for her at 103 Brighton Road in 1975. The poolside party even featured a live band. CARLEEN SPENCER, PRIVATE COLLECTION

ABOVE: *Barry Spencer, Carleen's ex-husband, relaxing poolside.* LEFT: *High fashion prevailed at the party.* CARLEEN SPENCER, PRIVATE COLLECTION

Facing the camera was usually a lobotomising experience for New Zealand presenters, especially newsreaders. Often personality was expunged, and what remained was an affected BBC voice and stiff uninteresting persona. While this had been mediated over the years, Hudson and Halls were not only relaxed and real, they were themselves. David would discuss his 'half-inch nozzle' and call on Peter to 'bring me his nuts', while Peter announced, 'There's a fly in the studio, wouldn't you know it.'[10] They were lewd, crude and irresistibly spontaneous. Their relaxed, accidental style, their bitching and bickering on screen, their spontaneous unchoreographed movements across the stage that left the entrails of cameras and startled production staff exposed, would break taboos and melt formalities.

*

Neil Burke remembers catching a glimpse of an elated David strutting down Queen Street. When he inquired after his ebullient friend, David shouted out to him: "'I'm a star! I'm a star! I'm a star!'"[11]

He and Peter had passed the audition. They were contracted to make six 10-minute segments of a cooking programme for $20 an episode. This was substantially less than the cost of an expensive pair of boots in Julius Garfinkel, but it was a beginning. David knew now that opportunities would open up because they had a formula that worked.

Four days later, filming began. The first few 10-minute slots went flawlessly and the magic kept happening until Peter, while looking into the camera, splashed port wine over the heat and set the pot alight. In a panic, but still smiling 'unflappably', David threw flour into the flames in an attempt to extinguish them. Instead, the flour accelerated the fire; the situation was beginning to get serious. The cameras kept rolling, however, and the drama was captured live on film. David's benign smile combined with his useless flapping of a tea towel at the smoke and flames sent everyone into hysterical laughter. The floor manager standing off camera and ready with a fire extinguisher was doubled over, tears running down his face. This, together with Peter's alarmed but still dry repartee, made it one of the 'funniest 10 minutes of television most of us had ever seen', Marcia Russell remembered.[12]

Marcia knew David and Peter privately. She and her husband Tom Finlayson lived around the corner. But the professional was always personal for Peter and David, especially when Auckland in the 1970s still felt like a small town and everyone knew each other. Marcia had given them their break in television, but she also assumed the role of relationship counsellor, as so many of those close to them did.

'One of my favourite memories,' Tom Finlayson recalls, 'is when they were living along the road from us, in St Marys Bay; when they had a row – not infrequently – one would come running to Marcia for solace and drink gallons of gin to salve the pain. Eventually the other would turn up and either the row would continue, or they'd make up and stagger into the night.'[13] It didn't matter who was watching or whether they were on or off stage; the theatre of Peter and David's relationship continued regardless. Their union was volcanic, and once an eruption started, neither was in control until the conflict had run its course. But the fire on set in the Studio Two kitchen and the heat of Peter and David's private lives did nothing to lessen Marcia Russell's enthusiasm to have them on *Speakeasy*.

They enchanted afternoon audiences. The majority were women: mothers at home with children, and retirees. But there were men as well among the shift workers, university students, people between jobs and pensioners who watched. They were a discerning audience when it came to food and cooking, and in dull-grey suburban New Zealand everybody needed a laugh.

As Peter and David's fiery kitchen chaos settled, they began to establish their characteristic style. The newness of television presenting was stressful, though, and they sometimes survived simply on nervous energy. They often ad-libbed, not just to be spontaneous and funny but because they were balancing on a tightrope above a precipice. They were untrained. They had no experience in front of a camera, and cooking was still just their hobby. 'They always play acted … It was sort of "fake it until you make it",' recalls their *Speakeasy* set designer, Lindsay Waugh. She watched their audacity in amazement. 'They decided they wanted to be celebrities … so they cooked … They didn't have a clue. It was hysterical. But it was a lovely flamboyance and confidence … and it was the time of emerging celebrities, I think that was the thing, and they absolutely nailed that … we'd just got over that BBC-type stuff and we were becoming our own and we were looking for our own personalities … I think Peter and David recognised that trend more than some … they almost targeted it, as a lifestyle … they manufactured themselves … and it was really smart and absolutely on the money.'[14]

South Pacific Television saw the duo's potential and wanted to re-sign them: initially for their own 10-minute slot, then for an hour-long afternoon show, programmed to go to air twice a week. Even David baulked at this idea. Their 10-minute slots already pushed them towards the edge of their capacity. How would they cope with an hour-long canvas? Well, a chat show component would be added, the network told them. They were to interview a guest. This terrified them more than the extended programme time. David would remember this as a huge dilemma. Should they take the opportunity or turn it down? 'We were good enough for 10-minute cooking programmes, but this show was a full-scale affair that included the interviewing of celebrities. We didn't have a clue about that side. We were frightened that the TV people would "produce" us, make us serious, make us work from a script.'[15]

As neither actors nor chefs, they believed the leap from one programme format to another was too great. They turned the offer down. But South Pacific Television was persistent and came back with a proposition: Peter and David would be trained in interviewing techniques.

The network was persuasive and the duo's ambition a massive motivation. This chance would never come again, and they knew it. With much trepidation and no small amount of histrionics, they signed up. Their 'fake it until you make it' approach would be tested to the maximum.

*

Later, Peter would recall his agonising stage fright. 'I wanted to die … I was ashen, just ashen. I had diarrhoea for weeks. I wanted to run away. I thought I would throw up on camera and I literally needed two hands to hold on to a kitchen whisk.'[16] The first hour-long episode of *Hudson and Halls* was beamed out to television audiences from 1.50 to 2.50pm on Wednesday 27 October 1976. The show had a new set design, its own theme song, racy graphics and catchy roller captions and credits. Their programme had a unique fingerprint, but both David and Peter wondered how sustainable the formula would be.

Their *Speakeasy* segment was filmed without an audience. The new *Hudson and Halls* was shot in front of a live audience to create a dynamic and promote the network locally. 'They sent some cards to my senior citizens' club, and a group of us went along to a show,' remembers Evelyn Balmforth, who was a regular in the audience from the very beginning. 'They used to record the show in the morning, take a break for lunch and then record another show in the afternoon.'[17] The cameras rolled almost continuously. The only formal structure was provided by the commercial breaks and how much cooking David and Peter had to achieve in each segment of the programme. 'There was a bit of … editing,' remembers *Hudson and Halls* designer Lindsay Waugh. 'But it was shot as if it was a live show. They tidied it up afterwards because there were things being dropped [on the floor]. Swearing had to be cut out at that time … they were very stressed.'[18]

David would remember the first shows as a disaster. 'I think we were semi-hysterical because we were afraid we would dry up.'[19] The critics were vicious in their response, and Peter and David understood why. Too many of the show's ingredients were literally up in the air and if they didn't regain their composure they would drop the lot. After some especially savage reviews, the pair went to the programmers and begged to be released from their contract. The show had failed. Their food was fumbled and frantic; their interviewing stiff and unnatural; and they were completely overawed by the calibre of their guests. 'There we were,' Peter would remember, 'rank amateurs talking to real pros like Vince Hill, Roger Whittaker and Eddie Calvert. We were meant to be in charge. It was just ludicrous.'[20]

South Pacific Television refused to release them from their contract. The network's ultimatum was that they either improved or they would go down as one of television's most memorable flops. So the show went on regardless of their reservations. Presenter Jeremy Payne was assigned to give them additional interview training, and eventually they settled into their signature style and became more chatty and relaxed with guests.

Even their studio audience entered into the fun. To bring the experience alive for *Speakeasy* viewers, Peter and David had had a strategy. 'We developed a thing where we would say hello to a little old lady,' recalled David.[21] Each time they recorded a show, a make-believe grandmother was in the room with them. Instead of staring into an impersonal camera lens, David imagined he was joking and laughing in his kitchen at home with Nanny Halls. It was a tactic that had given their *Speakeasy* footage its familiarity and sense of intimacy. *Hudson and Halls*, with its live studio audience, needed a different approach. They found a new grandmother figure in the flesh-and-blood character of Evelyn Balmforth, whom they picked out of the crowd early on. In many respects she could have been Nanny Halls.

Aged in her late seventies, Evelyn was a newcomer to New Zealand, which she called her 'little adventure'. Five years after the death of her husband she had left her home in Yorkshire to join her son in Auckland. 'It's things like "Hudson and Halls" that make the adventure live on,' she would tell a reporter for the *Auckland Star*.[22] Evelyn sat in the audience of almost every one of their shows. 'I am an expert clapper now,' she announced proudly. 'They showed us how to clap properly – short and twice as fast as normal. Makes a real din.'[23]

Familiar with English pantomime, Evelyn was the perfect lead for the rabble of reluctant Kiwis uninitiated in the ways of audience participation and exhibitionism. She would 'tut, tut' when the cooks were gratuitous with grog; laugh at their bawdy

Peter and David in their studio kitchen, 1976. COURTESY OF THE *NEW ZEALAND LISTENER*

jokes; register an audible 'Ohhhh' when the recipe called for too many eggs; and give a loud affirming sigh when the finished dish was revealed. Evelyn's unconditional enthusiasm was infectious – for the stars of the show, the studio audience and the viewers at home. And as Hudson and Halls felt more comfortable, they began to play the crowd. With experience, they became incredibly good at it.

'David would light up like a Christmas bulb' in front of the camera, remembers producer John Carlaw.[24] But it was more than the camera that excited him. He was a show-off, and the set of *Hudson and Halls* was a matrix of attention focused on him and Peter. On one level the duo played to the television staff: to the producer, stage manager, designer, props person and camera crew. Then to Evelyn, their 'good luck charm', as they called her; to the studio audience she prompted and led; and finally to the viewers at home.[25] All of them became increasingly captivated by Peter and David's banter and light-hearted humour as the shows went on. 'I went to a couple of their recordings in Shortland Street … in the studios there and they were hilarious,' remembers Murdoch McLennan. 'It wasn't a very big audience, but it was fun … and virtually non-stop … it was almost like live TV – it wasn't live TV, but it was, "We'll do this" – WHOOSH – and then – "We'll take it right through to that."[26] Cooking combined with speed and adrenalin made for exciting viewing, whether it was at home or live on the studio stage.

For a new station like South Pacific Television this was miraculous. Television One had established itself as the voice of media authority. Not only had it covered world news and all the major local events of recent times, but it had also wooed audiences with this new form of entertainment. Television One had the experienced staff, the budget and the history with viewers. *Hudson and Halls* was a happy violence that led to a sudden and surprising loosening of Television One's vice-like grip. It shook the more established network, and made the programmers at South Pacific Television realise they were on to a good thing. The ratings for *Hudson and Halls* were unprecedented. 'After two-thirds of the afternoon series had been screened, the show won 63 per cent of Auckland viewers', and was second only in the ratings to *Days of Our Lives*.[27] The shift to a prime-time slot seemed inevitable.

*

Hudson and Halls moved to evenings in 1977. Their format of 'cooking-cum-chat-cum-music show' was kept, but the evening episodes were scheduled only once a week for 30 minutes. The new start on a Wednesday evening guaranteed a broader audience of prime-time viewers, but to keep this programming position the duo would have to maintain their ratings. The competition was stiff. Television One had responded with some aggressive programming of its own.

To maximise quality viewing for New Zealand television audiences, the National government in 1977 amalgamated both channels under one controlling authority, the Broadcasting Corporation of New Zealand, or BCNZ. The spur for this was viewer dissatisfaction. Television One and South Pacific Television had battled for prime-time ratings, going head to head with one stellar programme after another. New Zealand viewers had never had it so good, but every night was a prime-time dilemma. And after firing the biggest rockets off simultaneously, there were only fizzers left in the box. Viewers wanted choice but they also wanted common sense. Competition might work on a bigger scale, but with modest budgets to buy overseas stock and create local programmes, unadulterated competition in television was simply wasteful.

This was a rationale resonant with viewer frustration, but the amalgamation also served the government well. The new National government was determined to restore the office of minister of broadcasting, which the previous Labour government had abolished.[28] A state-owned media was one that could be influenced, and the National government was more reluctant than its predecessor had been to lose this sway. The BCNZ brought both television networks together under joint control, with the intention that they would operate with the 'maximum practicable independence'.[29] While programmers began to approach scheduling more holistically across the two networks, competition between them remained more vicious than anyone might have imagined.

South Pacific Television was hungry for new talent. They wanted it raw, as this was inexpensive and they could shape it and make it their own. Their investment in *Hudson and Halls* was part of a larger plan that would pay dividends later. As long as well-established stars were a costly luxury, there was room for new lights to emerge – and shine *Hudson and Halls* did, with unexpected radiance.

But it was not the only outrageous show in the suite of new locally produced programmes. Even more improper was *A Week of It*. 'The first words of the opening programme were: "Tonight we answer the question on everyone's lips – what's [Leader of the Opposition] Bill Rowling like in bed?" … The second line was as naughty: "And here's the Prime Minister (Mr Muldoon) getting a lei." With repartee like that *A Week of It* shot to prime time. Contracts with the writing team (mainly Christchurch lawyers) and actors were renewed.'[30] *A Week of It* sent New Zealanders into hysterics. This was an unparalleled blossoming of satirical talent. Billy T. James was another remarkable performer, who initially came to prominence in the variety show *Radio Times*, then went on to star in his own comedy skit show.[31] He captured both the spirit and the issues of the nation.

This burst of comic energy was an act of self-determination as well as a sign of maturity. For years New Zealanders had laughed vicariously at British and American spoofs and comic commentary. The personalities referred to were not necessarily household names and the 'insider' jokes often needed explaining, but Kiwis were habituated voyeurs accustomed to pressing their noses up against someone else's window to catch some second-hand laughs. Now it was New Zealand personalities and institutions that were being made fun of. It was a coming of age. The country had an audience mature enough to throw off its worthy shackles and laugh at itself. *A Week of It* rocketed up the ratings to become a nationwide favourite. Viewers tuned in as if it were a blood sport to see who would be lampooned next. Similarly, Billy T. James trampled over tribal and interracial taboos to become a star. Out of anyone else's mouth a lot of his material would have been slammed as racist, but when *he* said it, it was funny and *everyone* laughed.

Comic satire and collective laughter were the great salve of the 1970s, and were also immensely unifying and commanding. 'The routine of television watching,' remembers Lindsay Waugh, 'structured your life … which gave television personalities a hell of a lot more power because everybody saw it at the same time, and so you would talk about it the next day: "Did you see whatever on television last night?" … *Hudson and Halls* rode the wave of … that celebrity stuff when television was scheduled, and that, when you think back, was a very short window.'[32]

With *A Week of It* and Billy T. James also vying for light entertainment slots, the local competition for *Hudson and Halls* was fierce. The stakes were high. The peak-viewing format had to be tighter and more polished than it had been. There must be a greater seriousness to the show. The summer days of South Pacific Television's beginning were also over, and when the pressure came on, some of the fun faded. Even Evelyn, their avid live-audience fan, noticed a difference. Reflecting on the shift in culture, she recalled: 'They used to hand round one of those big flat trays of chocolates [during the recording of the show]. If it didn't go round there was another box. Television really must be feeling the pinch. There's no chocs now, and we even have to pay 10 cents for a cup of coffee at break.' *Hudson and Halls'* recording schedule had also changed. 'This year,' explained Evelyn, 'they recorded the first [show] in the afternoon, had tea and then did a late show. I thought I wasn't going to be able to watch them because I wouldn't have been able to get [a bus] home, and I wouldn't stay out after dark. No fear!'[33] Fortunately Evelyn managed to find a ride home and continued her unbroken attendance.

The evening audience was also more diverse. Would the pair retain their universal appeal? When asked by a journalist to explain their popularity, Peter responded, 'I think our success gives the lie to this myth about the butchness of the average Kiwi male … It seems to us that most New Zealand men are gentler and more tolerant than most people realise. I wouldn't say we've been instrumental in breaking down sexual prejudice … but we've never suffered an unkind word in that area. Wharfies and truck drivers are among our greatest followers.'[34] This was the positive spin Peter, David and the studio bosses wanted to believe. Would it continue to be the case when it was tested against the relentless reality of prime-time ratings?

Reflecting on this issue, Lindsay Waugh believes they were actually under constant threat. 'It never occurred to me at the time because [the television staff] all knew [they were homosexual] and of course it wasn't a big deal … We knew it was illegal – but it didn't occur to me how vulnerable they must have felt.'[35] The most vivid demonstration of Peter and David's vulnerability was the so-called 'Moyle Affair'. In

1976 Prime Minister Robert Muldoon told parliament that the Labour MP Colin Moyle had been '"picked up by the police for homosexual activities" several months earlier. Muldoon claimed he had received a phone call from the police who told him that Moyle had been driving slowly past the Harris Street toilets, a long-established Wellington beat, with his car window wound down. An undercover officer suspected Moyle of soliciting, Muldoon said, and approached him for questioning.'[36] Moyle, who could offer neither the police officer nor parliament a satisfactory reason for his actions, was forced to resign.

The network had already anticipated the need for damage control in relation to *Hudson and Halls*. When the question of their 'gayness' was finally posed by media, they were ready with a prepared answer. 'Are we gay?' Peter asked. 'Well, we're certainly merry. No question about it.' The response was a reference to Noël Coward who, notoriously, was not very merry but certainly very gay. With all the clever duplicity of a sphinx, Peter had said 'yes'. So, how would the average Kiwi male respond? Peter was even prepared to admit, 'We still expect to be hit rather than offered a drink in the pub – but it doesn't work out that way.'[37] However, David and Peter – and the network – must have worried.

Crisp Fried Fish with Lemon Sauce

SERVES 4–6

If you are going to have fried fish in batter then you might as well do it right. This recipe we devised when we had our own Fish and Oyster Restaurant [sic] ... The dish was extremely popular and when we eventually tried to take it off the menu and offer some alternative there were violent complaints from our many regular customers. We also used to serve with it this delicious lemon sauce ...

1 kilo (2¼lb) of firm fish fillets
plain flour for dusting
peanut oil for deep frying
6 spring onions

BATTER
1 cup plain flour
pinch salt
1 tablespoon peanut oil
1 cup water, approx.
2 egg whites

LEMON SAUCE
2 cups chicken stock
2 large strips of lemon peel
⅔ cup of lemon juice
good 2-inch piece of fresh green
    ginger, sliced thinly
⅓ cup tightly packed soft brown sugar
2 tablespoons arrowroot mixed with a
    cup of water

Cut the fillets into fingers and coat lightly in the flour. Dip in the batter and drain off the excess. Heat the oil in a large pan or wok and lower several pieces of the coated fish into the hot oil. Fry until light golden brown, which only takes a few minutes. Don't be tempted to overcrowd the cooking pot or wok. Drain each batch on kitchen paper and keep warm until you have cooked all the fish. Place on a heated serving dish, chop up the spring onions and sprinkle on the top. Finally pour over the lemon sauce, and try and serve it before it goes soggy ...

For the batter, sift the flour and salt into a medium-sized bowl and add oil and enough water to make a fairly thick batter. Beat well and leave to stand for at least 20 minutes. Just before using, beat the egg whites until fairly stiff and fold into the batter.

The sauce is made by putting the chicken stock, lemon rind and juice into a heavy-based medium-sized pot, adding the sliced ginger and sugar. Bring to the boil, lower the heat, covering and gently simmering for 10 minutes. Strain the sauce to get rid of solids and pour back into the saucepan. Add the arrowroot mixed with water to the sauce. Stir until the sauce comes back to the boil and thickens. Simmer one minute more and serve.

7. *Hudson and Halls* & an Oyster and Fish Restaurant: 1976–79

The new-format, peak-time *Hudson and Halls* began on Wednesday 9 March 1977 at 10.10pm. A newly released *Hudson & Halls Cookbook* accompanied the launch of the show.

The sumptuously illustrated, 172-page, large-format book was heralded for months in advance by the media, and was widely reviewed. 'In typical H and H style,' wrote the reviewer for *8 o'clock* in May 1977, 'many recipes call for a generous helping of liquor – vermouth with sole fillets, sherry with sautéed mushrooms, marsala [wine] with Neapolitan onions, rum with chocolate soufflé and red or white wine with almost everything.'[1] The alcohol content, along with the elegant images by Auckland-based photographer Basil Williams, set the *Hudson & Halls Cookbook* apart from the more familiar church and social club fundraising cookbooks and cheaper industry publications.

The cover illustration showed a young and trendy Peter Hudson and David Halls – celebrity chefs – relaxed and at home. Their approach in the text struck a similarly breezy note, with more than a whiff of inebriation. 'Mistakes can make the perfect cook and we have made plenty, so will you, but in the end we all learn something. Be a bit flamboyant, take a risk, don't worry too much … you can always add more wine … or go out to dinner! Enjoy yourselves, that is what it is all about.'[2]

The new show was more composed than the earlier one. 'Gone are the frantic dashes from kitchen to salon. The pace is more controlled [and] at least cooks at home now have a chance of keeping up with the play,' wrote a reporter for the *Auckland Star* in 1977.[3] Better reviews. A cookbook. Peter and David had shattered the ceiling of celebrity at last. Their egos inflated with their exponential rise in popularity.

The cover image of the Hudson & Halls Cookbook *(1977) showed the young and trendy celebrity chefs relaxed and at home.*

Frosted Cheese Mould.

Basil Williams' photographs for the book were highly styled, as shown by the back-cover illustration of a Frosted Cheese Mould.

Crepe Cake (left) and Russian Crepes. Many of the recipes in the Hudson & Halls
Cookbook *called for 'a generous helping of liquor' – vermouth, sherry, rum – 'and red or
white wine with almost everything'.*

The Hudson & Halls' Double Chocolate Cake recipe came with a warning of sorts: 'This is very rich, and only small portions need be served … unless you really love chocolate, in which case get stuck in and enjoy.'

Fresh Fruit Flan

The heavily glazed Fresh Fruit Flan.

Riding high: on the cover of the New Zealand Listener, 2 April 1977.

In June 1977 they flew to Australia principally to promote the *Hudson & Halls Cookbook*. In their bags they had packed tapes of their new prime-time show. They, and South Pacific Television, were desperate to sell it to Australia. 'It seems the Australians are biting. They suddenly want to know who Hudson and Halls are,' Barry O'Brien, one of the network bosses, told the *Auckland Star*. Peter and David were guests on three television talkback shows: Nine Network, Ten Network and Channel Seven. They were also interviewed on three radio stations, including with their old friend John Law, who had Australia's top-rating talk show on 2UW in Sydney.[4]

The pair returned briefly to Auckland for the Telethon at the end of the month, touching down like a tornado before taking off for a two-month trip overseas. They were taking their cookbook to the international market.

Hudson and Halls were an obvious choice to join the line-up of hosts for the 24-hour television fundraising extravaganza that was Telethon. They were spontaneous, able to think on their feet, and keen for the extra publicity. At various points throughout the event, footage from the five main centres of Auckland, Hamilton, Wellington, Christchurch and Dunedin showed hysterical cheering about fundraising targets from the live studio audiences. The telethon jingle was 'Thank You Very Much for Your Kind Donation' and it was played to celebrate milestone targets or large donations. The atmosphere in the studios was one of manic excitement.

The 1977 Telethon raised an astonishing $2 million for the treatment of arthritis. It was judged a huge success by everyone except David Halls, whose experience was tainted by the public response to a gaffe. Slipping back into pantomime-cum-*Carry-On*-movie mode, he made a bawdy comment about his co-host Gabrielle Drake's breasts. David dismissed the furore: 'Three seconds of trivia out of 24 hours of brilliance.'[5] He excused his remark on the grounds that it was admiring. Maybe he felt exempt from censure because he was gay. Surely people would see it for what it was: a throw-away comment, a bit of light-hearted banter? He shared this kind of humour with Peter all the time. But when his risqué repartee was directed at a woman, not even he was exempt from criticism. Feminism had awakened the public consciousness to comments that objectified women. People were beginning to see them for what they were – inappropriate.

David was so heavily chastised, Gabrielle Drake felt she had to step in. She was 'horrified', she told *8 o'clock*: 'I took David's remark as a compliment, for that is how it was intended. All this fuss is utterly ridiculous – David is a nice person.'[6]

Peter and David left New Zealand for a two-month book promotion tour of the US, the UK and Europe a few days later. Before he left, David reiterated his consternation: 'I just cannot understand the fuss about my remark.'[7] Still, their departure was fortuitous, removing David from the heat and extinguishing all debate.

In every other respect, they were leaving on a high. 'We have to see Hamlyns, our publishers,' announced Peter. '[We] sold over 7000 copies of our cookbook in three weeks without advertising and are extremely pleased.'[8] This huge volume of rapid sales was testament to the impact of primetime programming. Hudson and Halls were a household name. The Telethon fiasco was a lesson learned, if only they could apply it to their own steamy moments of spontaneity under the spotlight. David was stung by the criticism. He felt misunderstood, betrayed even by the media, but the incident was also exposure to the fact that profile was everything and almost no publicity was bad publicity.

In the duo's absence the cookbook continued to sell, and they negotiated another contract with South Pacific Television for a second prime-time season.

*

Peter and David flew first to Los Angeles, then to London. David, especially, was stunned by what he saw. There was a new kind of youth on the streets. The psychedelic, head-spinning hippie lifestyle was making way for the nihilism of the head-banger generation. The cosmic guru was about to be covered in punk grunge. 'Punk rockers wearing safety pins through their flesh – ears, noses, necks and faces – are a common sight these days on fashionable King's Road,' David recorded in an article sent back to New Zealand. 'It's there they meet their common enemy, the Teddy Boys, to do battle, although the conflict is evidently not as aggressive as most of the newspapers report.'[9]

But this burgeoning new counter-culture barely touched Peter and David, who were much more interested in the fashion on King's Road. On Jermyn Street, Peter's favourite haunt from his OE days, 'we bought beautifully cut, best quality pure cotton shirts for around $25. Really worthwhile,' they chorused to readers at home.[10] They also published their own survey of ice-cream vendors. 'Prices here in London continue to astound us … A van outside the Houses of Parliament charged 90c, but the price went up to an all-time high of $1.20 outside Madame Tussauds.'[11] They loved the big-city buzz of London and celebrated its eccentricities. 'It's strange to see so many cyclists on the street here – not just people in casual clothes, but businessmen complete with bowler hat and briefcase. They are braver than us.'[12]

Peter and David with friend John Addey, a key public relations adviser to Rupert Murdoch and 'early backer of Vidal Sassoon', London, 1977.

Tony Larsen (left), John Addey and Peter.
JOHN FIELDS, PRIVATE COLLECTION

While still in London at the beginning of August, they 'gave a brilliant cocktail party … on behalf of Hamlyn's – the people who published our cookbook – at Searcy's', a restaurant they hoped would dazzle their London friends as well as their publishers.[13] They were on an alcohol-fuelled high at the Searcy's book launch, and at the more intimate dinner party with special friends afterwards. This was the culmination of all their hard work and good fortune. David scrawled an effusive note in the cookbook he signed for their close friend John Fields and his partner. The message was an ecstatic celebration of food, friendship and all that celebrity had brought them. The dedication listed in French the names of those at the dinner party, finishing with 'et the rest of the world!! et the E.E.C.–!!!! Pierre et David, Love us xxxxx'.

After London they went their separate ways for a time: Peter 'to see old friends in Paris', and David to go home to Epping 'and take me mum a copy of our new cookbook', he told reporters in New Zealand.[14] The cookbook and its association with a well-known London publisher and ritzy launch party at Searcy's were concrete proof for Hilda and George Halls that their long-absent son had finally made it. His television show might be screening only in New Zealand, but David had talked to them about syndication, about the chance of selling the show to Australia,

Britain and the US. It felt as if anything might be possible. He had come so far from his co-op days that even his parents struggled to maintain their opposition to him emigrating.

But there was still a silence around his sexuality. They had had their suspicions, and to some extent the image of Peter and David together on the cover of the cookbook confirmed their worst fears. But David's parents would reserve their words on the matter as long as David reserved his. Their reunion in Epping was, therefore, clannish. He was drawn back into the family, embraced like the prodigal son returned. It was a wonderful welcome for David, but without Peter there it also felt incomplete.

*

By the time they arrived back in New Zealand in the later part of 1977, the dust had settled over the Gabrielle Drake debacle. At the forefront of most people's minds was the success of Hudson and Halls' last series. John Carlaw, their producer, told readers of the *Auckland Star* that the 'show had done exceptionally well against stiff opposition on Wednesday nights'.[15] This was enough to secure them another 12-week series in the same time slot. David and Peter were delighted. It seemed that their run of good fortune would never end. Their growing confidence was matched by an increased commitment to New Zealand – and to New Zealand television, which had breathed sweet celebrity into their lives. Repeatedly in interviews they would say that their ratings kept them in the country. 'We don't want to leave New Zealand, of that we are certain,' they said individually and together.[16]

The underlying implication, however, was that if the tide of public feeling for them began to ebb, they would follow up leads elsewhere. They were citizens of the world, cut free from their roots by a restless desire to escape the limitations 'home' placed on their homosexuality. Having moved once, they could imagine moving again. However, these thoughts were well to the backs of their minds when they began shooting the second series, programmed to premiere on South Pacific Television on 21 September, again on a Wednesday night.

The following year's show, which began on 20 May and ended on 24 June 1978, was more innovative still. In this series they had a greater influence on the format. They felt completely invested in the programmes, which were groundbreaking because they took viewers out into the world beyond the studio: to the place where the food they were cooking and serving was found, farmed or grown. *Hudson and Halls* now combined the great Kiwi 'hunter-gatherer' spirit with a love of the

This studio set was designed by Roy Good for Hudson and Halls in the late 1970s.
ROY GOOD, PRIVATE COLLECTION

outdoors. This was what had appealed to Peter and David most about New Zealand, and they were keen to incorporate it in the show.

Hudson and Halls was programmed to take over the *A Week of It* slot. The *Auckland Star* promised readers that 'over the next six weeks [Hudson and Halls] will prepare dishes featuring venison, trout, cheese, crayfish, avocado and oysters … the first eight minutes of each programme were shot on location and provide a blend of information about that week's main ingredient and the area where it is found. They visit an oyster farm at Russell and a deer farm at Taupo, go trout-fishing near Rotorua, gather avocados and select a crayfish at Gisborne and visit a cheese factory at Eltham.'[17]

To accommodate the new shot-on-location segments, the *Auckland Star* reported that the show 'would not include guests and entertainment as it did last year'.[18] The series was now a lot more costly to make. 'Each programme took two days filming … The studio sequences were done in front of an audience which naturally included "Hudson and Halls" regular Mrs Evelyn Balmforth.'[19] Their first programme opened

Filming on location, 1978.
CLOCKWISE FROM TOP: *Rotorua, where they also tried trout fishing and explored the tourist town; a deer farm near Taupo; Rotorua; relaxing at an avocado orchard in Gisborne.* COURTESY OF THE *NEW ZEALAND LISTENER*

David and Peter pose in front of a statue of Captain Cook in Gisborne in 1978.
COURTESY OF THE *NEW ZEALAND LISTENER*

with Peter and David standing in front of a statue of Captain James Cook in Gisborne. 'If one Cook can go to sea, why not two?' they asked.[20]

Peter and David were delighted with the indoor–outdoor format, but studio bosses reeled at the cost. The new combination was far from the cheap and cheerful partnership that had made local programming possible. To send a camera crew around the country was a heavy financial commitment, especially for a half-hour's viewing. This was not cost-effective television. The next series, they decided, would be filmed entirely in the studio.

Peter and David were devastated when they heard the news. They believed in the show, and thought their rising star gave them clout with the programmers. They went into battle, only to find themselves beating at a brick wall. The network's decision also rubbed raw their feelings about reimbursement. More than once the normally good-natured David referred in interviews to the network's meanness. 'Not that we care so much for money … Well, we get so little from South Pacific Television,' he told reporters.[21]

141

The distance between the two parties became so great that in the end it was irreconcilable. '[Hudson and Halls] have parted company with South Pacific Television,' the *Auckland Star* announced at the end of July 1978.[22] The newspaper interviewed the network's light entertainment boss, Barry O'Brien, who was vitriolic about the separation. The company had three more series planned and the duo's behaviour felt like a body blow. 'They made totally unreasonable demands in respect of their next series,' he told a reporter. 'We couldn't comply with the finance and facilities that they requested.' His frustration with the couple wouldn't allow him to leave it there. Besides, he added, 'they were not rating very well either. In fact, they were only drawing half the audience, or less, than *A Week of It* did.'[23]

Peter and David were equally determined to defend themselves, putting their own case to media. The couple explained that when they were told that the next series beginning in August 1978 would be shot entirely in the studio, they offered an immediate solution. They understood the issue was money. The cost of making the outdoor film was $1000, Peter told the *Auckland Star*: 'that is $7000 for the next series. They said they could not raise that much and this is what we are angry about … we could have cut out the final series and used the money to make the best possible shows. But they said we could not do another outdoor show at this juncture. So what is the point of going on if we cannot agree on how the shows should be done?'[24]

Peter and David were completely committed to the outdoor segments. This was iconic New Zealand footage, they believed, set to bolster the burgeoning tourism industry. As well as being angry, they were hurt. But too much had been said, and neither side would budge. So Hudson and Halls took their brand, and their cookbooks, and left South Pacific Television.

*

Life on the other side of television celebrity was lacklustre. They had lost the audience that meant so much to them. There were positives, though. They still had their morning slot on Radio Hauraki with Kevin Black, 9–10am, which was well received. Their talkback-style cooking programme was relaxed and fun, and Kiwi audiences listened in and responded enthusiastically.

Radio cooking shows have a long history in New Zealand broadcasting. For years Maud Basham, or Aunt Daisy as she was known, began her broadcasts on public radio with a singsong 'Good morning, good morning, good morning … the sun is shining up my back passage.' Aunt Daisy was an institution. She had begun broadcasting about classical composers on the YA network in the 1920s. Her ZB cooking programme, which started in 1933, became rock-solid reassurance for New Zealanders during decades of Depression, war and unparalleled change. Her many followers listened avidly to her not-so-parochial recipes and advice. London-born Aunt Daisy was also a traveller, particularly to the US, where she picked up cosmopolitan culinary ideas and brought them back.

In her own middle-class, middle-aged way Aunt Daisy was a subversive. As both the comfortable voice of Kiwi cooking and a harbinger of change, she regaled New Zealand radio audiences with her recipes for more than three decades. Less than a week after signing off for the last time in 1963, Aunt Daisy died at age 83. Her departure overlapped with the beginning of the television era and a new form of cooking instruction. Radio, however, did not disappear as a disseminator of recipes and advice.

Television cooks Graham Kerr and Des Britten both began with or had strong connections to radio, but it was food presenter Alison Holst who was the true heir to Aunt Daisy's empire. She started in radio as the modest voice of the middle ground but, like her predecessor, she was a quiet revolutionary. Born in Opoho in Dunedin in 1938, Alison Holst was a dyed-in-the-wool New Zealander. Her father Arthur was a lecturer at Dunedin Teachers' College and her mother Margaret a trained nurse and notable cook: 'Cooking to her was a vital part of the house, of life, of love, of everything else.' Margaret passed on her skills to Alison, who then incrementally shifted the ground.[25] Through radio programmes, her cookbooks and, more demonstratively, her television cooking series which began in 1965, she changed people's ideas about cooking.

The director of the New Zealand Broadcasting Corporation actually went looking for Alison Holst. Grumblings about Graham Kerr's food being too fancy inspired the search for someone to demonstrate cooking for ordinary people using uncomplicated ingredients on a modest budget. Alison Holst fitted the profile perfectly because in essence this was her mission. She was invited to make a pilot and, she remembers, '"I was terrified. My hands shook. I picked up a lettuce and called it a lemon."'[26] The outcome, however, was that she was hired and would, over time, introduce her burgeoning audiences to exotic ingredients, new technologies, and life-changing approaches to food and cooking.

Like Des Britten, Alison Holst understood the New Zealand psyche around food as only a native could. She knew instinctively what the New Zealand diet needed, and by 1967 she was already perceiving a change. 'I think that more families nowadays enjoy well balanced, satisfying meals, and find that there is no need to "stock up" on the large morning and afternoon tea for which New Zealand is so famous – or notorious! Young women, too, no longer feel that it is necessary to provide a tea-wagon laden with food when their friends come around for a cup of tea.'[27]

*

As well as having the sweet tooth identified by Alison Holst, New Zealanders loved their butter and cream. Butter was sliced from the block and spread thickly like cheese. Cooking commentator and historian David Veart notes that 'in 1920s New Zealand butter and cream were like the Mediterranean's wine and oil – basic items, cheap and always to hand'.[28] To some extent, New Zealand developed its idiosyncrasies around food preparation because of the ready availability of primary produce such as meat and dairy. In 1951 Scottish food writer Eric Linklater wrote: 'The natural quality of the food is so good that it deserves both skill and reverence in the kitchen. What lordly dishes a French housewife would make of it! But the New Zealanders, like the Scots, think that baking is the better part of cookery, spend their ingenuity, exhaust their interest, on cakes, and pastries and ebullient, vast cream sponges.'[29] The naked ingredients available were so naturally good that baking became the true test of a Kiwi cook's kitchen craft.

But meat and dairy were not the only raw ingredients in plentiful supply. The colonial necessity for self-sufficiency meant many people in both rural and urban areas grew their own fruit and vegetables, which in season were often available in copious quantities. The large quarter-acre section on which most suburban houses were built begged to be dug up. Kitchen gardens were the norm and autumn was harvest festival time. Glass jars lined kitchen benches, and caseloads of fruit, vegetables and berries were bottled, pickled and preserved. Kiwi cookbooks provided instructions and tips for preserving as well as recipes for brines, syrups, jams, chutneys and relishes. The family vegetable plot was generally the man's domain, so preserving was not necessarily gender specific, as most other cooking was. Men sometimes joined women in this factory-style storing of food for the winter. Preserving was entrepreneurial, and the family who were the shareholders of this home-industry ate the profits.

In the same way that Americans added a dollop of ice-cream to every dessert, New Zealanders ladled out their preserves. They served meat dishes with relishes, chutneys, pickles and sauces, and to puddings they added preserved peaches, pears, plums, cherries or apricots. In items such as pies and crumbles, preserves became the fruit pulp. Whether bottled fruits accessorised or were fundamental to the dish, desserts in most households were mandatory. Meals were not complete without this flamboyant star.

Housewives, generally the unpaid domestic labourers, also cooked confectionery, cakes and biscuits. Eating in between meals was institutionalised in the form of morning and afternoon teas. Tea or coffee was almost never consumed in isolation. Coffee, especially during the first half of the twentieth century, was of variable, even dubious quality. One commentator wistfully watched as servicemen helped themselves to their own supplies of freeze-dried coffee from home. 'Americans here are provided with two excellent brands of instantaneous coffee. They travel about in New Zealand hotels with little bottles of fine brown powder. When coffee is offered them, they say, "May I just have boiling water please." They whisk a small teaspoonful of powder into the cup, and fill it with boiling water. The powder completely dissolves, leaving no grounds [and] making a lustrous brown liquid with an appetising flavour which, with the addition of cream, turns the required gold beige.'[30]

Cakes and biscuits were the mainstay of the Kiwi morning and afternoon tea ritual. Tins had to be full, particularly for a farmer's wife, whose job it was to feed the multitudes of hard-working farmhands. Everyone expected a choice, so local cookbooks contained a host of sugary recipes. This reflected New Zealand's Scottish and Anglo-Saxon heritage, as it did current practice around home-based hospitality.

The imbibing of strong drink was equally surrounded by social sanctions. Teetotallers the majority of New Zealanders certainly were not; however, their behaviour around alcohol was very different to that of their forebears. In Britain in the nineteenth century, children in industrialised urban centres such as London grew up drinking flat beer and cider from an early age because it was the only refreshment pretty well guaranteed to be free of cholera or typhoid. Although the public house was the place where much liquor was consumed, many households kept their own supplies of alcohol. In fact, John Nott's *The Cooks and Confectioners Dictionary*, published in 1723, provided recipes for homemade wine, cider and beer. Alcohol was consumed domestically, and used in cooking to subdue the smell of rank meat and to tenderise old birds and leathery cuts in dishes such as meat and game pies.

New Zealand's drinking culture developed differently. Māori were one of the few peoples in the world who did not ferment inebriating drink. The post-colonial impact of alcohol on Māori culture was devastating and cautionary. The drunken debauchery of early whaling, prospecting, mining and forestry communities was also sobering. This history, plus the fact that the water was pure and many of the earliest white settlers were Christian missionaries, gave rise to a very different culture around alcohol. Drinking was generally done in the men-only public house between the finish of work and the serving of last drinks just before 6pm. Until the end of six o'clock closing on 9 October 1967, it was often a race to consume as much – mostly beer – as possible in the shortest time. Men then stumbled home in varying states of intoxication.

Modest quantities of fortified wine such as ports and sherries were the official tipple of the middle classes. In the early days of the Dominion, these were imported and expensive, and in the home were often measured out by the thimbleful. With this kind of preciousness around liquor it was almost impossible to imagine squandering it on a prime cut of meat that didn't require much tenderising in the first place. If this reticence needed bolstering there were also the pioneer's puritanical scruples, which made the concept of cooking with alcohol seem somehow lasciviously wanton. The use of wine or beer in a recipe broke some austere moral code in the Kiwi DNA.

To avoid the temptation to slop a cup of demon drink into a dish, cooking wine was not kept in the house, and in true settler style both the flesh and the dish were mortified with vinegar. Housewives using recipes sufficiently sophisticated to include wine in the ingredients automatically reached for the DYC malt vinegar as if the two items were interchangeable. The virtuous home economist could congratulate herself as she glug-glugged the vinegar into her measuring cup: not only had she saved the household budget money, but she had saved souls as well.

Prescriptions around the consumption of alcohol and food overflowed into the world of public dining. As late as the 1960s, many restaurants in New Zealand were unable to serve liquor with food. Even versatile malt vinegar could not o'erleap the ambitious gap between the recipe and the wine glass. Kiwi restaurants remained largely dry zones and the casual link between food and wine was not clearly established. Eating out was rare in any case, and the majority of it done at the nearest pie cart, or seated on tubular steel, vinyl-covered chairs around Formica tables in the sit-in section of the local fish and chip shop. This area included atmospheric extras such as a fly eradicator, white neon strip lighting, a faded poster of New Zealand coastal fish and a dusty vase of pop-together plastic flowers.

More exclusive eateries did exist, but these had their limitations. There was a certain predictability about the menu in the late 1960s and 1970s. 'We still had restaurants in Wellington like Clichy's,' remembers Lindsay Waugh. 'You know,

Chicken in a Basket, there was Prawn Cocktail and Filet Mignon. Every place was serving the same and it was really tedious.'[31]

In spite of the fact that New Zealand is surrounded by sea, fish was an expensive item on restaurant menus and not a popular choice of many home economists. Seafood was regarded as a delicacy. The other gulp-making gap in the Kiwi diet was the salad. Although kitchen gardens could accommodate and had the climate to grow great salad ingredients, many did not. Traditionally, Māori had steamed their vegetables in subterranean earth ovens, and settler stock baked or boiled theirs to death on the stovetop. There was nothing in the collective Kiwi consciousness to raise the national heartbeat over salad. When an obligatory lettuce leaf or two were added to a meal, they were often finely cut like cabbage and copiously coated in dressing, which was blobbed on by the ladleful.

Salad dressing raised pulses. With a base of sweetened condensed milk, camouflaged by that most adaptable of kitchen condiments, malt vinegar, it satisfied New Zealanders' cravings for sugary sweetness. A marriage of favourites: shaken in a jar, not stirred, then seasoned with a little salt and pepper, this was the flavour on everyone's lips. Enough dressing on those strings of watery lettuce, and the salad-averse Kiwi could almost forget they were eating something raw.

New Zealanders mostly socialised over meals cooked domestically. Hospitality happened in the home, and mostly in the weekends. Those who entertained during the week were suspect. This was backsliding and hedonistic. Heartland people had guests over for a meal on the weekend. Cooks were also quantity surveyors. All ingredients had to be purchased well in advance of cooking because all shops except corner dairies closed in the weekend. Even then, large swathes of stock were covered with drop-sheets to keep covetous eyes from lusting after the stock banned from weekend sale. Last-minute purchases of all but the most basic items were impossible until store business resumed on a Monday morning.

Recipe items were listed and purchased down to the quarter-teaspoonful, especially if they were something a little out of the ordinary like mixed spice or curry powder. A miscalculation sent the supplicant cook cup-in-hand next door. There was a tacit understanding. Neighbourhoods ran their own co-operative food bank where cups of sugar, flour, malt vinegar and even eggs were borrowed and repaid, often with interest. This exchange of ingredients built communities at the same time as it baked cakes.

The ingredients that stocked the shelves of local grocery stores in New Zealand were a puritan's paradise of austerity. Basic foods such as meat and dairy were amply available, and seasonal fruit and vegetables were generally well stocked and reasonably cheap. However, nearly everything unusual or exotic had to be imported. The English diet dominated not only what could be grown but also what arrived from overseas. This, plus the distance food items had to travel, limited the variety of herbs, spices, sauces, cheeses, wines (and the list went on …) that came into the country. Curries were dangerously daring; a sprinkling of paprika atop a shrimp cocktail on its finely chopped bed of lettuce, swimming in sweetened condensed-milk mayonnaise, a rakish addition.

It was not until the incendiary impact of the eggplant and avocado that the 'meat and three veg' monopoly was finally broken. Home cooks in the 1960s and 70s had few reference points to understand how these vegetables might function in a meal. The eggplant's alluring skin with its purple-black sheen and the avocado's tantalising waxy green flesh prompted explorer cooks to risk untried recipes, and quite abruptly tastes began to change.

*

Peter and David relished their radio connection with listeners, but this was not enough. Not enough to support them, at least, in the celebrity lifestyle to which they had become accustomed. They urgently needed another source of income and more connection with people. Opening a restaurant of their own appealed from the start. Their contacts in the restaurant industry would be helpful, and they had a ready-made profile to attract people in. Their first thoughts were to make it strictly lunchtime fare. 'We don't like working nights,' David confessed to the *Sunday News*.[32] Late shifts were gruelling and a young person's game. Their opening hours had to allow them a more sedate pace. Not that they had slowed down, but they had lost the desperate edge that does anything for nothing. They were proven. Time now to cash in on their reputation.

One possible solution came from conversations with their friend Suzi Kitt, owner of the garden restaurant Oblio's (named, according to the newspapers, after her dead cat) in Ponsonby, one of Auckland's rapidly gentrifying inner-city suburbs. Oblio's, opening as usual in the evenings, would now be shared by Peter and David offering a lunchtime menu. There was quite some debate over the naming of their new establishment. Their initial preference was H & H's Paté Parlour, but they finally opted for Hudson and Halls Oyster and Fish Restaurant.

In the end, instead of sharing with Oblio's, in 1979 they bought their own restaurant premises at 170 Jervois Road. This couldn't have been a more convenient location. Just the year before, Peter and David had moved from their immaculate little cottage in Brighton Road to an upmarket apartment overlooking St Marys Bay. One of five and built on a dramatic cliff edge at 7 London Street, the apartment took up two floors on the right-hand side of the A-framed building. David and Peter were at the peak of their television celebrity when they bought the apartment, and time was in short supply. Now there'd be no pool to maintain, no grounds to care for. And this was an undeniably salubrious address.

Geoffrey Collins, a young Saatchi & Saatchi executive who lived on the floor above them, quickly became a friend – and their official food taster. 'I used to have a lot of meals at their place,' he recalls, 'because they'd be cooking stuff for their show and then want to give it to someone to try … so they would give it to me …'[33] Geoffrey spent many entertaining evenings eating and, especially, drinking with them; in time, they were joined by Geoffrey's fiancée, Abby Smith.

Wellington-born Abby had worked as a model for 11 years in Asia and the UK. Coming back to New Zealand in the late 1970s was a huge culture shock. Sheets continued to be drawn over banned weekend produce, and cafés were straitjacketed inside their premises, even in balmy Auckland. It took a brave Three Lamps café in Ponsonby to finally break the council's by-laws and cautiously move a few tables and chairs out onto the pavement. The few fashionable nightspots were frequented by a familiar crowd. 'They opened the Melba,' Abby remembers, 'and downstairs the Mirage Club, and everybody would have dinner at the Melba and go downstairs … It was a fairly small clique, but it was full on.'[34]

Because Abby had been working overseas while Peter and David were establishing their careers as celebrity chefs, she had no idea who they were. 'One day Geoffrey said to me we should have Peter and David for dinner, and of course I couldn't bloody cook. I said, "Oh, okay." … So they came up for dinner and I made the most disgusting chicken and apricot with peas and various things only to find out that David couldn't eat peas and beans and legumes … But they were just so thrilled that someone cooked for them – actually had them to dinner.'[35] Despite the substantial age gap between them, the two couples became firm friends, socialising and drinking together regularly.

Peter and David's St Mary's Bay apartment became a party place in a similar way to their Brighton Road cottage, but these occasions were less centred on meals. Cooking was work. Entertaining was relaxing with a drink. 'Because our business is food we are now inclined to lose interest in eating,' Peter told an interviewer. 'I go upstairs in the afternoon, read 10 cookbooks and type my way through recipes. In a sense we've already had a meal when it is time for dinner. So we just go up the road and get hamburgers.'[36]

The London Street décor was even more extravagant than it had been at Brighton Road. 'It was very gay inside,' recalls Geoffrey Collins. 'It was all painted a dark brown, chocolate brown, and Peter had some wonderful antiques.'[37] The kitchen was just as dramatic, with onions, garlic, herbs, and copper pots and pans hanging European style from the walls and ceiling. It oozed camp sophistication, confused slightly by the idiosyncratic collection of new and antique items. The apartment was quintessentially modernist in design and style, but its new owners were men whose roots reached back to the Edwardian era. They learned the modernist motto 'less is more' rather than lived it instinctively.

Peter and David were living at London Street when they bought their enormous, three-ton 1962 Bentley S3 for $26,000. Abby Collins remembers them driving round in stately style like lords of the manor. The Bentley was part of the act, and part of them: how they wanted and imagined themselves to be. It was outfitted with two cocktail bars, which 'opened out from the backs of the front seats'. There were 'two picnic tables, attached to the bars and another … fitted on slides below the car's radio'. The interior, including carpet and leather upholstery, was rich red. The sun visors, too, were red and could be 'moved to the side windows … There are adjustable armrests on the front doors, sloping foot rests at the base of the back seats … [and] the interior woodwork is walnut.'[38]

While the Bentley was an extravagant establishment status symbol, David and Peter's ostentation was always balanced against their audacious disregard for rules and conventions. They drove drunk and neither of them had a driver's licence the whole time they owned the car. The Bentley was a dalliance and an act of defiance. Their celebrity, plus the fact that they came from other places, gave them the freedom to feel they were above the law.

But not every outing in the Bentley was a success. Geoffrey Collins and Abby Smith were married not long after they moved out of 7 London Street. Peter and David attended the wedding in their Bentley. 'They hopped in the car after the reception at my sister's house in Seaview Road,' Geoffrey remembers, 'and Peter's knee hit the handbrake and it took off down the road and crashed into a lamp-post. We all thought it was hilarious but Peter didn't … and of course they were both as pissed as owls.'[39] Even gossip columnist Felicity Ferret had something to say about the occasion in Auckland's *Metro* magazine. '*Abby Smith*, what an angel, finally made it legit, with marketing maestro of Blue Skys, the scrummy *Geoff Collins*. Abby's

Gossip columnist Felicity Ferret mentioned Abby and Geoff Collins' 1982 wedding in Auckland's Metro *magazine.* ABBY COLLINS, PRIVATE COLLECTION

glorious dress was designed by none other than the petit but very marvellous *Patrick Steele* … and *Hudson* and *Halls* got so carried away with the frivolities that they wrapped their Benters around a lamp-post on the way out. Tsk, tsk boys –'[40]

*

Peter and David wanted a cultured European-style ambience for their new restaurant. It was to transport its patrons to a foreign destination without leaving Auckland. Customers should feel like they were sitting at some secluded table on a cobbled street in London, Paris or Rome, or at a waterfront café on the French or Italian Riviera. The outdoor seating area was a Sissinghurst of perfumed flowers, and was themed spectacularly in white. There were white classical statues of water-carrying women; white wrought-iron furniture; and white busy Lizzies and waterfall petunias bursting forth in profusion from hanging baskets and planters. A water feature added the relaxing sound of trickling water and Vivaldi's 'Four Seasons' played in the background on a repeating reel.

'They had a gardener, Bill, who used to come in and do the gardening and everything was impeccable. Just beautifully, beautifully presented,' recalls Stephanie

Hall, one of the restaurant staff. 'It was all covered in … and everyone wanted to sit in the garden. "Please can I have the garden?" "Sorry the garden's booked, it will have to be inside" – the demand was constant.' Like their apartment, the interior of the restaurant was a magnificent chocolate brown, 'very dark, big mirrors and beautifully lit', and was full of Peter and David's antiques, collected over many years: 'Georgian silver candlesticks, Blackamoors – the old-fashioned little black boy holding the candelabra – Victorian chandeliers. All the porcelain was German Arzberg … and heavy, heavy crystal. Not cut crystal, but smooth. Beautiful water glasses … beautiful wine glasses. It was the 80s so it was lavish,' she remembers.[41]

Stephanie Hall got her job at Hudson and Halls Oyster and Fish Restaurant when she was just 18. She had been working at Tony's Britannia on the North Shore, and a friend, Tim Warren, who was working for Peter and David, urged her to apply. She was desperate to get the job, partly because they were so well known. 'I went over for the interview absolutely beside myself with nerves … "I've only ever worked in this big barn-like restaurant where they do steaks and stuff. But I can carry three plates,"' she reassured them.

"Love, love, we don't want that, that's fine,"' David told her, '"but we like someone who can work under pressure … that sort of restaurant means you can handle the pressure."'

Stephanie was hired on the spot, and it wasn't long before she was both hostess and on-site security, occupying a second-storey flat above the restaurant to keep the downstairs area safe. All Peter and David had was a simple push-button lock to secure thousands of dollars' worth of antiques. Occasionally, Stephanie would forget to push the button, go to bed, and awake in the early hours of the morning with the security guard shining a flashlight in her face and saying, 'You've forgotten to push the button in again, love.'

'What is it with you and that security guard?' David would ask her teasingly the next day.

'They taught me everything. I knew nothing,' Stephanie recalls. She had never eaten in a restaurant before she worked for them, only waited on tables. Peter and David would take her out to dine at The Bronze Goat, Oblio's and Bistro 260. 'They were all the really big popular restaurants on Ponsonby Road,' she remembers. 'The first time I went out for dinner … I ended up going out to Antoine's [an upmarket Parnell restaurant] in the back of the Bentley. So they're sitting up the front … I'm sitting in the back with this solid silver Georgian ice bucket between my thighs, with a half-bottle of Moet, for me, in the champagne bucket.' Antoine's had tripe and pigs'

Radiant in their white bower of delicious decadence in the garden area of the Hudson and Halls Oyster and Fish Restaurant, c. 1979. JANET PUTTNAM, PRIVATE COLLECTION

trotters on the menu – daring dishes which they loved. With the staff immaculately presented and on their best behaviour, David and Peter were still their irreverent selves.

'Have you got any bread and butter out the back?' Peter asked the waiter when he was halfway through his bowl of tripe.

'Oh, no sir, we don't serve that.'

'Come on, you must have a loaf of Tip Top out there.'

Then, after a brief hesitation …

'Yes, I'm sure we can manage to find you something.'

Finally there was Peter mopping up the sauce with a cheap bit of bread, and David, with the gravy running down to his elbows, sucking on the pigs' trotters.[42] They loved food. Their principal rule was that eating had to be pleasurable.

Peter was the backbone of Hudson and Halls Oyster and Fish Restaurant. He was a gentler, more refined presence than David, and hated going out to the restaurant. The kitchen was his sanctuary. He acknowledged people as they went past the door, but seldom ventured out. His vice was a little 5cm television on which he watched the afternoon soaps. The kitchen was hard work and his glasses were perpetually slipping down his nose in the heat, but this was his domain and he was in charge.

David was the razzle-dazzle dance man and his exuberance made working in the restaurant fun. When his foot wasn't bound up with ice inside a tea towel because of his gout, he would tap-dance or waltz through the restaurant, performing choreographed stage routines.

Among the promotional photographs for the restaurant is one of Peter and David sitting, beaming, in their white garden. They look happy; they were happy. Their restaurant was proof to all the doubters that they were not dabblers but a genuine part of the food industry. They were not just selling ideas about food but selling the food itself.

The image they projected publicly and the reality of their business practice were nonetheless at times some distance apart. While David was on the restaurant floor taking orders, Peter was often stressed and sweating to deliver meals. He swore and cursed audibly in the kitchen. They struggled to keep up and baulked at the 'customer is always right' philosophy – the first commandment of the restaurant industry. But when the pressure was off slightly and they were feeling relaxed, they slipped into the banter between themselves and their customers that had made them so appealing to New Zealand radio and television audiences.

Richard Matthews remembers going to their restaurant 'with Keith Lichtenstein, a great friend of mine, and we were about five minutes late and David shouted across the room, "Late again, Matthews," and I shrank.'[43] He was a friend, so Richard didn't take things too seriously, but not everyone appreciated the duo's cavalier style and Fawlty-esque approach. Geoffrey Collins remembers a story that did not finish happily. There was an illicit aspect to the restaurant's lunchtime service. Part of the attraction of the time slot was that long furtive liaisons could be conducted during business hours, away from the house-spouse and family. On Fridays, especially, men would bring their mistresses or wives to enjoy private time in a private space with great cuisine and wine.

One lunchtime a man accompanied by either his wife or mistress came into the restaurant carrying a BYO (bring-your-own) bottle of expensive rosé champagne. The lunch was clearly an important celebration. Before he was seated, the man handed the bottle of rosé over to David with the reverence of a priest passing a chalice. David put the bottle in the fridge while Peter prepared their food. But when David opened the fridge door to take the bottle out, the vacuum sucked the champagne onto the floor. It shattered on impact, gushing sticky pink liquid everywhere. A mortified David couldn't believe his bad luck.

The lighthearted fun that had preceded this catastrophe evaporated. What was he going to say? How was he going to explain it to the owner? The way to avoid all this was to find a replacement so the customer would never know the difference. David flew from one local liquor outlet to another in search of the rare pink drink. He found nothing even vaguely resembling the bottle that had been lost. Finally, he decided to mollify the customer by buying something even more impressive than the BYO bottle he had broken. The one hitch was that it wasn't pink.

He was breathless by the time he got back to the table and presented his *pièce de résistance* substitution. The patron, however, was livid, abusing David and telling him loudly and in no uncertain terms that he wasn't leaving the restaurant until he was served the bottle of wine he had brought. Crestfallen, David scuttled back to Peter in the kitchen to tell him what had happened.

Peter was furious. Flinging a napkin over his arm, he grabbed the exorbitant replacement wine and a bottle of red bitters and put them both on a silver tray. He carried the tray over to the table, and said to the man, 'If you insist on having rosé instead of this superb champagne, you can mix it your fucking self.'[44]

Crepe Cake

SERVES 4

(savoury filling)

This makes a lunch, supper or first course for dinner. First take a batch of crepes, one recipe of a simple, quick bechamel sauce and some fillings for layering between the crepes.

QUICK BECHAMEL SAUCE

1 tablespoon butter
2 tablespoons plain flour
1 cup milk
1 bay leaf
pinch each of grated nutmeg, salt and
    ground black pepper

Melt butter in saucepan and add flour, stirring until well blended. Add all the milk and stir until it starts to thicken. Add bay leaf, nutmeg, salt and pepper. Cook slowly on reduced heat, stirring all the time, for five minutes. Cool. If it should go lumpy, beat with wire whisk or beater until it looks as smooth as silk.

FILLINGS

½ large or one small lettuce
2 cups cooked chicken or leftover
    meat sauce
4 tablespoons tomato paste (not
    tomato sauce)
1 cup cheddar cheese, grated

Boil lettuce for five minutes in water to which you have added one teaspoon of sugar. Drain, cool, squeeze dry and chop. Mix with four tablespoons of bechamel sauce. Add same amount of bechamel to the cooked chicken or meat sauce.

Heat oven to 200°C. Place a crepe on to a heatproof serving dish. Cover with some of the lettuce mixture and sprinkle with some of the grated cheese. Place another crepe on top of this and cover with some meat mixture. Another crepe, and cover with a thin spreading of some of the tomato paste.

Continue layering until fillings are used. Top with a crepe, add the remaining cheese to the bechamel and spread over the top. Brown in oven for 15 minutes. Serve hot, cut into wedges.

***As this can slip sideways while cooking, stick several toothpicks in from the top to anchor it. Remember to remove them before serving or if they get lost, at least warn your guests!

8. Cooks, Farmers & Entertainers: 1980–82

Back in the limelight of television in 1980 after months of waiting, Peter Hudson and David Halls could not help firing one last round over the bow of their old television boss, Barry O'Brien. Their absence from the small screen had been a self-imposed exile, but they were still very bitter about their treatment. Peter blamed the standard of production on their final shows. 'We felt it was slipping,' he explained. 'For one, during the recording of the last two programmes they … let children into the audience. We had babies crying and children getting restless.'[1] But it wouldn't have mattered what miracle recipe South Pacific Television whisked up, the relationship had soured. The parties had become overfamiliar. They had settled into a comfortable mode of taking each other for granted, which became exploitation, then a hardening of attitudes before the final break.

Peter and David had lived in the dull world of ordinariness for 18 months and were desperate to get television back in their lives. Tom Parkinson, director of light entertainment for Television New Zealand, recognised their talent – and their ratings potential. 'He knew they were going to be hot property,' remembers Roy Good, head of the design department. 'Tom Parkinson … was great at sensing what would be an audience winner. He knew that these guys were going to do it.'[2] With the full weight of an amalgamated Television New Zealand behind him, Parkinson could drive *Hudson and Halls* in a new direction.

The couple's return to television necessitated a fresh look, and Peter and David were thrilled with his ideas. 'Tom Parkinson … wants to lift the show into the category of peak-hour evening entertainment. That means evening dress and an intimate restaurant atmosphere,' they told an interviewer.[3] They had been uncompromising about retaining outdoor locations with South Pacific Television, but with Parkinson they relinquished this demand. He offered them something that appealed even more than the great outdoors: a dress shirt, dinner jacket and bow-tie. They were going upmarket.

It is slightly ironic that Peter would say of this new series that he felt more comfortable than when he and David had been 'directed to be "show-bizzy". I just wanted to be natural, relaxed and me.'[4] But dress shirts and dinner jackets were no more them than any of their other television incarnations. The difference was perhaps that they were now more at ease in front of the camera, and the show format was familiar.

The first of the more dapper and sophisticated *Hudson and Halls* series, which began in March 1980 and ran for 28 episodes, continued the chat-cum-music-show component. They were looking for a similar combination of notable overseas guests and local personalities. The opening episode featured British film and television star David Hemmings, who was in New Zealand for the filming of *Beyond Reasonable Doubt*, a movie based on the trial of Arthur Allan Thomas, and the British pop group Racey.[5]

Even though Peter and David came with the warning label 'Handle with Care', thanks to their reputation for being 'difficult', they were also a brilliant bet. They had been around long enough to know the importance of timing, and they understood the complex relationship between the camera, the studio audience and viewers at home. They had plenty of experience yet were not stale.

Hudson and Halls were at their peak, and Tom Parkinson knew it would be worth navigating the crises to get the best prime-time footage from them: their drinking on camera, loosening proceedings to the point where they might dangerously unravel; the wild horse of their relationship still bucking and seething with anger and irritation. There was nothing gilt-edged about their behaviour in front of the camera or towards each other, but if he could successfully deliver them to viewers, Parkinson believed they would be winners.

Tom Parkinson had a very able producer in Jeff Bennet, who ferreted around the set looking for stashes of alcohol to confiscate. He also put out some monumental flare-ups between the pair. He remembers one episode when the atmosphere between them got so heated, and David so utterly incensed, that he burst off the stage in the middle of the show, sped along the corridor to the Green Room and sat there fuming until Jeff himself managed to coax him out so that filming could continue. Parkinson's other secret weapon was Carleen Spencer, wild horse-whisperer and great friend of Peter and David, who had a special knack for calming them down. If she was in the country, he would ring her up and ask her to come down to the studio to settle sore nerves.

Also in his favour was the fact that Hudson and Halls had just spent time chilling in the salt mines of celebrity neglect. They had learned about the fickle nature of television. David told a reporter: 'You never know with TV, you can be top of the tree today and dead as a dodo tomorrow.'[6] Opportunities could be withdrawn, and Peter and David had already pushed their luck. By falling out with South Pacific Television, they had sealed off possible career paths. Hudson and Halls were officially on their best behaviour – at least for now.

There was little time to think once the contract was signed and they began programme production. And they still had the restaurant to run. They started each weekday at the restaurant about 6.30am and finished about 5pm. 'Around that they [would] have to write their material for the TV series, prepare the dishes they [would] use that week, rehearse, then record.'[7] Their schedule was physically punishing, and there was a relentless demand for content. If David was the flamboyant ideas man, Peter was the deliverer. He developed recipes and made sure that there would be an edible product at the end of each show. Away from the glamour of television this was a laborious job. 'Their cooking was strictly limited to dinner parties for friends. Now it controls their lives,' gushed an interviewer. 'They are always on the lookout for new ideas and recipes. They have a library of over 300 cooking books.'[8]

Peter was the bedrock researcher. The introduction to their 1977 *Hudson & Halls Cookbook* states: 'This book has been brought to you at considerable personal expense. Namely, two pairs of middle fingers on two pairs of hands that have bashed their way over miles of typewriter ribbon!'[9] Peter's fingers were usually the ones that banged away on the typewriter to bring their new food combinations together. His task was to turn froth and fun into fruition. Without his shrewd awareness of what was required, there would have been substantially less body to the Hudson and Halls brand.

David's skills lay in the look of things. First and foremost he was a designer and a performer – a show-pony who dragged himself reluctantly upstairs in their London Street apartment to labour over rewrites and the refining of recipe ingredients. His communication skills, however, stood out. He was almost a natural choice when Kevan Moore, former head of programmes at South Pacific Television who now owned his own production company, was looking for a front man for the new television game show *Blankety Blank*. Moore chose David because he needed a presenter 'with quick repartee, who could also work with panellists and contestants'.[10] David had honed these skills during hard, gaping moments of silence with guests on his own show. Despite his extroverted personality, when younger he had sometimes sat literally speechless in interviews, not knowing what to say or ask next. Bluster and bluff were not enough to survive an interview but by the time he was offered the *Blankety Blank* contract he was adept at managing other people's egos and stage nerves, and was a master of the wisecrack. While Peter was thumping out their recipes, David was studying one-liners. On television, particularly, he was chasing the brilliant quip that would bring the house down. He stole jokes, developed his own, and practised routines and the timing of his delivery. There was nothing natural about what he brought to television at this point other than his own delight at being on stage. He was now, as Kevan Moore explained to an interviewer, 'a showman in his own right, but with the intelligence not to upstage other show people'.[11]

The taping of *Blankety Blank* began at the Hobson Street studio on 23 February 1981. There were 26 programmes in the first series, aired within weeks of *Hudson and Halls*. In 1981 they ran from 3 March to 25 August, and in 1982 the programme appeared in two chunks from 2 March until 18 May and 29 June to 14 September.

Blankety Blank was a game show that required a tricky balance. A 'front person reads out a sentence to one of the two contestants … but there's one word missing,' Kevan Moore explained when outlining the rules of the game to a reporter. 'The contestant has to guess what that word is and if their word agrees with the words written down by the six panellists they get points.'[12] The regular panellists were Debbie Dorday, Tina Grenville and Wally Lewis, who were joined each week by special guests such as Angela D'Audney, Annie Whittle, Chic Littlewood and Ray Columbus. All had their own robust egos and attention-seeking strategies.

David made a radiant presenter. He was 45 years old and still in his prime. Tall, with a full head of silvering hair, he was commanding yet also calculating in his efforts to drive a difficult herd of stars together to the finish. For two years *Blankety Blank* had a good solid run, but there were problem moments when energy lapsed and humour died an unnatural death. The concept was part of the problem – filling in blanks was not an undertaking that automatically sent the blood surging – but at times there was also something missing in David's performance. Despite his preparations, he was strongest in his familiar duo. Without Peter's cues and satirical wit, there was less opportunity for David to shine. He satisfied the brief of being an able facilitator, but did not establish himself as an outstanding front person.

His profile was certainly enhanced, however. This was record exposure. That year, viewers could hardly avoid seeing either David Halls or *Hudson and Halls* on either Television One or Television Two. The time spent languishing in the wings between contracts had been a valuable chance to strategise, to rethink their priorities. Now Peter and David's star was truly on the rise.

*

The demands of their television commitments made running the restaurant more of a challenge. They solved some of the problem by taking on additional staff, but there was still the onus of having to be there as the major attraction, and the time-consuming business of restaurant management. They were understandably reluctant to give it up. Television had proved a precarious earner in the past and the restaurant could be lucrative.

The clientele 'were very moneyed', remembers Stephanie Hall, the restaurant's maître d', and few were spared when David, in particular, was in the mood for poking fun. 'People like Lady Caughey would come in and sit there with her ladies' lunches. She'd have the big round table at the front of the restaurant.' Lady Mary Caughey always wore a hat, one of which had a peculiar crease down the middle. As Stephanie was reaching over to serve the table, with three coffee cups in hand, David leaned in beside her and whispered, 'Lady Caughey's hat looks like an arse.' The coffee cups began to jiggle in their saucers. 'I had to just dump them and run … His laugh. I can still hear him shrieking with laughter.'[13]

On a good day the staff liquor allowance contributed to the haze of hilarity. Peter and David drank buckets of Coruba rum mixed with Coke, and employees were allowed to drink Old Pale Gold sherry poured over ice while they were on duty. One of the more memorable staff members was Jill. This was the 1980s, and Jill had elasticised strapless dresses with slits up either side. 'She would wear no bra, and she had flaming red hair, and her nipples used to stick out like a couple of cigar butts,' remembers Stephanie. Coming in from the garden area one day with her arms full of dishes, Jill's elastic top gave way, and by the time she was standing in the main restaurant she had one breast hanging out. 'If anybody in the front of the restaurant had turned round they would have seen Jill walking in.' David thought it was hilarious, and he and Jill just laughed and laughed. 'She would never wear any undies and she said, "It keeps the flies off the food" … she was fabulous in her platforms … tottering through the restaurant.'

Things were not always harmonious, however. Some days Stephanie came downstairs to find David drunk at 2pm. One day she said 'Drunk again' under her breath. 'I never forget to pay your fucking wages,' David snapped, then unleashed a tirade of abuse. Alcohol made both him and Peter aggressive. They began drinking early in the day, would drink during television filming and finish up the evening on red wine. The pattern of drinking took its toll: on staff relations and on their own.

'They had the most dreadful fights,' remembers Stephanie. 'You had to get out of the firing line.' The pair would throw anything within reach at each other. 'It didn't matter what it was … German china, the beautiful porcelain, crystal glasses.

'"You fucking old bastard."

'"I'm bloody going to leave you and I hate your fucking guts."

'But then other times David would go, "He drives me to distraction. I could fucking kill him, but I love him to death."'

Drinking dissolved their inhibitions and gave them their highs, but also threw them into confusion and despair. What kept the wildness from overwhelming them was their innate talent and generosity. However difficult they were, they held on to staff because they were great teachers and exhilarating company. Peter and David 'taught me how to sell food', says Stephanie. 'They [had] this apricot meringue cake, which was a pavlova … mixed with almonds and apricots, and I used to sell it. I literally oozed the description and … the whole table would buy it, and David would say, "That's my girl," rubbing his hands together.' To be in Hudson and Halls' orbit was to live among the stars. When a group of *Star Wars* actors, including Mark Hamill (Luke Skywalker) and Billy Dee Williams (Lando), visited Auckland, they were interviewed at the restaurant. 'We were allowed to watch from the side. It was pretty huge,' Stephanie recalls.[14] For those caught up in it, life in Peter and David's jet stream was a turbulent ride laced with deliciousness and anxiety.

Carleen Spencer's trip to New Zealand at the end of 1980 was thrilling for Peter and David. She was visiting with her son Chris Spencer, who had just graduated with a degree in town planning from New York University and had come to celebrate with his grandparents. Carleen and Chris went to Hudson and Halls' restaurant for lunch where Stephanie waited on their table. She recalls it was 'one of those ridiculous – wow – lightning bolt' meetings. The attraction between Stephanie and Chris was instant and mutual. They spent the summer together, 'hanging out and having the most wonderful time with all Chris's old friends from King's College. I was the girl from the sticks, so I was living the high life,' remembers Stephanie.[15]

When Peter and David heard about the romance between their friend's son and their maître d', they couldn't resist getting involved. Chris remembers the day vividly. 'They said to me and Stephanie … "We're going for a drive and you guys are coming with us." So Peter and David showed up in the Bentley with a champagne bucket in the back with two glasses and a bottle on the ice. They're in the front and we're in the back and they popped the champagne. So they were driving around Auckland, driving along the waterfront drinking … Peter was on the wrong side of the road for half of it … They ran out of interest about Mission Bay and said, "Let's go back" … and in this Bentley they did like a 14-point turn and they had traffic lined up on both sides and they were cursing out the window and telling everybody to "piss off" and the horns were going … It was just this fabulous circus everywhere they went.'[16]

Towards the end of summer, when Chris was returning to New York, Peter and David took the couple out to the airport to say goodbye. When they saw how heartbreaking the separation was, they offered to pay for Stephanie's plane ticket. 'I was blown away, because back then a trip to New York cost $2000.' (This is almost what it costs today, when incomes are a great deal higher.) 'They wanted me to experience a bigger life, and they really did treat me as their daughter.'[17]

Peter and David paid for the ticket and Stephanie left New Zealand two months later. Their gift was unconditional, and astonishingly generous considering the restaurant struggled at times with high overheads, and television was never well paid. There was an underlying attitude that presenting on television was both a vocation and a privilege, and remuneration was only part of a package of rewards, many of which were intangible.

Over time, the duo struggled increasingly to cope with the demands of the restaurant on top of filming schedules, their weekly radio show and celebrity appearances. They were getting restless and wanted a change of pace and more time to themselves. Their London Street apartment with its views of the bridge, the yachts and the harbour was magnificent, but the attraction of having only minimal land to look after had worn off. David, especially, hankered after a substantial property. His father had worked the land around Epping, and now he could afford to own land himself. Property signalled success in his world. He and Peter had already purchased the ultimate status symbol – the Bentley. Now they wanted the estate to go with it.

*

Around the time that Peter and David had purchased their Bentley, Abby Collins bought a 63 Studebaker Hawk. Now they took any opportunity they could to go on picnics together on the weekends. Ultimately, the purpose of these excursions was to look for property, and eventually they found the perfect spot on a breathtaking stretch of coastline an hour's drive north of Auckland. 'This was up at Ti Point,' says Geoffrey Collins. 'For about $70,000 … they bought this 14 or 15 acres [6ha] of cliff front … an absolute bargain.' It was an ideal fit for David's aspirations to be a gentleman farmer. He told a reporter for the *Auckland Star* in September 1981 about their 'new business interest': 'They are establishing a Romney stud farm north of Auckland. David says it is their protection from the perils of television work.'[18]

The pressing issue now was to sell the London Street flat as quickly as possible. 'But the whole apartment was chocolate brown and they couldn't sell it,' Geoffrey Collins remembers. The pair decided to paint it a less flamboyant *Architectural Digest* white. 'When Peter sold it, I went to help them move … I walked downstairs and all they'd done was painted the walls white, but they'd painted around everything so the brown silhouette of all the paintings and the grandfather clock and the sofa and everything else was on the wall. They hadn't even bothered to move the furniture!'[19]

Their house at Leigh, on Ti Point, was built in almost the same haste. A two-storey modular Lockwood house was erected in a little over six weeks. The interior space was open to the roof, and upstairs at either end were bedrooms. The downstairs was open plan: 'The kitchen was in one corner with the dining room in the front … A big living room went around to a snug … and later they built a swimming pool.'[20] In just over a year they had the interior the way they wanted it as well. 'Whoopee! … Ordered all the furniture for the dining-room, very elegant cane, fully woven, daisy floral like we had in the restaurant. Elegant dining chairs, the Chinese Chippendale look with navy blue cushions, navy blue table cloths with soft yellow overlay cloths, dark green enamelled walls (almost black) all on an acid green carpet … should look ever so chic!?' David wrote excitedly to Carleen Spencer and Jerry Podell at the beginning of 1983.[21]

This was the perfect property from which to entertain, and instead of just coming for dinner close friends often stayed overnight, avoiding the 80-kilometre trip back to Auckland after too many drinks. When people arrived for one of Peter and David's weekend parties at Ti Point, which became known simply as The Farm, they were handed a drink the minute they walked through the door. 'There was a rum and Coke in your hand at 9.30 to 10 o'clock in the morning and then they'd cook lunch and we'd drink and we'd play 500 or Last Card … It was just hilarious, we'd

Peter and David's house (The Farm) at Leigh, on Ti Point in the Rodney District. CARLEEN SPENCER, PRIVATE COLLECTION

get drunker and drunker … and we'd go to bed and the room would be spinning.'[22] They went for walks, played cards, but there was never any television unless there was something special on.

At London Street Peter and David had acquired two Burmese cats. The big additions to their fur family at the new house were two Rottweiler pups. 'They were going to call them Fluffy and Poofy but decided Bullet and Nero were a lot more butch,' Abby remembers.[23] The Rottweilers were dubbed the 'two Rotties', after the 'two tenors', Pavarotti and Domingo, because they loved singing. Initially the two Rotties accompanied singers on television, even hitting opera singers' high notes. David and Peter videoed them, and the dogs would howl in unison with their television selves in a kind of canine quartet.

Chris Spencer, Stephanie Hall and Carleen Spencer covered in sun-tan lotion after a day in the sun at Fire Island, Bay Shore, New York, 1981. STEPHANIE HALL, PRIVATE COLLECTION

In August 1981, just over two months after they moved to Ti Point, David wrote to Stephanie Hall and Chris Spencer in New York. Peter had gone to bed and David was dashing off a quick note before he turned in himself. 'We like it [here] very much,' he told the young couple, 'but get the odd twinge of "have we done the right thing" every now and again – possibly because we feel so guilty about having it all – beach, super house, pool, spa, dogs, cats, car, mint three wheel motor bike – THE LOT!' David and Peter were living their rural idyll and were still in rapture. They drove into Auckland reluctantly most days to work in the restaurant, and certainly didn't miss the traffic. 'It's just lovely peace and quiet and what with the pair of kingfishers we have on the property, the fantails and wax-eyes – it is superb. The other day witnessed a school of dolphins chasing fish along the shoreline.'[24]

The only 'depressing and frightening' thing was the weather, which had been unseasonably settled for the first few weeks after they arrived. Their exposed spot with its magnificent views had begun to show glimpses of its tempestuous potential. Even on fine days the sea-wind blew relentlessly. Sometimes their wooden home creaked and groaned under the strain, like an old sailing ship in a storm. Occasionally it felt as if the roof might be lifted off by a sudden wild gust of wind.

Peter had been outdoors, David wrote. He 'bought a type of hoe thing today to dig out thistles on the property, plus a long rain proofed parka with hood. He went with the dogs to try both out (digger thing and parka!) in the pouring rain … silly bugger.' Peter came home, drank a number of Coruba rum mixers, ate a rabbit pie that David had 'knocked up' while he was out, and disappeared off to bed exhausted. Peter was now nearly 50. 'There are still no half measures with him – must get him some more of those slow down pills and pop them into his coffee!!!!'

FROM TOP:
David with Bullet and Nero, early 1980s. CARLEEN SPENCER, PRIVATE COLLECTION

John Fields and David Atkinson relaxing in the lounge at The Farm, mid-1980s. JOHN FIELDS, PRIVATE COLLECTION

Peter (right) relaxes with David Atkinson and John Fields, mid-1980s. JOHN FIELDS, PRIVATE COLLECTION

David the pool cleaner. CARLEEN SPENCER, PRIVATE COLLECTION

Joan Weirn, Carleen and Peter enjoying the view from The Farm. CARLEEN SPENCER, PRIVATE COLLECTION

Peter had been dieting and had managed to lose weight and keep it off. David too had lost weight but then put the 'whole bloody lot on again – never mind I can have my "Blankety Blank" suits let out I suppose if they ever come up with the cash to do another series'.[25]

Although David still hankered after his own independent stardom, the couple's partnership in television was their most important asset and food their mainstay. They were always casting around for innovative ideas. 'Stephanie, you must write a few short letters describing food trends, restaurants (cuttings from *N.Y. Times* or food articles),' David told her in a letter. That year they were not taking a trip overseas, so Stephanie was to be their international 'eyes'. Keeping up to date with changing food styles and fashions was crucial. New ideas could be used for their restaurant, in the new cookbook they were perpetually compiling and, if the concept was spectacular enough, on television. Novelty was always an important ingredient, to keep people coming back. They would only maintain their positions as doyens of the kitchen if they had new ideas to promote.

Their property at Leigh was not on the pulse – that was the point of it, it was a getaway – but that worried them slightly, especially when David still had red-hot television ambitions. They had no intention of selling their restaurant. 'Although it's a bit quiet, it's not doing too badly,' David told Carleen and Jerry.[26] Hudson and Halls Oyster and Fish Restaurant was their foothold in Auckland, but there would have to be changes. 'We will be stopping night times at the end of this month, as we won't be able to cope with lunch and dinner,' David explained to Stephanie and Chris, saying 'it will be for the best'.[27] They would need a chef to replace Peter in the kitchen, and a front person and manager-cum-dessert maker to stand in for David. Stephanie's brother Brett was employed as a chef and manager, and her mother Carole also worked in the restaurant. Coming to terms with the idea that it was simply too difficult to run an elegant central-city restaurant while commuting long distance would be a gradual process.

On The Farm they ran a breeding flock of Romney ewes and rams, as well as ducks, peacocks and cockatiels. Peter kept cages of white doves. While hosting a pool party, David, against Peter's express wishes, released the doves into the brilliant blue sky above their heads. In a gore of ravaged feathers, the doves were picked off by local hawks, like food scraps thrown to vultures. By the time they had finished their killing, not a single dove was left alive. Infuriated, Peter rushed inside. Item after item of David's possessions – a television, a microwave, pieces of furniture – were thrown from the second-storey balcony into the pool. Peter was inconsolable.

Their fights at Ti Point had all the razor-sharp rancour of earlier conflicts. Frequently one or other of them would go and stay with friends, or Peter would 'take off and stay at the Regent in Auckland'.[28] When in a rage they fired paintings, pottery and silverware down the cliff. Afterwards, they would inevitably be down at the bottom to pick them all up again. Then it was a matter of taking the dents out of the silver, fixing things that could be mended and restoring to the cupboard those items that had survived their flight unbroken.

Crockery had a life expectancy in Hudson and Halls' kitchen similar to that of a fighter pilot in World War One. Items might be returned to the cupboard once or twice, but the odds were against them and ultimately there was likely to be a mishap. Sometimes the damage was quite spontaneous: a wilful but wonderful expression of the couple's right to be free. Geoffrey Collins remembers when Peter decided he didn't want to do the dishes one night: 'He picked up all the crockery and went down to the cliff edge and sailed it out to sea.'[29]

'We have done more entertaining up here in the last few months than we did in town in the last few years,' David wrote in October 1981. As well as having friends over, they began hosting 'very posh lunches here for overseas guests'. This was their strategy for the future. 'Well, television won't go on forever and we have to think of something to keep us in booze.'[30] Their plan was to build on to the Ti Point house and run an exclusive restaurant, not open to the public, but strictly 'prior bookings that have been recommended by friends or business acquaintances. If it all fails, then sell the place off, have a good trip around the World and pop ourselves off with a couple of pills (only joking).'[31]

Their moods swung dramatically. One moment they were ecstatic and the next plunged into despair. 'We have gone into a decline, and are just managing to walk the dogs and try and kill the thistles on the place which seems a never ending battle.'[32] Sometimes Peter got so depressed he had to take himself away. 'Peter has gone to the City for a few days as a break away from here and I hope he comes back in a better mood. Anything can trigger him off, so I thought it best that he goes down alone and has a break for at least a few days.'[33] The drinking, the stress of running the property on top of their other professional and social commitments, and their sense of powerlessness in dealing with television bosses all contributed to their mood swings.

Their financial circumstances always ran close to the edge. They were spenders. If they had money, it sat in their pockets hot and burning to be thrown away, and this, along with the way television scheduled its programmes, was not a good

Peter and David's television audiences were spared this style of cooking attire.
CARLEEN SPENCER, PRIVATE COLLECTION

David with Jamie Cormack in the kitchen at The Farm, early 1980s. JAN CORMACK, PRIVATE COLLECTION

combination. 'So we wait once more on someone's whim as to whether we eat or not,' David wrote in a letter to Carleen and Jerry.[34] They worried about money, and about getting enough work. To stay positive they dieted, went on the wagon, started exercise programmes and visited an acupuncturist and fortune-tellers; but always they struggled to shake off their fits of depression.

Ironically, 1981 proved to be their greatest year in entertainment yet. They were honoured to be invited to be part of the 'entertainment for Her Majesty whilst she was in Auckland at the Royal Variety performance'.[35] Ratings for their shows were also bubbling along at an exceptionally pleasing level. *Hudson and Halls* was almost always one of the top three shows, and more often than not at number one. This was an outstanding achievement for a cooking show pitched against strong local competition and the best of overseas material. When the news came through that they had been voted Feltex Best Entertainers of the year for 1981, they were knocked over.

This was tangible affirmation after their years of hard work, and it was payback time for South Pacific Television who had so publicly dumped them. O'Brien's parting words that 'they were not rating very well' had haunted them. The award, won over other well-established talents such as Ray Woolf, Tina Cross, Ray Columbus, Billy T. James and McPhail and Gadsby, was concrete proof of their popularity.

But more than this, *Hudson and Halls* had lasted, and nothing lasts for long in television without substance. If Darwin's theory of evolution applies anywhere, it is on the small screen. To stay alive requires adaptation. By the 1980s successive governments had pulled and pushed television along opposing pathways, from draconian-styled control to relative autonomy, and the prevailing theme through the 1960s and 1970s had been evolution and change. Against all odds, Hudson and Halls had survived this brutalising backdrop and flourished to become the most popular entertainers in New Zealand. The New Zealand public had taken them into the heart of their living rooms and their lives. Hudson and Halls were loved not in spite of their foppish foolery, but because of it. They had turned food into theatre and made it an entertainment.

Peter Hudson and David Halls were desperate for that approval. They wanted to be successful sons of their adoptive country. 'I'm not sure if two Kiwis with our image would get such a welcome from the public ... I don't know if New Zealanders would be so kind to their own,' David once said.[36] He felt they had an exemption, that they were guests with freedoms not extended to home-grown talent. Now they felt as if they belonged, and that New Zealand was their home.

*

The publicity around their success created its own dynamic that continued to attract viewers and kept *Hudson and Halls* dominating the ratings. The line-up of proposed guests announced towards the end of 1981 seemed more entertaining than ever. They were bidding for well-known names, such as American actor Kristy McNichol (Buddy in the TV series *Family*), as well as local performers Tina Cross and Billy T. James, the Auckland Boys' Choir and harpist Rebecca Harris. In terms of food, their pre-Christmas special that aired on 23 December 1981 had everything you needed to take away on the great Kiwi exodus to the beach or the bach. 'Hudson and Halls will demonstrate two summery drinks (one of them very alcoholic),' promised the reporter for the *Auckland Star*, plus 'a ginger soy marinade ideal for barbecue cooking, a chicken and sugar snap pea salad served in a pastry case, and a dish to use up any left over Christmas turkey.'[37]

They had got inside the New Zealand psyche, understood its changing orientation towards Asia and the South Pacific, and had added their own twist. After their Christmas special screened, Jeff Bennet, their producer, received around 2000 requests for copies of their recipes. He had never seen such a response and was not sure what made the recipes so popular. 'Perhaps there are lots of people who still have turkey left over,' he quipped.[38]

Hudson and Halls had been guests in New Zealanders' lounges, and trainers and motivators in their kitchens, for six years now. Although many saw them primarily as entertainers, they also shifted people's ideas and changed their habits around food and entertaining. At an elemental level, they made it not just fun but hilarious.

Alison Holst's approach to food was level headed and serious. She was a graduate of the School of Home Science at the University of Otago, and there was something of the home economics teacher in her measured delivery. Graham Kerr was trained in hospitality and was ex-military; he also erred on the side of caution. Des Britten, with his 'bounce' and his 'fun, fun, fun' byline, was the loosest of a staid crowd. But still cooking in front of the camera was generally regarded as didactic rather than a theatre sport. If the presenters made it interesting, that was a bonus; if it entertained, they got another series.

Serial viewers such as Sheila Mickleson watched Hudson and Halls because they took the mundane and the everyday and made it pantomime. 'I can't remember anything really about their cooking. I can't remember what they cooked because I was always actually a fan of Alison Holst, and I can remember what she cooked … things always seemed to go wrong [with Hudson and Halls] but it was probably on purpose … I laughed a lot because it was so amusing … It was a really nice down time … because the kids were in bed … They were more amusing than anything else.'[39]

They aired their dirty tea towels on television and showed a brazen disregard for convention. While Kiwis were still keeping up appearances and covering over their flaws, foibles and especially failures, they celebrated mistakes and outrageousness. *Hudson and Halls* fan Michelle Osborne remembers watching a show when they accidentally put salt in a sponge instead of sugar. 'The sponge rose, absolutely perfectly, and looked immaculate. They creamed and jammed it, and then sliced it … one layer on top of another … and they dished it out and David took a spoonful … put it in his mouth … and you could see the face change. He could have just chewed and been quiet and that's a wrap. But, no! He got this shocked look on his face … and of course Peter got a bit grumpy that he had admitted that it was wrong … but David was all for letting the cat out of the bag … and Mum and I thought it was *hilarious*.'[40]

The boundaries they pushed went further than just the kitchen. 'They were like a typical married couple together and with all the things that go with domesticity,' Michelle Osborne remembers.[41] These were gay men and the nation was in their kitchen. If viewers in the 1970s were naïve enough to think they were just pals, by 1981 the penny had dropped with a resounding clunk for most people. And by the time New Zealand realised its surrogate sons were properly queer instead of just acting, it was too late. The majority of the country had already switched on to them. They made gay men not just look good, but feel familiar. Hudson and Halls laughed, they appeared to enjoy life, and they were fun to watch. Suddenly homosexuality was not something out there and 'other' – to be feared and hated – but something friendly, admirable even, and positive.

Television cooks and cookbooks were symbiotic, and Peter and David planned to have another cookbook out by the early 1980s. Their restaurant business and hectic way of life, however, made finding focused time difficult. Fortunately the *Hudson & Halls Cookbook* of 1977 had the staying power of a lasting publication. Its mouth-watering illustrations put it in the category of collectable cookbooks that had begun to occupy the divide between cooking manual and coffee-table book.

Basil Williams' photographs were not just informative and enticing, they were also artistic. The back-cover illustration of a Frosted Cheese Mould (see page 131) is a brilliant still life of cleverly composed Hudson and Halls food. A luminescent green cheese mould, two austere white goblets, blue decanters and a lighted white

By the end of 1982 Hudson and Halls' ratings had dropped to alarming levels.
COURTESY OF THE *NEW ZEALAND LISTENER*

candle in an aqua-blue candleholder are placed in front of a painting of white lilies. This merging of life and art elevates the subject – food. Similarly elegant images are peppered strategically throughout the book to evoke possibility and keep the flagging cook inspired. Many photographs feature either a glass of wine or an open bottle, communicating not only David and Peter's own preoccupation, but also the idea that food is festive and alcohol is intrinsic to celebration.

*

Since the 1960s, celebrity chiefs had endorsed a relationship between food and alcohol. As households reluctantly loosened their grip on the DYC vinegar bottle, new items were added to the shopping list. You still couldn't buy alcohol at the same place you bought food, but a new bond was being established. Alcohol didn't just accompany food: it could be the magic ingredient in it. Those who didn't buy liquor specifically to cook with were more vigilant about what happened to the dregs of the beer bottle or the last glass and a half of cheap red wine. Now they could add it to a recipe.

Des Britten used alcohol the most generously of the celebrity chefs, but it is likely that no one in the whole of New Zealand baptised their food in liquor as liberally as Hudson and Halls. Alcohol was added to almost everything, including the most unlikely of dishes. They had recipes with beer, red and white wine, port, dry and medium sherry, brandy, bourbon, gin, rum, Cointreau, cognac, vermouth, tequila, madeira, Grand Marnier and Marsala. The additive lifted ordinary ingredients to a new level. Once, cooking had been too mundane to waste good drink on; Hudson and Halls' dishes required their own grog cabinet. Their instructions for Boeuf Bourguignon were clear: 'The burgundy used has to be the quality that you would normally drink yourself as a table wine, you cannot use cheap plonk.'[42]

Alcohol made cooking more ostentatious, and many of the social and legal taboos around it were being lifted too. The six o'clock curfew on bar sales in public houses had gone, along with much of the stigma associated with drinking. The pursed lips of puritanism were beginning to look outmoded, and already there were drugs around that seemed far more insidious than liquor. Society was freeing up its attitudes. Hudson and Halls were both a product of these changes and a driver and consolidator of them.

Still, drink remained just that little bit naughty, and it tickled most New Zealanders that these renegade chefs used so much of it. Their Chicken Tarragon Cream Sauce called for two cups of dry white wine, their Coq au Vin for a quarter of a cup of 'good' brandy and two cups of red wine; their Boeuf Bourguignon required two cups of 'good' burgundy, and their Oxtail Casserole one cup of port. Desserts were also charged with alcohol. Their Chocolate Rum Souffle used one cup of dark rum, and black grapes were soaked in brandy for three months before they went into the Mixed Fruit Flan. 'Potent, but WOW!' they wrote.[43]

Alcohol gave their food difference. The more they used it with the least likely ingredients, the greater that difference became. They put brandy in onion soup, made 'scrambled eggs with vermouth, duck cooked in red wine, chicken cooked in Calvados, liver cooked in Dubonnet, claret jelly, nectarines in vodka, and pears cooked in white wine'.[44]

Such dishes had an air of exotic flamboyance. Not in the sense of being foreign, but rather of hedonistic indulgence, which was the closest thing to foreign that most New Zealanders knew. Peter and David's food was an antidote to the settler practice of self-denial. The 1960s saw the first wave of baby boomers 'turn on, tune in and drop out'; the 1970s was the decade they wasted in finding themselves after dropping out; and the 1980s, up to the financial crash in 1987, was an unprecedented period of self-indulgence. For many, the social conscience picked up on picket lines or at protest marches was slickly subverted. This new generation looked at their frugal forebears with suspicion. Surely there must be more to life than going without? They were hungry for luxury, for flashy food to entertain with that matched their fast car, escalating salary and gigantic mortgage. They were upwardly mobile, and elegant eating was an outward sign of success.

Hudson and Halls' recipes ran on alcohol and drove like their Bentley. The engines were complicated and the parts sometimes hard to get, but driving them made you feel like a millionaire, and best of all they turned heads. Although the *Hudson & Halls Cookbook* begins with the disclaimer 'Mistakes can make the perfect cook and we have made plenty, so will you', and introduces readers to basic kitchen equipment, common herbs and culinary terms, its recipes are far from easy. Each dish has a considerable number of ingredients and the instructions are complicated. These are grandiose recipes not intended for learner drivers.

As well as being quite specific about the type of liquor used, such as Jim Beam bourbon because 'some brands can be too perfumed', Peter and David were particular about other ingredients. Instead of using generic materials like mustard, mushrooms or cheese, suddenly the home economist and cook had to bypass the handy mix-as-you-go packet of powdered Colman's mustard, the ubiquitous block of super-soapy colby cheese, and the next-door neighbour's paddock full of leathery old earwig-infested horse mushrooms, and spend some real money. Hudson and Halls specified Gruyère, Blue Vein, Parmesan and Swiss cheeses; and Mushrooms in Mustard Sauce called for Dijon mustard '(if unavailable, use a mild one and some cream)' and large dried or button mushrooms. They were also highly specific about the cooking oils they used. Hudson and Halls were after the finer flavours registered by a more discerning palate.

Along with their celebrity colleagues, they drove the demand for diversity on supermarket shelves. Generic food bought in bulk to save both money and multiple trips to the store became less desirable almost overnight. Bulk all-purpose food did not satisfy a public that was beginning to see itself as more complex and heterogeneous. Hudson and Halls also helped create the environment for domestic manufacturers to expand their product ranges and directed importers towards new product lines overseas. The traditional family unit – mum, dad and two-point-five children – was beginning to change too. There were singles and solo parents, childless and career couples, under-the-radar same-sex partnerships, along with vegans, vegetarians, pescatarians and new immigrant groups. As well, a greater awareness of international cuisine was being encouraged by overseas travel.

Faster container ships and a burgeoning number of long-haul flights brought more choice, and food began to confound the seasons. Grocery and produce suppliers added extra aisles to carry new and year-round stock. Manufacturers sent staff into supermarkets to set up food-sampling stalls to promote new product lines and innovative ways of using them. The weekly grocery shop became a samplers' paradise of used paper serviettes, empty toothpicks, wooden skewers and tiny plastic cups. Although it was frowned upon to line up in the queue more than once if you were over five years old, many people did.

Overseas cookbooks had always listed foreign brands and ingredients that were impossible to get at the bottom of the Pacific. Local celebrity chefs like Hudson and Halls, however, were obliged to list ingredients that could be sourced locally. They might be expensive, strictly seasonal or in short supply, but they could not be impossible to find. *The Des Britten Cookbook*, which also appeared in 1977, was published by supermarket giant Woolworths, making clear the important relationship between recipes, ingredients and suppliers.

Des Britten tackled Kiwi cooks' grey ideas and habitual economies. 'Can there be anything worse than a floury, soggy lump of batter wrapped around the usually stale piece of fish?' he asked his readers. 'Sadly, a big percentage of our fish and chip shops serve that sort of thing up. Sadder, however, is the fact that most of us accept and eat it.'[45] He was challenging New Zealanders to reflect on what they were eating and to improve it. 'Hamburgers are those inviting things that you buy when driving home late with the kids,' he shared with parents. 'It seemed like a good idea until you take that illusion shattering first bite.'[46] He urged New Zealanders to use the best basic ingredients 'simply'. 'Good food is not necessarily elaborate food nor need it be expensive.'[47]

He offered helpful solutions to old problems. 'This is a good recipe for starting off the week, with the leftovers from the weekend. I devised this … because one of my

The Des Britten Cookbook *appeared in 1977, the same year as* Hudson & Halls Cookbook. *While Britten had the Kiwi nuclear family in his sights, Hudson and Halls shamelessly targeted the emergent yuppie.*

pet hates … used to be having to eat the leftover part of the lamb or hogget from the weekend roast every Monday … I'm all for getting out of routines.'[48] He encouraged his readers to try new things, to give green beans a go instead of tired old watery lettuce, and to eat Ingredient X – garlic. 'My use of garlic has caused me and TV1 many problems,' he admitted. 'How well I remember the thousands of two-dollar notes and postal orders coming in after I offered, on camera, to buy a garlic crusher for a lady who lived in the country. It seemed the whole country wanted garlic crushers and I was the one to supply them.'[49] While garlic was a daring addition to a dish, the eggplant in his Aubergine au Gratin had to be formally introduced. 'Eggplant or Aubergine (it's one and the same) is a vegetable which I'm pleased to say is becoming more and more popular … I'm sure you have all seen them in the green-grocers – they look like large pears and have a most beautiful bright purple skin.'[50]

While Des Britten's insights were home grown, the *Hudson & Halls Cookbook* was more detached. Not having that intimate understanding of New Zealand eating patterns from an early age influenced their approach. Their recipes did not worship at the shrine of that sacred New Zealand institution – the nuclear family. There was no guilt for the childless cook, no sense of family being the default social relationship. While Des Britten sensitively accommodated cooks' qualms and insecurities about alcohol just in case they lost their nerve – 'wine, red or white (stock if you are out of cooking wine – water if things are tough)'[51] – Hudson and Halls good-humouredly reprimanded their readers to harden up their liquor, and use only the best. Their cookbook targeted people like themselves — an emergent animal who would be called the yuppie, or Young Urban Professional.

Hudson and Halls' recipe for Russian Crepes called for lumpfish or a small jar of caviar. 'If the latter, hand napkins around or you will get caviar over your "shagpile",' they warned.[52] They used kipper fillets, anchovy fillets, smoked roe, prawns, shrimps, tongues and trotters, and in the vegetable line courgettes, aubergines, capsicums and avocados. They knew how these items worked in a dish because they had sampled them overseas. Their cuisine challenged New Zealanders to search a little harder in the deli or gourmet section of the grocery store and dig deeper into their pockets to pay for it.

Their recipes came from all over Europe. From France they had French Peasant Soup, French Onion Quiche, Onion and Anchovy Tart, Ratatouille, Chicken Livers with Orange, Coq au Vin, Boeuf Bourguignon, Lamb Roast French Style, and Tarte Tatin. Italian-influenced recipes were represented by Minestrone, Neapolitan Onions, Italian Style Cauliflower, Bolognese Sauce, Ossobuco, Pizza, Gnocchis and Zabaione. Spain was present in Spanish Style Peas with Ham and Spanish Omelette, and the United States with Southern Fried Chicken and Pot Roast. According to David Veart, 'there was even a recipe for Lemon Stuffed Boned Leg of Lamb which descended directly from Eliza Acton's [English] ... mid-nineteenth century' cookbook.[53]

But not every dish in *Hudson & Halls Cookbook* came from a Eurocentric tradition. They also included Japanese Style Chicken, Chinese Green Beans and Chinese Duck, and some helpful advice about using the new-fangled soya sauce. They recommended cooks use only the thickest, darkest varieties: 'Not the wishy washy thin ones as they are useless for this or anything else.' They also endorsed Chinese Five Spice which 'is generally readily available from most Chinese food stockists. If you fail to locate one, phone your local Chinese restaurant.'[54]

A Pacific Rim cuisine had already made debutant appearances in other cookbooks. Des Britten, for instance, included Stuffed Green Peppers (Chinese Style), and Poisson Polynesian. But his experiences with Asian cooking had not always been positive. 'I decided to do a Chinese type dish on television, but made a few slight variations here and there to give a wider appeal,' he explained to his cookbook readers. 'The day after the telecast, every Chinese in my home town of Wellington, and no doubt in yours, was gunning for me, telling me it wasn't a real Chinese recipe.'[55]

But neither Hudson and Halls nor Des Britten's books was a match for Alison Holst and Richard Silcock's 1974 *The New Zealand Radio & Television Cookbook*, in which most of the recipes came from radio and television audiences. The response from contributors was phenomenal and the outcome illuminating. 'The Pacific Rim had taken over from Europe as the supplier of the "exotic other" to be eaten on special occasions, and many of the continental recipes, ingredients and cooking methods had been absorbed into the mainstream chapters.' Chinese, Malaysian and Indonesian food was featured and the book had a substantial section of recipes for game.[56] This represented a major shift in orientation away from Europe towards Indo-Chinese and South East Asian theatres of cooking. *The New Zealand Radio & Television Cookbook* solicited its contributions from a changing public. Waves of immigration first from Europe, then Asia and the South Pacific had already begun to influence what people wanted to eat. Immigrant groups brought their own restaurants, importers, wholesalers and grocery stores. The cultural footprint of New Zealand food consumption was shifting.

By the time Hudson and Halls released their first cookbook, they had already changed their ideas about technology in the kitchen. 'We don't use equipment like electric mixers because they aren't found in most viewers' homes,' they told a reporter in 1977.[57] This may have been true at the start, but after two years on the small screen they had come to recognise the tangled relationship between television and marketers. 'They were sponsored by Kitchen Wizz,' Geoffrey Collins remembers. 'They used it all the time in their house (they used their food processor for everything). That made it easier for TV New Zealand because basically every ad break was the Kitchen Wizz during their show.'[58] Hudson and Halls advocated the appliance with gusto, even after once failing to put the lid on properly and having the Wizz spray its contents around the room. They also now used electric frying pans, mixers and woks.

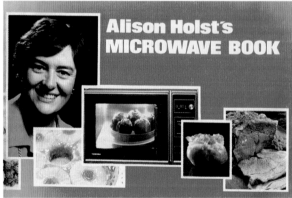

Neither Des Britten nor Hudson and Halls was a match in sales volume or longevity for Alison Holst's The New Zealand Radio & Television Cookbook *(1974) and Alison Holst's* Microwave Book *(1982).*

Ovens, electric elements and gas rings were universal, but the 1970s was the decade of the deep freeze. Not everyone owned one, and celebrity chiefs proselytised and instructed people in how to use them. The prohibitive cost undoubtedly delayed their entry into many households: in February 1975 an average 311-litre freezer cost $240, the equivalent of $2270 today.[59] Hudson and Halls were determined to help cookbook readers use their freezer as more than just a bulk subantarctic storeroom. Readers could 'spoon the leftover tomato purée into an ice cube tray and freeze' it; store excess pancakes in packets of eight with paper between them for a savoury or sweet stand-by; freeze the overflow of a large batch of Rich Meat Sauce, 'then divide it into smaller quantities … for later use'; and freeze all kinds of meat. It was important to label and date these because no one wanted to find a centuries-old piece of meat at the bottom of their chest freezer.[60]

By the end of the 1970s the microwave was just coming onto the New Zealand market. Hudson and Halls used the microwave sparingly while Alison Holst was more expansive in her research. She began microwave cooking in 1979 with a Toshiba that had two settings and a turntable, and had this advice to her readers: 'Microwave cooking is a completely new type of cooking with a completely different set of rules … In microwave cooking, especially when you are starting, you must make notes of what you did, the times you used, the dish you used.'[61]

*

Not only were Hudson and Halls promoting manufacturers' products but they were also involved in making commercials and advertising. Their visibility and instant brand recognition made them ideal promoters of a variety of cooking and kitchen products. 'Here's Big Boy,' Peter announced while David, standing close behind him, squirted a thick white substance onto a stovetop. The sexual innuendo made this tantalisingly risqué, but also bordered on bad taste. The boundaries between paid advertising, cooking programmes and celebrity endorsement became so blurred that in 1982 the director-general of Television New Zealand, Allan Martin, made a statement to the media. He wanted a clearer separation: 'The Television Standards and Rules booklet says advertising must be separated from programme content otherwise both programme and commercial can be viewed as a complete effort to sell or publicise items.'[62]

Through 1982 Peter Hudson and David Halls maintained their run of successful shows. Their guests continued to be outrageous and unusual, among them the young trick-unicyclist Glen McIvor whom promoter Lew Pryme suggested for the programme. He caused a sensation on stage. In the studio audience, still, was 82-year-old Evelyn Balmforth. She had watched Peter and David make every show, except one, since they had begun filming in front of a live audience in 1976. Evelyn still carried the guilt of taking a holiday to Pakatoa Island in the Hauraki Gulf and missing that one show: 'They wondered what had happened to me,' she told an interviewer in her broad Yorkshire accent. 'I'll never do that again. I think they're both darlings. I call them "my boys" – I have a son about their age.'[63]

At the beginning of filming in March 1982, the duo greeted Evelyn 'with a peck on the cheek and a "hello darling"'. After a show that included Derek Metzger, winner of the Pacific Song Quest, Richard O'Sullivan from *Robin's Nest* and *Man About the House*, and the jazz-comedy band known as Uncle Albert's Orgasmic Orchestra, they called her back. '"Get the booze out," they said when the pint-sized grandmother came on stage for a photograph.' In the midst of all the dazzle was Evelyn, whose loyalty had given the audience its familiar face. She was one of David and Peter's great allies and a huge promoter of everything they did. She told a reporter afterwards she had been to Hudson and Halls Oyster and Fish Restaurant. 'It's not a common fish and chip shop. It's classy. It's a bit pricy, but they have very nice china.'[64]

Tom Parkinson and Jeff Bennet were ideas men. Parkinson particularly recognised the need in television for constant novelty. They called him the 'barrow boy' in television, recalls Roy Good, because of his Cockney accent, and the fact that before you knew it he had conned you into doing something previously unimaginable.[65] In the case of *Hudson and Halls*, Jeff Bennet was left to implement the impossible.

Hudson and Halls needed a new gimmick to reinvigorate the formula before the show became stale. It had potential yet for development, and the decision was made to take the show to Singapore to explore the main types of Asian cooking found there. Television New Zealand envisaged four, maybe five programmes 'to be made there over 10 days from July 31'. The extravaganza would begin with Malaysian-style cooking. They would visit the renowned 'Aziza's restaurant which is run by a woman called Hazizah. It seats about 30, is in a back street, but has an international reputation.' Chinese food was next, and this would take Hudson and Halls to a major restaurant at the Oberoi Imperial Hotel where 'chicken in lotus leaf stuffed with preserved vegetables' would be prepared. They would also explore North Indian cooking by watching tandoori chicken being prepared in tandoori ovens. The final cooking style featured on their itinerary was 'indigenous Singapore "nonya" food [that] will be prepared by chef, consultant and cookbook writer Terry Tan with his family in his home'.[66] Nonya food brought together a number of popular Singaporean cooking styles to create something unique.

Filming was brilliantly timed to coincide with Singapore's National Day celebrations. National Day is 'a festival for all the races and religions which goes on day and night,' Jeff Bennet explained to a reporter.[67] The streets would be a blaze of colour with food and drink everywhere, providing a startling backdrop to filming. This authentic Asian food footage would be canned in Singapore; in the studio back home Hudson and Halls would demonstrate 'New Zealand versions of the dishes, banana leaves will double for lotus leaves'.[68]

The concept seemed unbeatable: the bustling markets full of exotic foods, the glittering nightlife and the multitude of stalls and tiny restaurants could be nothing but a success. Peter and David, however, found the intense heat, crowding, noise and incessant flies too much. There was something gruesome and grubby about the marketplace, the food preparation and the condition of the kitchens. They sweated profusely and whined almost as much. Asian cooking was not their passion, and it showed. While these programmes pointed to new directions in which the duo could move, they were never revisited. The cost of making the programmes once all the accounts came in would have been exorbitant. Such spending might have justified an occasional fling, but there was also the surly response of the show's two stars to contend with.

Fruit Flans

sweet pastry shell
pastry cream
tinned, poached or fresh fruit
whipped cream or nuts for decoration

The pastry cream described in the recipe for Dolce alla Piemontese is very useful in constructing a fruit flan when you haven't much fruit. Bake ahead a sweet pastry shell, or defrost one from your freezer.

Fill almost to the top with pastry cream, and chill. Place some tinned, poached or fresh fruit on top, and glaze over with a fruit glaze.

GLAZE
½ cup fruit syrup
1 teaspoon arrowroot

Mix half a cup of syrup with one teaspoon of arrowroot, and bring to the boil. Let cool, and brush over the fruit. Top with whipped cream or nuts.

PASTRY CREAM
1 cup milk
2 tablespoons vanilla flavoured castor sugar (if none available add ½ teaspoon vanilla essence)
2 tablespoons plain flour
2 egg yolks
finely grated rind of one lemon
1 tablespoon butter

Bring three-quarters of the milk to the boil. Meanwhile, mix sugar and flour in a bowl, add egg yolks and lemon rind, and mix with remaining quarter of milk. Pour boiling milk on to mixture in bowl, then return mixture to saucepan. Reheat until it boils up once, stirring all the time. Remove from heat, beat in the butter, and cool.

ADDITIONAL IDEAS FOR FRUIT FLANS:

* Fresh strawberries sprinkled with sugar and glazed with port and arrowroot. Add two teaspoons of sugar to this glaze when boiling.
* Canned peaches or apricots. Use the juice from the can with the arrowroot and one tablespoon of rum or Cointreau.
* Gently poached sweet apples cut in slices. Do not let them go to a mush! Use a glaze of two tablespoons apricot jam, half a cup sweet white wine plus arrowroot.
* Poached pear slices, glazed with blackcurrant jam, sweet white wine and a tablespoon of sugar.
* These, and many other combinations, can be made quickly and easily. These recipes make the fruit go further, and look really impressive. To make the glaze look at its best, push it through a fine sieve with the back of a spoon before brushing over the fruit.

9. Ratings, Rejections & the BBC: 1983–87

Television is gladiatorial and the mob fickle. Such is the nature of ratings and programming that a series like *Hudson and Halls* could plummet in the space of a year. By the end of 1982 the show's ratings had dwindled to a shocking 10–16 per cent of the viewing public. Tom Parkinson was quick to communicate the reasons for this to the press. The principal problem was programming. The shows had been tailored for a Friday-night, stay-at-home audience who were older and more sedate. For them the black tie, white dress shirt and black dinner jacket were perfectly pitched. They were Hudson and Halls' constituency. But a last-minute change to another time slot put the pair in front of a younger, more selective Tuesday crowd.

This mismatch was exacerbated by the fact that they were pitched against some of the biggest gladiators in the ring. 'They were weighted against the big Tuesday night American blockbusters like *Evita* and *Beggarman, Thief*,' Parkinson explained to the *Auckland Star*. He admitted to being worried about ratings: 'If the show didn't have the necessary razzmatazz and seemed a trifle tired', there were strategies he would introduce.[1] The audience and the competition were contributing factors, but there was also the fact that the last two years of almost uninterrupted screen time had left Hudson and Halls overexposed. Perhaps this influenced what happened next.

The hour-long programme was slashed to a tight 30 minutes. The guests in this abridged format would be 'people in the public eye'.[2] Instant recognition, rather than the slow reveal of an unknown talent, was crucial. As well, there would be fewer programmes. In the past they had shot 28 programmes annually; in 1983 they would film only 14, seven of which would be held over to the following year. David confided to Carleen: 'That means [Tom] will have had us out of work for 7 months

TOP: *Alison Holst on the* Hudson and Halls *set in Auckland. The celebrity guest list before the format change in 1983 included the doyenne of Kiwi cooking.*
BOTTOM: *Miss Universe 1983, New Zealand's Lorraine Downes, also made a guest* **appearance.** COURTESY OF THE *NEW ZEALAND LISTENER*

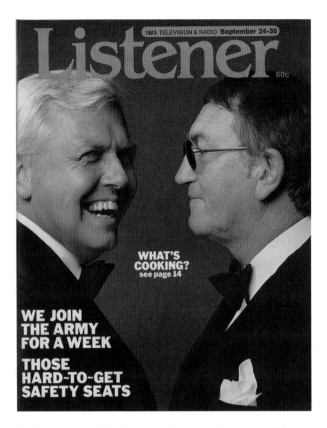

By September 1983 they were back on the cover of the
New Zealand Listener.

this year and a further 5 months till February, thus cutting our income from 28 shows in a twelve month period to 7 … [it] is an insult to expect us to hang on … for a salary that we could hardly exist on anyway. We are furious to say the least, and we got conned into doing Singapore for nothing by Tom … Jesus dear you can't trust anyone these days.'[3]

Television bosses had lost absolute faith in the formula. They were dipping rather than submerging themselves in risk because *Hudson and Halls* was no longer a guaranteed success.

The celebrity guest list before the format change in 1983 included Alison Holst, and Bruno Lawrence, star of the phenomenally successful films *Smash Palace* (1980), *Goodbye Pork Pie* (1981) and *Utu* (1983). Alison Holst's experience of working on the show left an indelible impression: '"Bruno was charm itself," she remembers. "We did our rehearsal and everything was just fine … Then I went to get changed and do make-up and I think Bruno went off to the Green Room … There was time to spare and there was *a great deal of wine* … there was absolutely nothing else to do. And when he got on the show, he couldn't say a word" … Lawrence was tanked, hammered, legless. "Some people would have been thrown completely, but [Hudson and Halls] coped magnificently."[4] David and Peter even answered Lawrence's questions for him and he just nodded mutely.

'The new trimmed down and tightened up Hudson and Halls series', as the *Auckland Star* described it, began on 29 September 1983 with a brand-new set design. *Hudson and Halls* had had the same brown and green set for five years, so Kerry Shone's new design was overdue. The new plan added visual drama while eliminating the area that had previously accommodated guest performers. The kitchen, which cost $7000, was black and white with touches of red coloured steel or glass. The idea came from Hudson and Halls wanting a black chopping board to show off the food. The colour theme continued through the rest of the kitchen: 'white potato peelers, store eggs in a fancy red wire egg basket, wash up in a scarlet sink and chat to guests over dinner while reclining in black and white zebra chairs. A green silk fern and coloured place mats to … complement the food … black lacquered table, French stainless steel cutlery with black or white handles, and white plates interchangeable with black hexagonal dishes.'[5] David was delighted. The 'new set … looks stunning', he told Carleen and Jerry.[6]

The seven-part series would have six New Zealand-based personalities as guests. 'To boost sagging ratings', producer Chris Cooper told the *Auckland Star*, 'Hudson and Halls will now cook three family budget courses instead of whipping up a single fancy dish.'[7]

By now there was an underlying negativity towards *Hudson and Halls* from both television bosses and the media. Peter and David, the two exotic peacocks, had lost some of their sheen. They had shifted from surrogate sons to titillating targets. Even their move to Leigh was constructed adversely. An article written in March describes it as 'reclusive', and their 'small farm at Warkworth' as being 'far from the probing public eye, behind double-locked gates. Their telephone number has changed and is unlisted.'[8] The warm, friendly, flamboyant image projected in previous articles was changing.

Change as a concept was becoming television's mission statement, and the race for ratings would be used to justify everything. Hudson and Halls were in their 'dazzling' new black, white and red studio for only one series before they were out again on location. 'Hudson and Halls will camp outside for their salad days series', the *Auckland Star* told its readers, 'and shift into their own back garden for the next batch of summer shows … Peter Hudson and David Halls want to cook meals for all those summer holidaymakers who set up camp with a television set. This means plenty of salads, brunches and picnics all prepared on authentic gas stoves with camp chairs, sun hats and casual summer substitutes for their dinner jacket costumes.'[9]

Using their own home as the backdrop to the show would once have been the realisation of a dream for Peter and David, but they were not happy with the dramatic drop in screen time. Their show had been halved, then cut again. They had been looking for more time to relax, but this was far more than they wanted or could afford.

The salad days series aired in the summer of 1984 from 5 January to 9 February. But modification was back on the menu again. '*Hudson and Halls* is going straight,' the *Auckland Star* provocatively announced in August. 'The next series will revert to the studio – none of this alfresco nonsense – and guests will be cut out. The show will be 30 minutes, following the trend of recent series.'[10] Everything was being condensed. When *Hudson and Halls* lost its guest budget, it lost one of the cornerstones of the show. The duo had become more than just cooks on a cooking programme; they were entertainers. Removing the guest component was taking them backwards. Inevitably, it would also have an impact on viewer numbers.

Ironically, the programme series Hudson and Halls filmed to celebrate their tenth year on television was stripped down to what they were when they began: no guests, just 24 minutes of cooking. 'The extra time will allow us to put a "bit extra" into the cooking side of things … [and put] greater emphasis on presentation and style,' Peter told the *New Zealand Herald*.[11] He didn't mean it.

In October 1984 the *Auckland Star* warned television viewers: 'Don't hold your breath for the *Hudson and Halls* cooking programme next year. Present plans include the two zany cooks but the series won't be included in TVNZ time slots until much, much later in the year – maybe even as late as next spring.'[12] This meant *Hudson and Halls* would have been absent from the screen for over a year. 'After ten years with the bastards [in television] we have come to expect every mean and dirty trick in the book. They really do hate our guts,' David unloaded to Carleen and Jerry.[13] Only when Tom Parkinson resigned from Television New Zealand in 1984 did Peter and David understand how much he had actually done for them. 'Since his departure, we have been virtually dumped,' David wrote; and in another letter, '[N]ow Tom has resigned, we have no one at court to give us a guiding hand.'[14]

Although Television New Zealand's actions were ominous, serious negotiations were under way to sell the show in the UK. 'We may still get our wish of overseas television after all these years yet, already!!!!' David excitedly told Carleen and Jerry. The pair had also 'signed a long term contract with Sanyo to promote their microwave ovens … to start at $50,000 per year', as well as a contract 'with Ralta electrical and … with the gas board' which, with the 'pissling $14,000' from television, would 'bring it up to $40,000'.[15] So while their New Zealand show was being cut and pared back there was a growing income from endorsements, plus the very real hope that they might finally break into another market.

*

To maintain currency, the new series took a more contemporary tack. Hudson and Halls were now in front of a time-starved generation of cooks whose one missing ingredient was space in the day to whip up anything elaborate. The new episodes were programmed for Television One on Tuesday evenings from 7.30 to 8.00pm. Beginning on 23 October and finishing on 4 December 1984, the show was set to tackle 'stress in the kitchen by offering recipes which are time-saving and inexpensive', Ricky Stratful, their new producer, explained to the *Auckland Star*. 'Hudson and Halls are very serious about the intent behind the series – food is expensive and there should be no waste. They are also insistent on safety in the kitchen.'[16]

Nothing in this dismal summary of promotional 'highlights' sounded like Hudson and Halls. By the mid-1980s, 'user-pays', budget-cutting and corporatised austerity began to rise out of the free-love and dope-smoking ashes of the 1960s and 1970s. The new ethos was clipped and pared back, and its soon-to-be unchallenged god was the work ethic. Cooks could be women and they could be men, equally; they could be moneyed, middle class or hard up; they could be young, old; possibly even gay, lesbian or bi-sexual; but above everything else they were a unit of work that must pay its way.

Time in the kitchen was becoming a greater luxury than the wine you splashed in the Coq au Vin. Repatriated in a new, more palatable guise, puritanism returned after a brief absence as a natural extension of corporatisation and global capitalism. Suddenly, things had got serious, and every bean was counted. Hudson and Halls are going to 'create a delicious meal using offal in their second programme', sang the food writer for the *Auckland Star*. '[L]iver, onions, raisins and pinenuts, chicken liver with ham and sage, and posh lamb kidneys.'[17] The kitchen was the same black, white, grey and red they had had in the previous series, the article told readers.

'Hudson and Halls are responsible for the design of their studio kitchen, and the two refrigerators in it have been with them since the first series.'[18]

Gone was the heady flamboyance that had been the hallmark of their earlier shows. The article, entitled 'Clowns of the kitchen', said a lot about changing attitudes. The mid-to-late-1980s take on the two maverick presenters was that they were ridiculous. Instead of being seen as unique and original, Hudson and Halls were perceived as tired and outdated. Their on-stage drinking no longer registered as 'bad boy' bohemianism, but as an embarrassing weakness emanating from addiction. The chances of their lasting much longer on television seemed slim.

*

The turbulence that pitched *Hudson and Halls* from one format to another was building into a treacherous storm. Never before had things been so unpredictable. Always, television had been tossed around by successive governments, but the 1980s heralded a decade of draconian change. The 1970s had been a decade of creative endeavour. Amid the mayhem, ideas became programming and careers evolved with unprecedented momentum. The medium of television was maturing with a sense of unbounded potential. Roy Good remembers having to tell his art staff to go home at night because the work they did was so engrossing. Exuberance over the work rather than the ethic drove them on.

The new era began positively enough in February 1980 with the formation of Television New Zealand (TVNZ). This was a centralising strategy to make viewing a more streamlined experience. Instead of audiences choosing channels, they would select programmes, allowing a great deal more complementary viewing. At this point 'local content was estimated to be running at something like 50% of primetime viewing – 48% on TV-1 and 15% on TV-2'. With a completely integrated relationship between the channels, quality programmes that were not populist 'were able to be moved into accessible primetime hours, doubling the audience for shows like [the arts programme] *Kaleidoscope*'.[19]

While amalgamating the networks did provide clearer viewer choices, this was arguably the beginning of an unprecedented level of centralised control and economic austerity. Robert Boyd-Bell writes of this period: 'Staff morale also took a steady battering as the newspaper critics and politicians constantly debated the major question in broadcasting politics during this time – how to give *effect* to the National Government's election manifesto which promised progressively increased involvement of private enterprise in New Zealand television.'[20]

Opponents fired across a no-man's-land of indecision regarding private enterprise until the more fiscally free-marketeering Labour government came to power after a snap election in 1984, and television was rocked again. A commission of inquiry was established 'to investigate alleged irregularities and corrupt practices within the TVNZ entertainment department'. Overnight the barometer dropped, and the atmosphere chilled ahead of a storm. 'Although the reports of two accountants found no significant financial malpractice', the commission of inquiry was set on publicly censuring the accused. It strongly criticised 'the role of Ian Cross as full time chairman and chief executive of the Broadcasting Corporation, and castigated Television New Zealand director Allan Martin and controller of programmes Rod Cornelius for lax management and administrative procedures.'[21]

The Labour government would completely change the nature of broadcasting in New Zealand. Under the State Owned Enterprises Act of 1986 it planned to deregulate 'broadcasting and the related telecommunications industry … and to set up a Broadcasting Commission which [was] to be funded by a broadcasting licence fee'.[22] The intention was to move New Zealand television from being a division of the Broadcasting Corporation of New Zealand to being a state-owned enterprise (SOE). There was to be no protection, and TVNZ would have to 'compete for programmes, audiences, and advertising dollars in a deregulated market environment'.[23] The way to achieve this transition was through contract funding. In this brave new environment, all contenders for funding would be treated equally.

Fear of the future was used as the stick to drive change. Always New Zealand's isolation, its small scale and protectionist monopolies were held up as factors that increased the country's vulnerability. As New Zealand had prepared itself during World War Two with a network of coastal gun emplacements for an attack from Japan that never came, so too did television.

Dread of digital technology, globalisation and the looming threat of a privately owned television channel changed New Zealand. Competition from a more aggressive, market-savvy third overseas television channel hovered like Banquo's ghost at every gathering. This spectral projection of a national sense of inadequacy was used to re-shape television in a commercial manner.

*

Peter and David's shift to The Farm meant there was always lots to do – fences to build and repair, and '350 metres of metal drive edged by grass which must be cut'.[24] There was livestock to feed. To the Romney sheep were added a herd of steers, and there were peacocks, Peter's renewed flock of doves and the domestic pets. The pair continued to entertain dinner guests at their house parties, which often spilt over into the pool. Abby Collins remembers that one weekend her brother-in-law Marty Collins brought along scuba gear: 'We were in the pool for hours … Going up and down along the bottom, pissed. Very lovely time, very funny.'[25]

Running a farm was a huge commitment, and there were traps. 'The weather here is disastrous,' David wrote in desperation to Carleen and Jerry in February 1983. 'No feed for the stock, wool prices at an all time low. We sent our sheep off in January to be sold, and they all came back the same day … $10 per head under what we had originally paid for them, so we didn't sell, like everybody else … so it is down on the knees every morning, praying for rain.'[26] The Farm was supposed to be a money earner like their restaurant, but frequently it cost them more than it earned. None of their plans seemed to realise any real cash. 'Peter and I keep hoping that we can strike it rich so that we can be looked after in our old age, that's if we ever make old age.'[27]

In their first year or so at Ti Point they came home one night to find they had been robbed. Burglars had got away with $16,670 worth of their possessions. The house's remote location was only part of the reason. When the perpetrators were finally apprehended, charged and found guilty in court, it was revealed that the burglary at Peter and David's house was part of a spree of thefts that occurred across an area from Ellerslie in Auckland to Warkworth, Snells Beach and Mathesons Bay. The culprits, who were just 17 and 19 years old, had been cheeky enough to use a Triumph sports car stolen in a robbery in Remuera as their getaway vehicle, which they left in a ditch along with a .22-calibre rifle taken from David and Peter's house. One of the burglars was injured in the crash and a trail of blood marked their escape from the car. The daily commitment to feed and move stock and care for domestic pets, and the worry about home security, now meant Peter and David seldom left the property without a caretaker in charge.

Bullet and Nero, their two dogs, had been locked in the laundry when the thieves forced open a sliding door to the house. 'An angry Mr Hudson said today it was a pity the dogs were shut up. They are Rottweilers … [and they] would have torn them to pieces.'[28] Peter was certain the thieves must have been watching the house, because this was the first time it had been left without anyone there to look after it.

As their television appearances dwindled, Peter and David travelled widely and more often as part of a manoeuvre to maintain their celebrity profile. In 1985 Hudson and Halls did not appear on New Zealand television. Instead, during the

14 or so months from mid-1984 to late 1985, they met and shook hands with 'more than 200,000 … They hosted shows in Palmerston North, Hamilton and Wellington, where they attracted thousands to The Great Wellington Show and The Hudson and Halls Food Fest.'[29]

At a trade fair in Palmerston North, probably in September 1985, they put in long days, working '10am to 10pm daily for five days, bloody hard graft … Had to assist in an act where a guy was sandwiched between two beds of 8 inch very sharp nails and then we both stood on top of him, we nearly freaked the first time. He survived and so we did this little act three times a day on stage. Peter was then made to smash huge concrete blocks whilst he was still sandwiched with the help of a huge sledge hammer.'[30] At his final performance David had to assist the magician, who had lost his voice. In Hamilton they did another stint of long demanding days.

In August 1986 they were booked to appear at the Wiri Show, and in October they hosted 'another Hudson and Halls Food Fest in Wellington'.[31] Food festivals were set to combine with fashion and foreign travel. Hudson and Halls had on their itinerary for that year the plan to host an exclusive Cook's Tour which would be taking in Singapore, Frankfurt, Paris and London, with a visit to Maxim's in Paris and fashion houses in London.[32] David was also booked for a stint in the theatre: '[Halls] will go solo for a short time … as Detective Inspector Porterhouse in the play *Run for Your Wife*, then on tour in New Zealand. The play also stars Eddie Yeats, of *Coronation Street* fame, and Robin Asquith, star of many *Confessions of a … movies*.'[33] The invitation had come directly from Robin Asquith himself. 'He has bought the rights to a play and … offered me a part in it for 10 weeks here at a very good fee (2000 a week plus expenses),' David told Carleen and Jerry.[34]

Peter and David's real passion was to be on the small screen in New Zealand, the UK, Europe and that great bastion of entertainment, the US, but negotiations to sell the show overseas were slow. In the meantime, there was comfort in knowing they had plenty of engagements in their diary to keep them busy, and a new cookbook coming out.

*

•

In 1985, 10 years after they premiered on *Speakeasy* as Hudson and Halls, and eight years after publication of their first cookbook, Peter and David brought out *Favourite Recipes from Hudson & Halls*. At 192 pages, it was published by Whitcoulls in Christchurch, and later picked up by Century Publishing in the UK and released in London, Johannesburg and Melbourne.

Peter and David in the promotional jackets they wore for their live shows in Wiri, Palmerston North, Hamilton and Wellington in 1985–86. JAN CORMACK, PRIVATE COLLECTION

The book's camp cover said it all. Peter sits sartorially in black jacket, white dress shirt and black tie. Behind him, leaning on the back of his chair and fractionally over him and into the photograph, is his partner and consort, the equally dapper David. The picture is one of ageing aristocrats, in the library after dinner perhaps – satisfied, smug, even slightly superior. Gone are the 1970s body shirts and that hint of an 'alternative lifestyle'. This is David's Theydon Hall and Peter's Iona Avenue, recreated as an illusion and the cover for something very different. It is a *mise en scène* of old money and affluence. To the left of them an antique clock ticks away time, and behind are books in abundance, including two substantial tomes on wine.

This is a celebration of Englishness at a time when Television New Zealand, and local book publishing too, were shifting their focus to all things Kiwi. Hudson and Halls' fabrication of foreign elegance looked decidedly out of place. However, on the back of the Whitcoulls edition is a picture of David and Peter on their lifestyle block at Leigh. The centrepiece is a hurricane-wire fence, which David holds casually, a rifle propped over his shoulder. He is dressed in shorts, gumboots and a cut-off-sleeved

197

FAVOURITE RECIPES FROM THE BESTSELLING COOKERY DUO

Hudson & Halls

NOW A MAJOR TV SERIES

Favourite Recipes from Hudson & Halls *(1985) marked a change in style. The 1970s body shirts had given way to aristocratic attire.*

t-shirt. Peter, posed with his foot on a spade, has a floppy Fred Dagg-styled hat, dark sunglasses, gumboots and a purple grandpa-buttoned t-shirt. The Rottweilers, Bullet and Nero, sit to the right of the frame in panting obedience.

These juxtaposed bookends communicated Peter and David's experience brilliantly: a front cover that projected a faux-aristocratic formality and, behind it, the real-life experience that was hands-on, haphazard and homosexual.

While there are everyday recipes sprinkled among the 'evening entertainers', this book is really about possibilities for the grand dinner party. It is flamboyant and unapologetically exorbitant in calling for lavish ingredients. Cooking had changed, they noted in the foreword. There was 'a greater variety of vegetables … available than was the case in the not-so-distant past, cuts of meat have become more interesting, and cooking equipment has taken on a new aspect.'[35] All of these things are reflected in the commentary, recipes and handy hints, but the coding of this cookbook is solidly Hudson and Halls.

There was still a firm grip on the grog bottle, and they still advocated that the alcohol you cook with should be no different in quality to what you drink. Their new advice acknowledged New Zealand's changing food styles and eating patterns, however. The influence of Indian, Chinese and East Asian cooking, particularly, had altered the rubric: 'Once there were rather snobbish, strict rules about white wine with white meat and red wine with red meat … [now] simply, if a dish is highly spiced, to our taste a good heavy red is appropriate, and with delicate, light food, a white. How could you drink wine with curry? Try chilled beer instead. A chilled sherry goes well with soup, a sweet Sauterne with fruit and cheese.'[36]

Favourite Recipes reflects a more avid engagement with Asian food, especially Chinese cooking. After filming their shows in Singapore, David and Peter knew more about it: 'The best thing about Chinese-style food in most cases is that it is quick to cook, very tasty, and easy on the waistline,' they wrote in the meat section. Chinese cooking introduced exotic vegetables and spices – such as sambal oelek which they had to explain and source for their readers – and utensils: 'A wok is still the best thing to cook Chinese food in, although we sometimes use a large, heavy-based pan, and we now have a wok-shaped pan that has a slightly flattened base so that you can use it on an electric cooker as well as on the gas.'[37]

While the new cookbook was more multinational than its predecessor, there were the usual French and English dishes intended to stir up a sense of the exotic in far-off New Zealand. The idea of their Marinated Leg of Lamb with Anchovies was, they explained, to 'recreate the taste of sheep which have been grazing on salty grasses by the sea, as in Normandy'.[38] Tomato and Onion Pie, based on a dish from Mrs Beeton, the famous nineteenth-century English cook and recipe compiler, was a gesture in the direction of traditional English cooking. Hudson and Halls' food took cooks out of the kitchen and transported them across time and culture – and this was the intention.

Favourite Recipes includes a substantial fish section. After a number of years of owning their own fish restaurant in Ponsonby they felt well positioned to advise readers about freshness and best practice for barbecues, and they also drew on their experience of cuisine from Singapore. Nonya cooking provided them with their recipe for Spicy Wrapped Fish Cakes: 'The original is all prepared and pounded in a pestle and mortar, but we have adapted it to the modern kitchen by using a food processor.' And there was another modern improvisation: 'Should you have access to banana leaves use them to wrap the mixture, as the result looks very oriental. Failing that, squares of foil are perfectly adequate.'[39]

The game section was sizable, and their approach more cultivated than wild. 'No, you won't find Bear Burgers or Possum Pie here, just venison, duck, pheasant and rabbit – tame game, that can be fairly readily purchased in a lot of stores,' they wrote. 'Hedgehog covered in clay and cooked on an open fire has never been something that we could try, having over the years rescued many of them from the swimming pool with the aid of a large sieve, dried them out a little, fed them with a saucer of warm milk and set them on their merry way to eradicate pests from the lettuce rows.'[40]

There was just one vegan-style vegetarian dish – Fresh Green Salad with Fresh Herbs – and the only real use for a microwave they advised, other than for defrosting meat (as long as it didn't sizzle in the middle), was to cook vegetables, which it did 'magnificently'. They remained passionate advocates of the food processor, which could crush, chop, slice or blend anything.

There were practical suggestions for the home economist with a pretty decent budget and robust culinary imagination, and handy hints, also, for luxury revisited, *Brideshead*-style. About their Truffle Sauce, they told readers: 'The Italians use white truffles, shaved very thin, with pasta, and it is quite expensive. You can use black truffles if you wish. At first we were not going to give the recipe, then we thought, why not, you may get lucky and find someone rich has given you some and you don't know how to use them.' If you were cooking Tandoori Murgh, they advised, 'the millionaire class use saffron threads (at the time of writing, they cost more per weight than pure gold). If down to your last million, use saffron powder.'[41]

One of Hudson and Halls' most mystifying combinations has to be Fresh Strawberries with Cabbage – a startling combination even for the most hedonistic 1980s dinner party. They reassured cooks that although it sounded like a culinary paradox, it was a delicious combination. Their instructions were to take a largish cabbage and cut it across about a quarter of the way down with a sharp knife. 'Carefully hollow out the bottom to form a bowl, wash the strawberries (with their stalks on), dry them and place them in the cabbage bowl. Replace the top of the cabbage as a lid. You may have to hollow out a bit of the lid so that it sits snugly on top. Cover in foil and chill in fridge.'

The cabbage's partnership with strawberries was not purely functional, nor was it just a visual pairing of complementary colours. The marriage was about taste: 'The cabbage seems to bring out the flavour of strawberries unlike anything else.' Strawberries stored in a hacked-out cabbage promised drama on the dining-room table. However, to throw away a serious cabbage simply for a subtle change in flavour, even if it was an important part of a culinary pantomime, went against every Kiwi caution. Hudson and Halls knew this. 'Don't, of course, throw the cabbage bits away – use them for slaw.'[42] One can only wonder how many of these extravaganzas in green and red were ever made.

Try the precise type of cooking oil; use the correct mustard; tip in the exact hard-to-find sherry or expensive liquor: there is an uncompromising fussiness about their cookbook that oozes two incomes, including the pink-dollared variety about which society was beginning to talk openly. *Favourite Recipes* was a cookbook for a new breed of comfortable couple. They had a choice about children and could be gay or straight. These pairings were powered by careers and salary, and they still had just enough leisure time in the kitchen and around the dining-room table to celebrate their emerging identity.

*

Homosexual law reform had been a work in faltering progress since the early days of gay liberation. In 1974 National Party MP Venn Young made a first attempt at decriminalisation with the introduction of the Crimes Amendment Bill. This would have legalised sexual behaviour between consenting male adults 21 years and over. But even this decidedly discriminatory amendment was defeated 34 to 29, with a massive 23 abstentions. Warren Freer, another National Party MP, proposed amendments again in 1979 and 1980, with a similar age restriction. By this time gay rights groups had become more uncompromisingly aware of implicit homophobia in the age of consent and did not support the amendment, which was again defeated.

Homosexuality polarised people as it always had, but the arrival of Aids was the catalyst that reheated the debate, especially for heterosexuals. The first signs of the virus could have been symptoms of something else: 'Men were falling ill with fevers, weight loss, pneumonia, skin lesions and unusual cancers.' But then a trickle of cases became a pandemic. 'In 1984 scientists announced that Aids … was the result of the HIV virus.'[43]

Suddenly gay issues became everyone's issues, because although the majority of the identified cases were among the gay community, the disease was sexually transmitted and therefore no respecter of sexuality. Aids worried everyone, especially married men who enjoyed homosexual liaisons on the side. Safe sex to prevent the spread of Aids, as well as notification and early treatment, were essential. But who was going to seek a diagnosis or treatment for themselves or their sexual partner if in doing so they were confessing to a crime? There were still jail terms, fines and, via *Truth* newspaper, public humiliation.

Aids education around safe sex shifted many people from the middle ground towards reform. A new sympathy and compassion arose in those who understood that the disease was wiping out a generation of young men. People saw the tragedy in quilts made for Aids victims, and were moved by them. But there were others, especially among evangelical Christians, who saw Aids as God's judgement: a divine plague among the damned to create a living Hell. For those whose homophobia took a less theological bent, there was the terror of infection. Aids was the new leprosy. Fear ignited paranoia. People were frightened to kiss, touch, even breathe the same air as someone with HIV or Aids.

These mixed responses to Aids threw together some unlikely combinations. Those who feared Aids and wanted early notification so the leper's bell could be rung joined the broad-minded and the newly educated to support homosexual law reform. The vanguard of this groundswell were young gay activists and their supporters, who had been seeking a change in legislation for years. Aids gave their political agenda an urgency as well as a focus. In 1985 a new initiative was sponsored by Fran Wilde, a junior Labour MP. Wilde's Homosexual Law Reform Bill consisted of two parts: one that sought to legalise sex between males over the age of 16, and another that outlawed discrimination against gay men and lesbians. The Homosexual Law Reform Bill generated the hottest public debate in New Zealand since the Springboks' rugby tour of 1981.[44]

The collective vote was still in the negative, but the fundamentalist foundation on which homophobia rested had shifted. 'Yes' or 'No' to legalising homosexuality became a conscience vote for all New Zealanders, and everyone voiced an opinion on it. Votes for and against were solicited as in an election campaign.

All the rhetoric, however, would not change the political imperative. In 1985 Aids was a new and unknowable disease, and it had to be tackled. Human rights might be subject to conscience and referendum, but pandemics and public health were not. Regardless of the people's mandate there was a crisis to avert. Reformers finally had a degree of success. Parliament voted to legalise sex between males over the age of 16, by 49 votes to 44, but the clauses relating to discrimination were lost 49 to 31.[45]

The fact that the section of the bill outlawing discrimination against homosexuality failed to pass is telling. If Hudson and Halls needed any more evidence to prove that their caution about being anything more than an 'open secret' on television was well placed, this was it. Entertainer and celebrity commentator David Hartnell believes the couple's continued existence on television depended on their discretion. 'Coming out as gay back then would have finished their career. The public would accept them camping around as a couple of funny chaps but didn't want the reality of two gay men prancing around on TV.'[46]

New Zealand loved Hudson and Halls because they weren't out. Outrageousness could be endearing and campiness titillating but, like politics in rugby, there was no place for sexual politics in celebrity cooking because it would spoil a good bit of entertainment. Happy with the hypocrisy, television bosses were only really interested in the 'thumbs up' or 'thumbs down' of the ratings arena. As David Hartnell put it: 'The public loved their campy style but the homophobic men at the top who were running TVNZ didn't like them and certainly didn't know how to deal with them.' But 'they were bringing in the ratings and the dollars re advertising revenue.' This, he said, was 'all the heads of TVNZ were interested in', and when Hudson and Halls began to wane they were happy to see them go.[47]

Peter and David would not have missed the irony that just as they were being phased out of New Zealand television, homosexuality was finally being legalised. They had been 'out' in the public eye for 10 precarious years. Their partnership and living arrangements had been the subject of many a feature article in magazines and the press. Yet just when they had less to fear from this sort of exposure than ever before, they were deemed redundant.

The devastating news that their contract would not be renewed came in 1986. Malcolm Kemp, head of entertainment at Television New Zealand, believed 'they had gone slightly off the boil'.[48] Television wasn't closing the door conclusively, but in its eleventh year on air *Hudson and Halls* was terminated. Television bosses felt their decision was justified by a range of reasons. The duo were loose cannons, Kemp believed. They drank too much on set and this led to gargantuan rows; they were outspoken about their treatment by the network, and demanded too much money. There was a level of emotional turmoil and toxicity there that Kemp just wasn't used to dealing with.

Hudson and Halls were as mortified as they were mystified. Again they felt betrayed. They felt the switching around of formats and the turnover of producers had caused as much damage to their ratings as anything they might have done on or off screen. They had a big fan base and believed there would be a revival of interest in the programme, especially after the next cookbook came out.

David Hartnell knew Malcolm Kemp was sincere in his belief that Peter and David had lost some of their mass appeal for Kiwi audiences. Kemp's move was not prompted by homophobia but by a realistic assessment of where the duo stood in the market. Hartnell believed, however, that Television New Zealand missed a valuable opportunity, and that *Hudson and Halls* could have been reconstituted as a late-night chat show, Graham Norton-style, with panellists or guest interviewees. Peter and David, he suggested, had the ability and the following to evolve, but were never given the opportunity: 'They burnt every bridge they crossed with TVNZ simply because they were so grand and demanding in playing the star role.'[49] The bosses, especially, remembered the tantrums over contracts and remuneration.

The duo had generated enemies. As Peter said in an interview with the *Auckland Star*, 'We crossed someone in TV with a very long memory.' He and David understood that 'TV is a fickle world', Peter continued,[50] but they were still deeply saddened by the outcome, and would always hold on to the hope that New Zealand television would have them back.

*

In 1986 *Hudson and Halls* appeared for the last time on New Zealand television. The show aired on Television One on Friday nights from 8.00 to 8.25pm. The series was just five episodes long, running from 3 to 31 January.

As David finished the final show with the words, 'Until we meet again, and we don't know when that will be', Peter interrupted him: 'It won't be long. It won't be long'. David continued, 'Very good health, a long life and every happiness.'[51] Peter's final 'God bless you all' ended their years on television.

The drama of their dropping from the small screen was followed by another ending. They decided to leave Ti Point. 'Television cooks Hudson and Halls have sold their rural retreat north of Auckland,' announced Lester Kidd in *Truth* in 1986, 'but their agent denies that the pansy pair are planning to leave New Zealand.'[52]

There were numerous reasons for the move. The wind that lashed the place was at times unbearable, as they told friend Richard Matthews when he was visiting: 'the only day it wasn't blowing a gale was the day they bought the house, and after that it was incessant'. Five years of managing the property had also taken its toll. Caring for the animals was time consuming; running the farm was constantly demanding. Peter was 55 years old and feeling the pressure. He was a perfectionist: he wanted every detail to be right. Windswept, out-of-control nature was just too unpredictable.

Their agent, Suzi Kitt, handled the publicity around their move. 'They certainly haven't lost their appetite for country life,' she told *Truth*, 'and Hudson and Halls would not be parted from their two big Rottweilers, which they raised from pups. They would also take their two Burmese cats to the city, but the steers and chooks will be left behind.'[53] 'We like the area and the people,' Peter reassured readers. 'We have decided to hang up our gumboots, but I would certainly consider returning to the country life-style when I retire … We have been here five years and it seems we have got busier and busier … It's when you have to hump bales of hay around in the teeming rain or on Sundays [that] you think twice.'[54]

The issue that clinched it was that at long last they had work overseas. They would be commuting between Auckland and the UK. Television New Zealand had sold the summer series, which had already aired at home, to the BBC. This was outdoor cooking on The Farm, featuring a mix of stunning scenery, barbecue cooking and salads. For the British viewers it showed an exotic idyll. It was a South Pacific travel programme with food, and the series had been well received.

During the protracted period of negotiations around the sale of the series David had approached a British television producer called Georgina Abrahams who had 'a formidable track record', and whose production company had connections with the BBC. Their first meeting was disappointing. She told him she wasn't interested and was looking for something new: 'someone to cook Japanese and Chinese food on television'. 'So I told her to her to go and find someone [else],' David remembers saying.[55] Nonetheless, they kept in touch and a few years later the unbelievable happened: they were offered their own programme on BBC television.

This was confirmation of their self-belief, and the last laugh they were looking for. To them it made a mockery of a programming decision that they thought was largely vindictive. '"They reckoned we had all the flavour of last week's left-overs; we were as flat as old pancakes!" chortles David Halls wickedly.'[56]

With smirking satisfaction they announced their good news publicly: 'We are going to be working overseas off and on for the next few years and won't be able to maintain the farm.'[57] The media relished the irony: 'They may not be seen in this part of the world but BBC cameras [will] beam them into late afternoon lounges on the other side of the world for three or four months each year,' wrote a journalist for *Sunday*.[58] The apparent callousness of television bosses made great copy, especially when it involved iconic celebrities.

The sale of their property at Ti Point was astonishingly quick. It was due to go to auction but they got an offer from an Auckland businessman '24 hours after it was advertised'.[59] The buyers were Ken and Jenny Wikeley, who became friends. 'We only got to know them because they bought "The Farm", we love them both,' David told Carleen Spencer when later he wrote urging her to show the couple around New York.[60] The spot was prime real estate, and the global domino effect of slumping markets had not yet begun to affect land values in New Zealand. Coastal properties, especially lifestyle blocks, were still in hot demand, and Peter and David made a small fortune.

The new home they bought at 58 Roberta Avenue, Glendowie, in Auckland's eastern suburbs, had its own drama. The house 'snuggles at the bottom of a wide, winding driveway bordered by manicured lawns,' wrote Les Wilson for *Sunday*; 'views from the mansion go on forever across the Hauraki Gulf'.[61] Once again, Peter and David had put their money to good use. The property had all the features they loved, as well as its own particular character. 'Their home is moody and somehow relaxing,' Wilson continued. 'Two prim bedrooms lead to a library and a modern study with steps down to the pool. As you might expect the kitchen is ultra-workmanlike and the lounge, overlooking the pool, serene.'[62]

After four years of hard graft, Peter and David had also sold the restaurant. The demands of The Farm and the long commute had made running the business increasingly difficult. While they were glad not to have the heavy commitments of the restaurant, they missed the income it generated, and now took paying guests into their home for intimate dinner parties. 'Our do's are small affairs where people dress properly, drink the best wines and relax on good conversation,' they told *Sunday*.[63]

In December 1986 the pair found themselves in a private hearing of the Auckland High Court regarding the sale of Hudson and Halls Oyster and Fish Restaurant. Michael Ewens, 'new owner of the fashionable Papillon in Jervois Road, Herne Bay,

In 1986 Peter and David moved with Bullet and Nero to 58 Roberta Avenue, Glendowie, in Auckland's eastern suburbs. JANET PUTTNAM, PRIVATE COLLECTION

A well-tanned Peter with John Fields.
JOHN FIELDS, PRIVATE COLLECTION

David and Peter with Carleen (right) and an unknown friend at Roberta Avenue, late 1980s. CARLEEN SPENCER, PRIVATE COLLECTION

who bought the restaurant from the duo', wanted $30,000 worth of damages and exemplary damages. 'It is believed the case concerns seating in a garden area at the restaurant, for which a levy must be paid to the city council in lieu of parking space.'[64] Michael Ewens had bought the business on the basis that the garden was a legitimate extension of the available restaurant seating space, when in fact Peter and David's development of it had not been strictly legal. The outcome of the court case remains confidential.

*

Peter and David's life was as hectic as ever. In New Zealand they had income from paying dinner guests, their two-hour afternoon Radio Pacific slot with Sue Thompson, celebrity events and promotions, and product endorsements. Even though they had been dropped from television they still enjoyed celebrity status, which they used wherever they could. But their weekly radio broadcast was their only regular engagement with New Zealand audiences. Fans and followers like Evelyn Balmforth, mystified by the duo's axing from the small screen, wrote to Hudson and Halls' agent, to the radio station and to Television New Zealand demanding them back again. Peter and David continued to hope this kind of pressure might convince the network to re-think their position, but there was no movement.

Posing in their own kitchen, probably at Roberta Avenue in the late 1980s. JANET PUTTNAM,
PRIVATE COLLECTION

In July 1987, less than a year after being told they had been dropped by Television New Zealand, Hudson and Halls began filming in the UK for the first of the BBC-franchised shows. It was the start of a double life, split between a mansion in the garish new suburb of Glendowie and an ancient rental property in the sixteenth-century village of Prestbury, near Manchester. Along with the villages of Wilmslow and Alderley Edge, Prestbury, with its population of around 3500, was part of Cheshire's golden triangle, one of the most salubrious, sought-after and expensive places to buy or rent outside London. Their arrival in the village made quite an impact, and although they did not stay there long, they were larger-than-life, highly visible Antipodeans and were treated 'like lords', David would remember. 'It became our second home.'[65]

Publicly they were full of optimism. 'You can be a bit dirtier here', Peter told Tim Murphy. 'The English have dirty minds'. In fact, he said, 'the British … have the best sense of humour in the world'.[66] Before they left, however, they were privately much more conflicted: 'We have so many doubts about the show and how we are going to work in the guest bits … but have decided not to worry about that too much until we actually get there.' The one thing they felt confident about was the food, which would all be drawn from the current book.[67] '[W]e set off either to become "Stars" or dead losers … say a little prayer for us and wish us well', David begged of Carleen and Jerry.[68]

The arrangements for their journey had been monumental. 'There's so much to do, the mechanics are just unbelievable. It hasn't really hit us yet', they told Frances Levy of the *Woman's Weekly* in May.[69] As well as remembering everything they would need to bring from New Zealand for the filming, arrangements had to be made for the pets. 'The budgies and the cats stay [at home with the house sitters], but the cockatiels have been taken care of by Suzi's friends … The dogs go away up to the Larsens near The Farm and as they love them and he is also a vet we are quite content … but we are still going to miss them like crazy. It's all a bloody great upheaval at our age for all this to be happening.'[70]

But it was necessary: they were beginning to recognise that there was nothing left for them in New Zealand. They still felt the rancour of their dismissal, but began to understand it in the context of other writers, artists, academics and sports people who had been forced from 'God's own' by the lack of support in a small market. They still thought it ironic that 'they must travel 22,000 km to Britain … to film their latest culinary offerings. "I guess we'll be like so many others who have had to leave to further their careers," Peter told one reporter.[71]

For David, it was more than just exile from New Zealand. He was coming home to the 'old world' that had shaped and nurtured him as a young person. And he was coming home victorious. This was 'Essex-born David Halls' … chance to win fame in his home country', wrote Tim Murphy, reporting from London in September 1987, 'which is something he has thought about for years'.[72] All of their British guests on the show in New Zealand had urged them to take the series abroad, saying it would go down especially well in England. At last David could respond to his mother's continued plea for him to come home.

Their wild public positivity was fed by the big talk of BBC bosses who had high hopes for their offbeat banter and quirky behaviour, including the occasionally dissonant dish. The line-up of potential guests for the show looked like an invitation list to a royal wedding. Alan Walsh, the series producer, mentioned Princess Anne, the Duke of Westminster, Margaret Thatcher and Jeffrey Archer, as well as 'stars like Michael Caine, Angela Lansbury, Joan Collins and Barbra Streisand as distinct possibilities. "Anyone of note you've ever heard of was on that list. It's a bit daunting!"' Peter told the *New Zealand Woman's Weekly*.[73]

The BBC aimed for the highest-profile guest list they could get because they wanted the programme to have a long reach. Dinner jackets and camp humour mixed with a dash of down-under realism would, the BBC hoped, be a sensation at home and abroad. They had already had 'interest from television companies in Australia, USA, West Germany, Scandinavia, Yugoslavia', and it was intended that the programme would be 'screened in Belgium and Holland while it was being shown in Britain'.[74] The BBC also talked in blockbuster terms about a cookbook to accompany the show, and figures like 100,000 copies for the first print run had been discussed.

The shift to a major global network set Peter and David's nerves on edge, in the same way that moving to longer stints on air in New Zealand had done. For years David had dreamed of the day when his parents might see him on their own television network. Now the reality was far more challenging than he had imagined. There was no Evelyn Balmforth to be his good-luck charm; instead his mother, father and wider family would be in the audience for the first show. He knew that when it aired, almost the whole village of Theydon Bois, where his parents still lived, would be sitting riveted to the screen, watching their prodigal son return as a star.

The BBC shot 13 of the 15 shows in the Birmingham Pebble Mills Studio and ended the series in New Zealand, where the crew taped two special programmes at Peter and David's mansion in Glendowie. The first series got off to a more modest start than the original mooted guest list would suggest: Basil Brush, an acerbic glove-puppet fox, was hardly the big-ticket entertainer their producer had promised. Basil was, however, instantly recognisable and well known in New Zealand, as was singer-songwriter Roger Whittaker.

Peter and David arrived at the glamorous premiere screening of *Hudson and Halls* at the British Academy of Film and Television Arts (BAFTA) in September 1987, Peter with a broken leg and David hobbling with what he claimed was a pinched nerve. Peter told the crowd how he broke his right leg in the middle of filming: '"We were having a walk up in Coventry,' he said. "And I was wearing bifocals. I tried to jump over a ditch and I misjudged and fell short. I heard this snap and I thought: I've broken my bloody leg." ... They still had four of the 13 shows to tape, so the 57-year-old kept up the cooking. "They tried having me sitting down," he said. "But I knew I could just stand against the bench supporting myself with the wine glass – and swivel around."'

The BBC's press release circulated at the premiere described 'their wicked humour and idiosyncratic style', promising they would soon be 'cult figures in Britain'.[76] Reactions from the BAFTA audience to the one-and-a-half shows screened were 'largely positive'. Peter and David waited with a sense of guarded optimism for *Hudson and Halls'* inaugural appearance on the small screen four weeks later. The time slot they were allocated, 3.05pm on a Monday afternoon, was not favourable.

Then came the long anxious wait for reviews which, when they came, were vitriolic. The most far-reaching and damaging attack came from *Did You See?*, BBC2's prime-time television review show. *Hudson and Halls* was 'spotlighted' by the show's presenter, Ludovic Kennedy. The assembled panel of experts included food writer Jonathan Meades, iconic radio and television entertainer Spike Milligan, and feminist publisher and co-founder of Virago Press, Carmen Callil. Their savaging was monumental, and when they had finished there was not much left for people to like.

'It is really dismal,' Meades told the audience. 'I would have thought if the BBC wanted a couple of ageing chorus boys who can open cans of lychees they could have found them closer to home.' They 'aren't camp', he told viewers, and 'they aren't funny'. Spike Milligan described them as a 'failed Laurel and Hardy combination' that produced 'working-class cordon brown cookery' in front of an audience that looked as if it was in a hospital waiting room. 'But they were doing their best,' he added. 'I wouldn't condemn it. On a scale of one to 10, I would give it a three.'[77]

The *Did You See?* review was bitterly disappointing, and might have been bearable if it had been the only negative one, but there were more. The *Guardian's* highly regarded columnist and TV reviewer Nancy Banks-Smith described Hudson as 'thin and tense' and Halls as 'plump and chummy'. She outlined the possibilities for disaster in the kitchen: 'Fire, knives and boiling oil combined with television cameras offer heroic possibilities and seem to induce in cooks a degree of panic.' Then she described the decorum celebrity cook Fanny Craddock once showed on film when a greased duck shot off the plate. Fanny 'leapt sideways and caught the fleeing fowl with a vigour and grace which would have brought any Twickenham

David sent this card to Jan Cormack in August 1987, telling her in a message on the back that he had 'found this post card in a shop!'

crowd to its feet, cheering. Then continued without a word.' Hudson and Halls' solution to every culinary disaster was to drown their food in alcohol. 'Sherry in the unbelievable peanut soup, Calvados over the calamitous raw pork and a [liqueur] on the diminished dessert.' The tone was mocking to the end. 'They then understandably ignored the food and had a drink. "Cheers dears, I've been dying for this all day."'[78]

Anna Raeburn, writing for the *Evening Standard*, described Hudson and Halls as 'two large gents who combine being professionally demanding with a nice line in bitchy backchat'. She went on to slate their upcoming book, which was 'about to make its debut with a selection of recipes including some you've never heard of, some you never would have thought of, and some you can't believe they've got the cheek to offer again'. Raeburn picked through their press release and commented with disingenuous derision, 'When they announced their British visit and its purpose, all their friends wanted to know what they were going to say if they were asked if they were gay? "Yes." Hudson is the crusty one but Halls is the most wonderful straight

213

man. Both can switch on the charm and are the farthest thing from New Zealand lamb you can think of.'[79]

The one critic who had something vaguely positive to say was Patrick Stoddart of the *Sunday Times*, though even this review was delivered with a more than a drop of sarcasm. *Hudson and Halls* was his 'highlight of the daytime week'. He described the programme as one in which 'two cooks who are very big in New Zealand bickered over the pork glazing and let Roger Whittaker help with the sweet. I can't wait for them to show us 101 things to do with a couple of kiwi fruits.'[80]

The *Auckland Star* delighted in the derision: 'The *Guardian* gives them a hideous panning. The paper's TV critic musingly notes that New Zealand could have no great entertainers if the cooking duo could be voted entertainers of the year … The fried pair will no doubt be happy to hurry home.'[75] There was a gloating aspect to much of the New Zealand coverage. In the vicious circle of dismissal – New Zealand television rejecting Hudson and Halls, then Hudson and Halls rejecting New Zealand – there were hurt feelings. The media feasted on these tender emotions.

That Hudson and Halls had failed when they had publicly expressed such high hopes was newsworthy, and reaction to it was symptomatic of the great Kiwi clobbering machine that sought to keep all people equal. New Zealand had room on its wall of fame for just a few stars: at the pinnacle was Edmund Hillary; most of the rest were rugby players. Many were quietly delighted that Hudson and Halls had finally received the pillorying they felt they deserved. This attitude, however, paled in comparison with the savaging they would receive from a relentlessly negative British media. It no doubt swayed attitudes and influenced the prospects for the show.

These first reviews were a mortification. Never before had they received such a sustained attack. Peter and David claimed it was 'all orange sauce off a duck's back', but of course it wasn't.[81] Their humiliation was public, but perhaps even more devastating were the comments of those who, out of retribution, jealousy or sheer dislike, cheered on the wave of criticism. Their only hope was the viewer ratings. The BBC had talked of audiences of eight million, which had seemed unrealistically high for a mid-afternoon slot on a Monday, even to them. Now they wondered, did *Hudson and Halls* have the numbers to convince the BBC to keep them on the small screen?

While Peter and David waited in New Zealand for the BBC's decision on whether to review their contract, Peter made a devastating discovery that changed things overnight. His health had not been good for several years as one virus after another defeated his immune system. 'Peter has had the flu for the last two weeks, but he won't stay in bed to shake it off properly,' David wrote to Carleen and Jerry in April 1985. In April 1987 he reported, 'Peter has been down with a series of cold and flu bugs for the last three weeks and on top of that he fell off the wall outside the kitchen window and split his head open.'

Full of foreboding, Peter went to the doctor who referred him to a specialist. He didn't tell David, because he knew he would be too upset. After meeting his specialist, Peter went to Antoine's restaurant to absorb the news he had received. His old friend and colleague, restaurant owner Tony Astle, saw him sitting at a secluded table on his own. When he approached, Peter urged him to sit down. Driven by a flood of grief, he told Tony that he had prostate cancer. Peter wept for himself, for fear of the upcoming treatment, and for his prognosis if the treatment failed, but above all he wept for David. Peter knew the news would obliterate his partner's steady ground. David's confident bluster depended on Peter.

The diagnosis introduced a paralysing doubt more debilitating than either reviews or ratings. This was a question of life or death.

Double Chocolate Cake

60 grams softened butter
180 grams castor sugar
6 large eggs
120 grams plain chocolate
180 grams ground almonds

Cream butter and sugar together until light and fluffy. Separate the yolks and whites of five eggs. Beat the yolks and one whole egg together. Stir into the butter and sugar mixture. Melt the chocolate slowly in a saucepan, and stir in the ground almonds. Mix this into the egg and butter mixture. Beat the egg whites until stiff but not dry, and gently fold into the chocolate mixture. Line the bottom of a deep cake tin and grease thoroughly. Pour in the mixture. Bake in a moderate oven, 180°C, for about one hour. Check after 50 minutes, don't be horrified when you see it start to drop. Remove, and cool on a cake rack, lifting off the paper. When cold ice with the following.

DOUBLE CHOCOLATE ICING
120 grams plain chocolate
1 tablespoon rum or brandy
6 heaped tablespoons icing sugar
1 heaped tablespoon sour cream
sliced toasted almonds, optional
whipped cream, optional

Slowly melt chocolate in a saucepan, add brandy or rum. Take off heat, and beat in icing sugar and sour cream. Leave to cool. Spread over cake, and decorate with sliced toasted almonds around sides, and piped whipped cream rosettes on top. This is very rich, and only small portions need be served … unless you really love chocolate, in which case get stuck in and enjoy.

***It is the best to leave the cake for one day before you ice it as this improves the flavour. To cool the icing more quickly, pop it into the fridge for a while, but do not let it get too thick before you start spreading it over the cake.

10: London & *Beginnings, Middles and Ends*: 1988–92

David was devastated for a time; a pall of anxiety and despair hung over them both. But Peter's treatment by urologist Dr Derek Rothwell of the Gilgit Road Specialist Centre in Remuera, Auckland, raised their spirits exponentially. He underwent radical radiotherapy, and his recovery was very positive. At the end of his treatment in late 1987–88, Derek Rothwell told them Peter was clear. The cancer had been removed and his prognosis was good. It had been a sobering warning to cherish life and grasp every opportunity. Time was precious, regardless of how much they had.

The good news coincided with the arrival of a contract for a new series with the BBC in 1988. This gave them hope and restored a good chunk of ravaged dignity. *Hudson and Halls* had not reached the fabled eight million viewers, but it had entertained more than three million people, who had become a regular audience. It was enough to convince the BBC that the programme's formula had not been all wrong. Ratings rather than reviews won the day.

The BBC planned a repeat screening of their 1987 series, and contracted Hudson and Halls for a further 13 shows – the same number they had filmed the previous year minus the two shows shot in New Zealand. 'We've been asked to go back and make another series and that looks like happening about July, August or September,' David told the *Auckland Star*.[1] When challenged about their dismal reviews, David responded: 'Everyone is entitled to an opinion but it is what the public think that matters and the viewing figures speak for themselves. It is silly to be upset – anyway we are the ones who are banking the money.'[2]

The highlight of 1988 for Peter and David, apart from their extended stay in Prestbury, was the launch of their new cookbook. This one was small and cheap, with low production values – no coloured dust-jacket and no coloured photographs inside. '*Beginnings, Middles and Ends* contains 77 recipes Hudson and Halls use on their BBC television series,' wrote Donna Chisholm for the *Sunday Star*. 'The book … is a far cry from the glossy, picture-packed coffee table hardcover which marked the pair's first foray into publishing.'³ New Zealand buyers had the additional disadvantage of not having seen the meals prepared on television.

Beginnings, Middles and Ends nevertheless contained some audience-thrilling sensations and bizarre combinations. Their Avocado Soup as a 'beginner' was bookended by a Sweet Avocado Pie. The Stuffed Squid and Squid Pie were a daring dive into uncharted waters for the average British housewife or househusband. There was Cucumber with Mushroom and Shrimps, Chilled Cucumber and Mint Soup, and Duck Pâté Using Partially Cooked Duck. There were ugly favourites to cause a fuss, and old favourites reconstituted. The foreword states, 'Too often food writers create new dishes or fads, purely for the sake of creating them. We have never subscribed to that theory. We prefer to analyze and change our favourite dishes that we have cooked over the last two decades, and up-date them if required, or if they still have the old appeal … leave well alone!'⁴

While the majority of their reliable recipes in *Beginnings, Middles and Ends* were indeed left alone, the long and detailed instructions lacked Hudson and Halls' usual personality and humour. The confidence and flair that had convinced cautious cooks to try something dangerous in the kitchen was no longer there. The text was even a little defensive in places: 'People tend to regard our recipes that have booze in them as exotic figments of our imagination. This is not true. Yes, we are known to have a tipple, but we rarely put alcohol into dishes just for the sake of it. We do it because there is a purpose for that alcohol.'⁵

As the blurb on the back promised, *Beginnings, Middles and Ends* was 'a collection of their favourite recipes, original and traditional, easy and exotic, from all over the world'. But by the late 1980s cooks wanted more. In the decade that Hudson and Halls had been cooking on television, the pace of culinary change had accelerated. An explosion of long-haul travel, food fads and new-fangled equipment, the widening of processed and non-processed food options, and the availability of previously hard-to-find ingredients had changed what people felt they could do in the kitchen. Hudson and Halls' 'scary' ingredients ceased to create even a flutter.

Beginnings, Middles and Ends *(1987).*

The public had changed too. They ate vegetarian or vegan dishes from choice, and ate them en masse. The two Vs had been adopted by the mainstream and weren't the exclusive territory of weirdos any more. Eating vegetarian and vegan, and preferably organic, would in time be closely followed by the rise of the farmers' market and eating local and fresh. As David Veart points out, never before in human history had 'people been so scared of what they ate … to this general belief that your food may be gradually killing you is added the curious conundrum that the rich, for the first time in history, are thin, while the poor are fat.'[6] While Hudson and Halls' *Beginnings, Middles and Ends* was a great record of what they had shown on television, it wasn't groundbreaking and it wasn't fresh.

*

Although Peter and David were cheered by their new contract with the BBC, the flurry of criticism in the British press proved unrelenting. Nothing they did, no changes to the manner in which they worked or presented themselves, seemed to stem the vitriol. They had become the whipping boys of a mob that could find almost nothing positive to say. As with earlier reviews, there were elements of ageism, classism, homophobia and anti-colonialism.

Daily Star critic Stafford Hildred described their performance on Terry Wogan's show as 'pathetically unfunny', but this was nothing in comparison with Jaci Stephen's derisive review of the second series for the *Evening Standard*. In September 1988 she wrote: 'On BBC1, viewers saw the unwelcome return of *Hudson and Halls* … Hudson … spends more time at playing camp than a girl guide … He also looks at the wrong camera, but this is not because he is being funny. Just stupid … "Oh! My little knob fell off!" [David] squealed. Oh, do tell us another … If ever there was a case of too many cooks spoiling the broth, this is it. Two too many.'[7]

A lone voice spoke positively: in the *Sunday Telegraph*. 'It is difficult to know how long Hudson and Halls (BBC1) would survive camping out in the bush,' wrote Christopher Tookey. 'Every week these two New Zealand cooks seem to dice with death as they camp about in their kitchen … I'm not sure about their cookery, but as divas of soap operas they take a lot of beating.'[8]

There was another gauntlet of criticism to survive in 1989, when Hudson and Halls were finally tackled over Peter's particular habit of throwing ingredients, waste and unsuccessful dishes on the floor. This cavalier act of showmanship, which was not so much an 'act' as an insight into Peter's nature, was more than just tolerated in New Zealand. Men saw it as a heroic gesture of male defiance; women as something they always wanted – but couldn't bring themselves – to do. There had been detractors, but Peter's actions appealed to the rebellious streak in many an austere Kiwi. His flamboyant flipping, tossing and chucking of items was a daring gesture of freedom that most cooks could only dream of. In Britain, however, Hudson and Halls' kitchen antics dismayed audiences from the beginning. There were rumbles. They were setting a bad example. Eventually the studio was 'inundated with letters'. By 1989 they had got the message loud and uncompromisingly clear, and the clean-up began. 'Kids copy us and mums have to clear it all up,' Peter told *Truth* contritely.⁹

Critical reviews of *Hudson and Halls* were sometimes out of line with the realities of the show. The British studio audience was older, but this matched the programme's constituency of viewers at home. Their ad hoc, apparently accidental style and slapstick tossing around of food was deceptive. Banter and behaviour that seemed spontaneous and unscripted had in fact been rehearsed on camera and were the result of years of practice. This was not a chaotic impromtpu delivery by a couple of amateurish 'Kiwi fruits' from down under but, by now, a performance.

The BBC's incarnation of *Hudson and Halls*, with its retro 1930s graphic and 1980s metallic set, was more polished than it had been in New Zealand. Peter and David came on stage with all the razzmatazz of vaudeville entertainers. Their theme song played jauntily in the background; they stood in front of a black curtain and acknowledged the stage audience and welcomed viewers at home. This was pure theatre. Hudson and Halls were immaculate impresarios rather than chefs. The dress code – white shirts, black ties and black pinnies that sat high up like cummerbunds – was dazzling. Peter's posh Aussie accent appeared nattily 'proper', whereas David's Cockney, skewed by a little Kiwi overlay, immediately located him in the English class system. The dress, the campiness, the music-hall glamour were very English, while their irreverence took at least some of its cockiness and verve from the Antipodes.

The usual kitchen accidents were there: the fish that breaks up in the pan when it's flipped because it is frozen rather than fresh; and the 'Whoops, there's a fly in the studio … never mind, we're cooking with raisins, no one will notice.' Peter's acerbic wit and David's clownish pranks remained, but the BBC show was more calculated and professional. To build tension and create humour, they raced against the clock and had to manage without the repertoire of pre-prepared dishes to whisk out from under the bench. Only very occasionally did Peter, who executed much of the exacting work, stare moon-eyed and frozen with fear into the camera, and at these moments David, a master of distraction, moved the focus to himself so that Peter could manage the disaster. The liberties they took for granted in New Zealand were not taken here. The heavy alcohol consumption was replaced with sipping on a glass of wine, in moderation. Correspondingly, their new sobriety limited the nature of their exchange, so that nothing became too personal.

Hudson and Halls were seasoned performers by now: they knew the food, they knew their audiences on stage and at home, and they knew each other. Many of the famous guests they had on the show were friends and acquaintances from London. Their celebrities, well-known actors such as Barbara Windsor, Gordon Jackson and Leslie Crowther, ventriloquist Ray Alan and his puppet Lord Charles, or singers and musicians such as Lynsey de Paul, Lorna Dallas, Cheryl Baker and Faith Brown, were perfectly pitched for their audience, their repertoires ranging from rousing music-hall sing-along numbers to songs that were sentimental or uplifting.

The revolving circular stage turned from the kitchen to the guest act, who might be revealed in plumes of billowing dry ice or dazzling lighting effects, depending on the mood required. Boxer Frank Bruno and a dance troupe were notable exceptions to the usual guest list: Peter made his entrance on stage wearing boxer shorts the day Frank Bruno was on the show, and they performed a routine with the dance troupe.

They were comedians and this was food for entertainment. Primarily it was fun, but there was also a constant stream of tips and handy hints about how to do things. The show informed but never intimidated. No one who watched the programme ever felt that they shouldn't 'try this at home'. Writing for the *Evening Standard*, Victor Lewis-Smith commented: 'You don't have to be skilled in the way of *Larousse Gastronomique* to realise that Peter and David would really be more at home in a bed sit with a can of baked beans and a Baby Belling. The charm of the programme is that, for once, you really *can* make it better yourself and they don't try to hide the fact.'[10] It was rare praise.

They celebrated their mistakes and were sensational in their strange food combinations and slapstick antics, but at the end of the programme there was always a solid, simple dish with a step-by-step recipe that anyone could follow. Hudson and Halls were criticised for their simplicity, their adaptations and substitutions of exotic ingredients with items that might be found in the average kitchen cupboard. But they were not gourmet chefs performing to impress food snobs and critics. They were entertainers filling an empty Monday afternoon and people's plates with something flavoursome and cheerful.

*

CLOCKWISE FROM TOP: *Peter on the BBC set with Gordon Jackson, star of* The Professionals *and many other television dramas; British comedian Ernie Wise (of duo* Morecambe and Wise*) appeared as a guest in the BBC series; Adding the essential ingredient; David was a trained dancer but Peter was decidedly out of his element joining in with a dance troupe on the show; Kidding around on the BBC set.*

JANET PUTTNAM, PRIVATE COLLECTION

Hudson and Halls' camp format, with its time-worn tradition of popular music-hall acts which had seemed fresh and funny in New Zealand, looked tired and faux in the UK. Even an Antipodean twist wasn't enough to convince critics that they were watching something distinctive and new. The *Times* reviewer, in one of the more balanced evaluations of the show, reflected on the merits of their approach. In 'Television Choice', Peter Waymark wrote: 'Hudson and Halls are a high-camp double act from New Zealand who, while going through the motions of mixing ingredients or stirring saucepans, carry on a carefully orchestrated routine of mutual bickering. Hudson … keeps half-threatening to put his coat on and leave, Halls … tells his [partner] to shut up and get on with it. [They are] like Keith Floyd, another in the line of larger than life television cooks.'[11]

But camp was not only yesterday's meal, it was today's disease. Amid the continuing paranoia around HIV and Aids, camp humour was a bad-taste flaunting of homosexuality. This despite the fact that in April 1987, Princess Diana put herself at the vanguard of support for those with HIV and Aids when she reached out and shook the hand of a young man desperately thin and dying of Aids at Middlesex Hospital in London. Although scientists in 1983 had declared that HIV/Aids could not be contracted by casual contact, many people were still swayed by irrational fears. Princess Diana's ungloved hand challenged the public hysteria. In 1989 people were once again shocked when she shook hands with another Aids patient before kissing him on the cheek.[12]

The slights and slurs of insidious prejudice and discrimination against homosexuals could crush lives and ended careers. Among other abuses, it is hard not to see an element of homophobia in the review by Jaci Stephen, published in the *Evening Standard* in September 1989:

> *Every time a new series of Hudson and Halls (BBC1) comes to the screen, I sit and wonder about the mentality not only of those who appear to enjoy it in the studio, but of the people who allow it to be broadcast in the first place. Peter and David are two cooks whose 'act' centres around their camp response to each other's presence and dubious culinary skills. Yesterday, they were making desserts … This scintillating wit makes greater use of innuendo as the show progresses, and if the ghastly dishes they concoct don't turn your stomach, then leave it to the jokes … No sane person would want to eat anything that either man had ever held; this kind of humour gives the impression that you couldn't trust where their hands had been.*[13]

*

The bad reviews were sobering for Peter and David. Although there was some softening, and over time a feeling of familiarity, this wasn't the happy homecoming that David had envisaged. A straddled life that offered them security in New Zealand while they took on the challenges and opportunities of the UK, Europe and even the US began to look more and more appealing. A foot in both camps, however, depended on their making a living in both spheres.

For three years they waited, hoping to make progress on a contract with Television New Zealand. As time passed this looked less and less likely. Their final meeting with television executives in 1990 was as fruitless as all the others. In spite of their pleas and protestations, and the fact their programme 'rated in the top seven for British women', no offer was made.[14] They said they weren't 'down hearted', but in reality they were shocked and hurt. 'We made cooking look easy,' they told Les Wilson in March 1990. 'We prepared and cooked wacky dishes with no more than a frying pan, a bench oven, a spatula and a carving knife. We'd cart around little boxes of veges and salads and we could knock something up at the drop of a hat.'[15]

They had worked initially in primitive conditions; they had done their apprenticeship. Their dismissal now felt like a final betrayal. They always believed that their popularity with audiences in New Zealand and their viewer numbers in the UK would sway the programmers, but it was as if they had become too hot for the establishment to handle.

'We can't understand it,' Peter told Toni McRae. 'We know the public wants us because of the mail and calls we get from our weekly Radio Pacific show.'[16] But the curtain had most certainly come down for Hudson and Halls in New Zealand. The only thing to do if they were going to continue to finance their exorbitant lifestyle was to leave: to relocate themselves where there was work. Not occasional or charity work like they got in New Zealand, but proper paid work.

Peter and David's final farewell on Pacific Radio, which was filmed for television and screened on *Holmes* on 6 April 1990, is testimony to how they felt about leaving their adoptive country. In the film clip, Peter's voice chokes with emotion; his lower lip quivers as he struggles to keep back the tears: 'We're sad at leaving what we have come to regard as our home, but we have to eat … New Zealand television doesn't want us and the BBC certainly does.'[17] By the time the programme went to air, Hudson and Halls had already left New Zealand – on 5 April.

In 1990 the small screen was still in a state of flux. The slippery surface of television contracts meant jobs, opportunities and programming were precarious. Few shows gained a foothold for long, and in the ethos of director-general Julian

225

Mounter's restructuring, *Hudson and Halls* seemed outmoded. Cutting with the past had a kind of heroism to it.

In the era of state-owned enterprises, and in the long shadow of the fear of a third, privately owned overseas television channel, Television New Zealand executives – with the blessing of the Labour government – murdered the baby and looked for palatable ways of serving up the bathwater. The threat of a third television network was a scaremongering exercise: a way of justifying an ideological shift.

The overseas competition turned out to be TV3. Its late arrival in the market combined with its low audience numbers and limited transmission coverage meant that it failed to gain the necessary revenue from advertising or the cashflow needed to survive, and as a result went into receivership on 2 May 1990.[18] In 19 months' time it was back again under new ownership and would go on to become a viable competitor. In this new regime of competitive, ratings-driven commercialism, there was no room for *Hudson and Halls*.

'Commentators and politicians have decried the commercialisation of television,' writes Barry Spicer, '[arguing that] there have been significant reductions in the quantity and quality of news and current affairs and in the mix and quality of locally produced programmes which reflect New Zealand's identity and culture.'[19] With hindsight, many New Zealanders would agree with them.

*

For Peter and David, some of the gloss had already gone from the idea of moving permanently to England. After three years of commuting, they had to come to terms with some of the harsh realities of the shift. One of the key issues was scale. In New Zealand they had been exotic blooms in a tiny plot of fertile soil; in the UK they would have to rise above a forest of talent and overarching egos to reach the limelight. Among a small population there was also accountability. This could be as basic as the fact that you might bump into the person you shafted in a review or article the next day, or know someone who would. There was a transparency and naivety in New Zealand that was missing in a bigger, more class-ridden population. The intimate scale of New Zealand had worked for Hudson and Halls on their rise, and against them as they tried desperately to renew their contract.

But all the discussions around work in the UK were positive. They had secured their contract for 1990 with the BBC, and other opportunities were emerging. Their London agent, Mark Hudson, was talking big. 'He said that he wished he could be our agent as he wanted to be a millionaire,' David wrote to Carleen in October 1989.

Happy times that were full of promise. COURTESY OF THE *NEW ZEALAND LISTENER*

'Then Mark said that if we lived in Britain it would be like a licence to print money.' They had already appointed him their agent worldwide, and told him at the time that they were 'virtually putting our lives in his hands'. They were confident in their choice. 'We both have this gut feeling that he is the right person to escalate our careers for the future,' David wrote. 'He already has interest in the new book from several publishers. He is going over to New York either the end of this month or the beginning of November to see if he can finalise a contract … [and] he has ideas for a game show for me and also radio for the both of us when we return to Britain.'[20]

There was a possibility of a national television campaign for a major car company, as well as 'starring roles in two pantomimes … [one] playing the ugly sisters in Cinderella, starring Barbara Windsor, in London, and [the other] the roles of the two policemen in Aladdin, which stars Cilla Black in Southampton.'[21] David, who had played Sergeant Porterhouse in the New Zealand production of *Run for Your Wife*, had been offered the same role in the forthcoming London production.

When Peter and David did their filming for the 1989 BBC series they had 'requested a flat in London and … got [one in] Arlington House' in exclusive St James's. Once they realised there was an opportunity to buy it, 'we asked a friend of ours over there if they would advance us the total cash to buy it, utter cheek on my part,' David admitted to Carleen, '[but] they said yes.'[22] The pair certainly rented the flat at Arlington House, but whether they used what was almost certainly Anne (now Simmons) and her grocery-magnate ex-husband Albert Gubay's money to buy it is unknown, because only a few months later they purchased an apartment in Jermyn Street. Possibly the purchase at Arlington House fell through when they saw a more desirable property, or perhaps for a time they owned two expensive London addresses. Regardless, they were taking financial risks. Even moving to the UK required a degree of daring. This was nothing new: they had built a career and reputation by being impulsive, reckless even, but they were now in their middle years, and borrowing all the money for the purchase of a central London flat was a substantial stretch of their resources.

Their habit of procrastination made the risk greater. By the end of 1989 the urgency was pressing: 'We now really have to decide where our future for the next 5 years lies,' David told Carleen. 'There really is piss all future for us here [in New Zealand] and certainly not the earning capacity … if Mark comes up with something sensational in the near future we will just bugger off to London and start working our little arses off to pay the excess back [to our friends] and make some money.'[23] He and Peter would have to sell their house in Auckland to pay for the London flat. They were overcommitted. Their future depended on everything working out: their agent, the sequence of promised jobs, and their good health.

Peter and David crated up all that was transportable, valuable or precious, and sent it off to London to be there more or less when they arrived. The cats had already died, but there were the ageing Rottweilers to deal with. The couple's divided life always made pets difficult, and they had already had to find accommodation for the dogs for almost half the year. By the time they left New Zealand, the Rottweilers were in someone else's care; Peter and David would take the cats' ashes with them.

At the end of 1989 they had purchased their Jermyn Street apartment, also in St James's and in the heart of the fashion district they adored. The last of their chattels and much that they had worked for years to accumulate was sold at auction in Auckland. The advertisement on fliers and in the newspaper read: 'Webbs acting on instructions from Hudson and Halls who are moving to London will sell the contents of their Superior Residence at 58 Roberta Avenue, Glendowie including their 1962 Bentley model S3 silver and black motor car and 1986 grey Subaru Justi four wheel drive on Saturday 31st March at 11 am – also includes Charles Eames chair and stool.'[24]

It was hard and humiliating. Although the media spin was always that they were going to something better, Peter and David keenly felt what they had lost. 'Yesterday's auction held by Webbs was to clear up any leftovers' of Hudson and Halls' lives, wrote a reporter on 1 April 1990, 'but judging by the spirited bidding, two men's trash is another man's treasure'.[25]

The consolation for Peter and David was that after everything was cashed up they were, fleetingly, wealthy. Their friend Carleen recalls David saying that 'when they sold the house in New Zealand … for a brief moment they had almost a million dollars'.[26] But the crippling exchange rate, which barely returned one pound sterling for three New Zealand dollars, and the cost of transporting their remaining possessions halfway around the world meant their financial windfall was instantly diminished. The sterling value after bank fees had been paid in both countries was nowhere near equivalent. Nor was the cost of living, which at that time was a great deal higher in London than in New Zealand.

These negatives, which would hit them more as time passed, were weighed against the almost hysterical excitement they felt for their new address and for the celebrities they would be mixing with. Once their destination was determined, and they were on the way, their enthusiasm was unstoppable. David was someone who didn't often look back; Peter, who was softer and held on to significant things more sentimentally, felt bitter; but both men agreed there was no room in their new life for regrets.

Their apartment at 60 Jermyn Street was the manifestation of their dreams. The advertiser's text described it as 'a beautifully appointed three bedroom flat on the first floor of this attractive period building. The flat benefits from having many original features and has been excellently maintained by its present owners'.[27] As well as three bedrooms, one of which was very big, there was an entrance hall, two substantial reception rooms, a kitchen–breakfast room, two bathrooms and one ensuite. The staircase was manorial in scale and grandeur; the ceilings were high; and the rooms spacious and well lit.

It seemed too good to be true, and in many respects it was. Their apartment was not freehold, but rather purchased at the fag end of a very expensive lease; they had approximately 12 years left before the property automatically reverted to its owner. In reality, Peter and David were living in an exorbitant rental property paid for with almost all their New Zealand capital. The lease was ruinous, and added to it were yearly building costs and portage fees.

The flat at 60 Jermyn Street in London was the manifestation of their dreams.

JANET PUTTNAM, PRIVATE COLLECTION

But Jermyn Street was the least of their worries when they arrived at Heathrow Airport in May 1990. This should have been a straightforward arrival like all the others, but the fact that neither of them was going home at the end of shooting for the BBC changed everything. David was English, with an English passport and British citizenship; Peter was immigrating and now needed a special visa to live and work in the UK. He had been employed by the BBC before, but as a foreign national. This time, when he was routinely stopped and asked what he was planning to do in the country, he said he was working for the BBC and intending to immigrate. The immigration officer asked to see his visa. Peter, of course, failed to produce one, and the officer could do nothing else but refuse him entry.

Peter and David were in shock, blasted by the news. They had left New Zealand believing everything had been done. Their lawyer, their agent, the BBC: surely one of them should have realised what was involved and sorted out the red tape? But among busy people – none of whom were as invested in the move as Peter and David – this crucial detail was missed. The couple were furious, and stayed that way. They didn't have a good word to say about any of them. Ultimately, though, the buck stopped with them, and stop it most certainly did.

Peter was graciously given a week at their Jermyn Street flat before he had to leave the country. If he stayed and worked in the UK, he would be deported. David was flummoxed, and found it impossible to contemplate a separation from Peter. Ironically, after a lifetime of mutual threats to leave each other, David was almost immobilised with depression at the idea of starting off life in London without him. An interim plan was devised, whereby Peter would stay for a time in Amsterdam. When filming for the BBC began, he would commute by ferry from a Belgian port near Bruges to Hull in the north of England. Hull was only a brief train trip away from the BBC studio near Manchester.

CLOCKWISE FROM TOP LEFT:
Celebrating snowy weather after the shift to London in 1990. CARLEEN SPENCER, PRIVATE COLLECTION

Richard Matthews remembers 60 Jermyn Street as 'grand but sterile'. JANET PUTTNAM, PRIVATE COLLECTION

With Jan Cormack and her daughter Danielle in the London flat. JAN CORMACK, PRIVATE COLLECTION

David the Londoner. JANET PUTTNAM, PRIVATE COLLECTION

There were many long-distance phone calls as sulphur and brimstone rained down on those Peter and David believed were responsible for their visa debacle. Peter waited between Holland and Belgium; David fixed the flat as their gear began to arrive; and in the background the guilty parties in the visa saga anxiously prodded the immovable British immigration service to speedily whisk Peter's paperwork through. John Fields, a London-based Kiwi friend of Peter and David's, remembers going around to the apartment for a meal with his partner. 'David didn't cope by himself at all well when Peter was in Amsterdam ... we went round there for lunch and he could hardly get the lunch together. He was in a funny state.'[28]

Peter coped slightly better, but the separation was costly. Living apart was expensive, and their numerous weekends together added to this. When it came to filming, there was the additional ferry and train travel to factor in. But working for the BBC in Manchester helped return some sense of normality to their lives.

The first of the 1990 series of 12 programmes featured boxer Frank Bruno. 'Coming from the macho-infested Antipodes,' wrote critic Sue Heal, 'the lads had no problems adjusting to dear old Frank Bruno's less than helpful southpaw in their Poussin in Hazelnuts. But heaven help the dithering duo if they ever get a pinny on Mike Tyson.'[29] Other guests in the line-up included actors Jill Gascoine and Wendy Richard, and comedian Bernie Winters.

The *Hudson and Halls* format was much the same as it had been, except that Peter seemed to diminish with each episode. Being refused entry into the UK, the extra travel, not having a stable base – even the move itself: these were all good reasons why he looked just that little bit thinner. He appeared to have beaten the beast of celebrity cooking – putting on weight.

Reviews of the 1990 show were less of a hate fest than they had been. Sue Heal, writing for *Today*, saw the programme for exactly what it was: a piece of light entertainment. 'Now the roasting guinea fowl seems incidental as today's gastronomic super-stars romp on drunk and perform conjuring tricks with sit-com stars. Middle-aged Kiwi chefs Hudson and Halls were back this week with their white dinner suits and camper than a row of tents approach.'[30] At last Hudson and Halls were part of the British lounge-room furniture. The familiar faces, music and graphics offered a reassuring backdrop to viewers' Monday mid-afternoon lives. The duo had not made the massive impact the BBC had hoped for, but by 1990 an estimated 8 to 10 million people were watching their antics. They had staged a quiet takeover of the afternoon audience, grabbing the undecided channel-hoppers and making them stick.

In spite of *Hudson and Halls'* ratings success, some critics still held on to their original opinions. Jaci Stephen had lost none of her viciousness or her implicit slurs about camp contagion. Her October 1990 review for the *Sunday Correspondent* was as nasty as her previous ones. 'Actually "cook" is a little on the optimistic side,' her article began.

> [It] would probably be more accurate to say that [Hudson and Halls] commit genocide on their ingredients. Recorded before a studio audience where the average age is 103, the enthusiasm, the laughter can only be due to the fact that everyone is deaf. References to turkey skewers and stuffing went down particularly well this week. There was even greater hilarity when the two men ('men' is also on the optimistic side) engaged in their familiar repartee. 'There's not much slips down your throat, is there?' said David as his partner performed what can only be called an oral genuflection on his glass of wine. Peter also had trouble 'sorting out his chilies from his nuts'. 'One's hot and one's oval,' advised David. The dilemma for viewers was not what they were but where they might have been.[31]

Offensive reviews still riled, but Peter and David were used to them. Their BBC bosses had always chosen to ignore them too.

The end of filming and the arrival, finally, of Peter's visa meant that for a brief time they experienced unbridled euphoria. At last David could truly enjoy one of the pleasures of having returned to London: he was now just a tube ride away from his family. David began taking Peter home to his family in Epping, although he was never explicit about their relationship. These were special times. David and Peter always brought their own alcohol, because they drank a lot, but the centrepiece of these occasions was food. '[My husband] Alan would always carve the meat,' David's sister Janet remembers. '[Peter would say to] Alan, "Can I have those bits?" and he said, "But there's fat on them," and he would say, "But I love it. I love it." And they would compliment you on your dinner and we would sit together as a family and obviously he [David] didn't have that [after] going to New Zealand. We would sit together as a family … They would offer to wash and dry up. Really good times. They had some really good times.'[32]

The pair had also turned up to family occasions before they began living permanently in London. When Janet and Alan's daughter Mandy had her twenty-first birthday party they had arrived early to decorate the hall. After drinking heavily at the Theydon Bois pub they came in 'three sheets in the wind', recalls Janet. 'Can

Three generations: David, sister Janet, Hilda and George, and Janet's son.
JANET PUTTNAM, PRIVATE COLLECTION

Peter and David during a visit to Theydon Bois and Epping. JANET PUTTNAM, PRIVATE COLLECTION

we help out?' the duo asked.[33] They did so, in spite of their wobbly beginning, then returned in the evening for the celebrations. The dancing was inter-generational and riotous fun. Peter and David were stand-out celebrities in the tiny village hall. Mandy was in the police force, and Peter spent the evening dancing with her sergeant's wife. She was delighted. 'You could talk to Peter,' remembers Mandy. 'Sometimes Uncle David was quite aloof. I remember Peter being lovely; a really nice gentle man.'[34]

David's family was the family Peter never had. Their get-togethers filled a need in him, and in David, to be part of a wider relational network. This was something a gay life often denied people. 'Coming out' frequently ended family bonds. Fathers and mothers rejected children; sons and daughters rejected their parents; and the wider family ostracised its gay members. Gay and lesbian lives frequently began after an expulsion from home.

Peter had no family left to call on, and David kept his intact only because he was not honest. Their place in the bosom of the family was possible because they never took the rite of passage open to heterosexuals, and that was to announce their relationship. 'He loved his mother and father,' remembers John Fields, 'but [their attitude to homosexuals] was the real barrier.'[35] Mandy's generation would see things differently.

*

David and Peter were based in London; they were among the famous friends and acquaintances they had been pursuing for years. Entertainment was to be their signature here, as it had been in New Zealand, and it was lavish. David Atkinson remembers 'some very fun parties at their flat in London … They never had a lot of people. Parties for 20 people or maybe 15. They were better for lunches than dinners.'[36]

The apartment, which had been decorated by David in Peter's absence, was all about hospitality. Richard Matthews remembers it as 'grand but sterile. They'd put some of the things that they had from New Zealand in it and it didn't suit. It looked like a stage set.' He recalls attending one of their parties: 'I went to their flat, which was a grand affair and there was a boy waiter, good looking of course, working there for the evening passing drinks around. He came from Otago and I engaged myself in conversation and I remember Peter saying, "Matthews, don't talk to the staff. He's here to work."'[37]

But their circle of London friends was in some respects disappointing. 'They'd entertain people that had been on their show,' recalls John Fields. 'Gorden Kaye from

Dining on stage with Lynda Baron, better known as Nurse Gladys Emmanuel in **Open All Hours.** *In the late 1980s Baron became a personal friend.* JANET PUTTNAM, PRIVATE COLLECTION

'Allo 'Allo! … Barbara Windsor … They would go to these parties where these people were … but it wasn't always reciprocated.'[38] If entertaining was how they planned to break into the world of British stardom, Peter and David soon realised that most of the stars they believed were friends were simply acquaintances. They did delight in the company of Lynda Baron, who played Nurse Gladys Emmanuel in the BBC comedy *Open All Hours*, and actor-comedian Christopher Biggins. Danny La Rue was also a frequent guest at their flat between matinee and evening performances when he was working at the West End.

Old friends like John Fields and David Atkinson, who introduced them to their own circle of acquaintances, made for more meaningful relationships. John had been a particular friend of Peter's before leaving New Zealand for London in 1973, and was a regular visitor on his return trips. When, after a few years in London, John wavered over whether to return permanently, David threatened never to speak to

On the BBC set with Barbara Windsor, who began her career acting in Carry On *films and became a household name playing Peggy Mitchell in the BBC soap* EastEnders.
JANET PUTTNAM, PRIVATE COLLECTION

him again if he didn't stay in London. John worked in cosmetics and there were few opportunities in New Zealand for advancement. In London he met financier David Atkinson and made a successful life for himself with his partner.

Although about 15 years younger than Peter, John was never conscious of a generation gap; if anything, Peter had sometimes seemed the more wildly unpredictable, on one occasion trying to whisk John off to Fiji on the spur of the moment. Now the balance in their relationship was shifting. In the spring of 1991 Peter went to John in confidence. 'I'd just like you to come with me,' he said. He was worried that the prostate cancer had returned, and he wanted his friend's support when he visited a Harley Street doctor. 'He didn't want David to have the shock … the reality of it all.' The appointment was in the morning, and afterwards, Peter and John went for a walk in Regent's Park where Peter admired the blooming beds of daffodils, wondering whether he would ever see them again. 'And that's when

Peter relaxing with a cup of tea while visiting the Halls family in Theydon Bois and Epping, late 1980s or early 90s. JANET PUTTNAM, PRIVATE COLLECTION

we knew it was terminal,' recalls John. 'I thought, he'll beat this in the end, but he just kept doing the shows and getting thinner. He was still working but you could see … how gaunt he was becoming. But he kept going. He didn't give up. The weight loss: he got very tired but he kept it going.'[39]

Peter kept working because they desperately needed the money. The cost and disruption of not having a visa had been financially crippling from the beginning. Then there were the disappointments. The biggest one was Mark Hudson, their London agent. While he had sold them lots of big ideas, he wasn't in his office when it came to making them happen. The cookery book which they had worked on for months vanished from the agenda. The pantomimes, the games show, the promotions, the radio slot: nothing eventuated. But the biggest blow was the loss of their BBC contract at the end of 1990 – and with it their dependable income.

The decision not to renew their contract was likely made for a number of reasons. The BBC possibly felt that after four seasons the show had reached the end of its natural life. The poor reviews would also have contributed. Another factor was the behaviour of the duo themselves. David did confess to his sister Janet that perhaps they had asked too much of the BBC executives. They could be difficult, as well as financially demanding.

With the folding of the majority of their work opportunities came a growing sense of desperation. They felt they ought to network with celebrities through providing hospitality at home and paying for dinners out, but in reality they couldn't afford it. Whatever money they had paid back to friends they borrowed back again bit by bit. They were sliding deeper and deeper into debt as the days passed. Bad decisions had followed good ones, and they ended up owing Anne Simmons, who had likely funded the purchase of the Jermyn Street flat, a substantial sum of money. They kept thinking it would be just until they found their feet, but the ground beneath them was actually slipping away. Nothing was certain, least of all Peter's health.

David was devastated when he heard the cancer had returned. Like John Fields, he remained in denial, believing that Peter had beaten the cancer before and he would do it again. Peter began a course of chemotherapy, but each treatment pushed hope further into the distance.

They were not alone in their misery. Going through the same hospital system with them was Edward McLeod, a beautiful young New Zealander. Peter called him Emerald. For a while all three – David, Peter and Emerald – supported each other in the hope that there might be a cure, or even a remission, for their cancers.

When all the National Health Service cures had been exhausted for Emerald, Peter rang Carleen and Jerry in New York. Would they mind having him to stay for three months while he received specialised hospital treatments? Carleen didn't hesitate. A phone call from Emerald followed Peter's. 'It's so lovely of you, but no, I'm not coming,' Carleen remembers him saying.[40] He didn't see the point; he had Aids. His diagnosis was terminal leukemia, and he had come to terms with it.

From financial necessity, and with thoughts of a possible recovery, Peter kept taking the jobs that came along. He looked terrible and sometimes felt worse – but this did not seem to dampen the enthusiasm of scouts for the BBC who invited them onto the Saturday night variety show *Noel's House Party*. David would later tell friends their London agent advised them to accept the offer to keep up their profile.

Hudson and Halls went on the show believing it was a legitimate invitation to cook. When the cameras rolled, David attempted to be his old showman self. Peter looked frail and fractious, as if he had only just escaped the oncology ward (which was just about true). As soon as they began their demonstration, the voluminous larger-than-life-sized Mr Blobby appeared with its asinine grin, repeating the words 'Blobby, blobby, blobby', and sabotaged everything they did. Peter found it hard enough to stand there, let alone deal with the destructive antics of a leering, yellow-spotted pink clown. 'Fuck. The BBC get worse every fucking day,' he exclaimed, supposedly off camera. His expletives were bleeped out. He was ready to walk off the set.

Noel's House Party was for them a merciless act of humiliation. The show wasn't their style; they couldn't see the humour in ridicule. At home in New Zealand many viewers watched in cringing disbelief at the bad-taste send-up. Their friends, especially those who knew that Peter was terminally ill, were thunderstruck. Abby Collins, their old model-cum-makeup-artist friend, remembers the show. '[*Noel's House Party*] absolutely destroyed them because they went on as serious punters and

Their appearance on Noel's House Party *was an exercise in humiliation. Contrary to appearances, Peter and David hated every minute it.* JANET PUTTNAM, PRIVATE COLLECTION

they had to suddenly do some cooking with [Mr Blobby]. Humiliating. They hated every minute of it.'[41]

David had been making much to friends about how the BBC had promised to whisk him and Peter off in a limousine at the end of the show so they could fly to the Isle of Man to spend Christmas with Anne Simmons. In retrospect, he realised this was the least the BBC could do.

The New Year of 1992 brought no great comfort. Peter continued to deteriorate, as the doctors had told them he would. Now it was simply a matter of waiting and making the most of the time he had left. Towards the end, David became more and more protective. Not everyone was a welcome visitor at Peter's bedside. John Fields remembers one woman living in the south of France who had been quite a good friend was left on the doorstep after ringing the bell. David had looked out of the upper-storey window to see who it was. 'Do you think …?' John began. 'No,' David said before he had a chance to finish, 'I don't want her in here.'[42]

Even in the hospital, where Peter went for a time before finally coming home, David's protective reach was long. One person who made it through the barricade was Michael Williams, their old friend and lawyer, now living in Sydney. 'I spoke with Peter when he was dying in a London hospital,' remembers Michael. 'I found out through friends which hospital he was in and I wanted to talk to him before he died and I got through to him. [There] I became a bit emotional and found it difficult to talk to him and … He sensed this and … said, "All you have to say is you love me, you silly old cunt." It was the way he said it, it was quite moving.'[43]

Peter was released from hospital and sent home. Now only their closest friends shared the last intimacies of a relationship that for nearly 30 years had survived every tumult but cancer. Peter died in David's arms on Saturday 12 September 1992.

*

David was inconsolable. He went through the preparations for the funeral in a state of numbness. Held at Putney Crematorium, the funeral was difficult for everyone. 'David read the poem,' recalls John Fields, 'but there was no eulogy or anything, it was quite formal … And we were all a bit on edge … and David was in a terrible state. But the lovely poem, which Peter put together … he said that's what he wanted.'[44]

David began talking of suicide almost immediately. His friends urged him to seek help. When John asked him how he was getting on with his grief counsellor, David said, 'It's no use at all. No use. No use.' But he was very friendly with a chemist around the corner, John remembers, 'and he had discussed various combinations of things. He had all Peter's surplus drugs, and he knew what he was doing.'[45]

David was a strong character, and he became progressively more determined that his own death was the only solution. John spent hours reasoning with him. He remembers one conversation:

'"I want to end it all. I want to be with Peter."

'"Well, what about your parents?"

'"They'll cope."

'"They're old. They'll never understand … Do they know that you and Peter were lovers?"

'"No. Never, ever, never discussed it … No, no, never."'

John challenged him. How well prepared would his parents be, then, for the media-bomb that would explode and expose all there was to know about this gay celebrity suicide? Journalists would pick over the wreckage until everything was revealed.

"'No, I'm not having any publicity," David said belligerently. "I'll just push it under the carpet."

"'You're a high-profile figure, there's going to be lots of publicity.'"[46]

But David was not thinking rationally, and he was unable to see the damage his suicide would do to his elderly parents and wider family. The only thing that was keeping him alive was his promise to Peter that he would look after Emerald.

When Emerald died, David folded. Two deaths in such quick succession was too much. John Fields believes that after Emerald's death, 'he was never ever happy again'.[47]

In 1992 there was also very little work to act as a distraction. The few engagements David accepted he struggled through on his own. There were some radio interviews and the re-runs of *Hudson and Halls*, which were now received far more positively than they had been on their first showing. Victor Lewis-Smith wrote for the *Evening Standard* in September 1992:

> *My jaw fell open when first confronted with two Kiwi fruits called Hudson and Halls (BBC1). Under the guise of presenting a cookery show, this pair … crack off-colour jokes, bitch and generally continue their private lives in front of camera while simultaneously preparing perfectly good food. Yet the confused and aged daytime audience (you can almost hear the deaf aids' whistling feedback) adore them. … Tragically, Peter Hudson died earlier this month so we shall not see this odd but likeable couple again. Why is BBC1 showing its most interesting programmes during the day? Who knows – perhaps Jonathan Powell [Controller of BBC1] … has decided to conceal his genuinely golden treasures in unlikely time slots, safe from the prying eyes of reviewers. Who cares? Set your video machines and catch some gems.*[48]

Just when it ceased to matter, *Hudson and Halls* was finally getting the reviews they had craved. But this did nothing to lift David's spirits. Making the shows with Peter was what had made him care.

John Fields continued to reason with David. In the future there might be someone else, another lover, he argued. 'It's not as if you've led a blameless life,' John reminded him. "'Yes, but I couldn't do it now. It was all right when Peter was there, but I couldn't do it now. I can't. I couldn't. No interest.'"[49] Everything had gone. The sexual energy, the wandering eye that mostly just looked but occasionally ended in a brief dalliance. There was nothing of the vibrant David left.

John and his partner invited David to dinner with friends, hoping to drag him out of himself. He spent hours with David at Jermyn Street 'striding up and down the living room together … with me grabbing hold of him', comforting him and talking him through the black forest of negatives that choked his mind. They discussed the possibility of suicide, but John believed it was just a reassuring door that David would never open. Merely knowing he had a way out would be enough.

Nevertheless, he agreed to keep a set of keys to the Jermyn Street flat. While this made practical sense, it also came with some uncomfortable instructions from David. 'He said, "I want you to find me." He didn't want just the cleaner or someone breaking in … so [I] took the keys … and he said: "Now, I'll ring you when I'm going to do it … I'll say something like, look John, could you come over tomorrow and we'll get together."' When John didn't hear from David he felt the crisis had passed. 'You think,' he explains, 'I'm never going to have to do this; he's not going to do it. We're going to get him through this.'[50]

11. Denouement: 1993

The *Good Morning* show produced by the BBC at the beginning of November 1993 could have been a turning point for David. Made under the spotlights that David loved, it could perhaps have helped to unravel his nihilistic thoughts and plans. Or maybe he was doing it as an empty gesture, going through the motions in the way that some people who are moving towards suicide have two contradictory realities working in parallel: one in which life is lived with the future in mind, and the other that plans its own death. If this segment of *Good Morning* could have made a difference to the outcome, it failed. The reason is in David's face when Nick, the blandly handsome 40-something presenter, says to him in his immaculate BBC voice:

'We all miss Peter.'

'Yip,' David interjects, as Nick continues without pause.

'It must be very difficult for you, your first appearance on screen, since …'

David has been broadsided. For an instant, devastation flickers across his face.

'Err … ahh … well, yes, I suppose it is really, yes, but the … ahh.' He shifts uncomfortably at the bench, trying to secure himself. 'It doesn't really worry me particularly,' he says in a monotone. Then he finds the laugh.

'He's still up there giving me the guiding thing.' He chuckles. 'If I do it wrong you'll know he's definitely up there.'

Humour recovers the situation for him, but David's spirit is broken. It is obvious to anyone watching closely that the presenter has touched something raw. Nick pushes harder.

'You're going to have to approach your work life differently,' he continues.

'Oh sure, yeah, sure,' David responds defensively. Trying to shut him down.[1]

David's performance in this guest slot was flat without his dry, satirical straight-man, Peter. On stage the duo had always been greater than the sum of its parts. In front of this camera lens, David saw himself reflected back, diminished by the loss of his partner and reduced again by grief. Nothing in this brutal equation took his sadness away, or made him believe he had a future.

*

The plan had been loosely there since before Peter's death. Occasionally, David had surreptitiously pocketed the extra morphine tablets that were used to manage Peter's pain. They provided comfort, the reassuring thought that he had an exit route, but there was also an element of the unknown. How would he know when he had taken enough?

There had been things to do, of course. Distractions. Looking after Emerald was one of them. There were also apologies to make, the squaring of things with old friends. He knew he had a 'please forgive me' note to write to long-time Auckland friends Jan and Gavin Cormack.

On 13 June 1993 he slipped a piece of fine-textured airmail paper into his typewriter, released the carriage back, then scrolled it up until the top of the paper was visible. He punched in the date. Outside on Jermyn Street it was a hot early summer's day. Just five days before, the barometers had reached a staggering 28°C. June would end up being the hottest month for the whole year. It was fumey and stifling, and no matter how hard David tried to shut it out, there was always that buzz of belligerent London life that refused to be silenced.

'Dear Gavin and Jan …' he began. He opened the letter by recalling a meal they had had at the Auckland Club. He wanted them to remember the occasion and especially Gavin's words, that 'no one other than the couple involved know what they feel about each other'. Then he told them how he felt about his relationship: 'Peter and me loved each other through thick and thin, good times and bad [and] … I miss and grieve for him more now than when he first went … I pray each night for my darling Peter, for Edward and that I will join Peter soon.'

David asked Gavin and Jan to forgive him. 'I was a real shit when I was out there last year … I just couldn't hack it and passing 39 St Stephens Avenue where we first met and fell in love really hurt me very much.' If anyone should mention his bad behaviour, he asked the couple to explain the reason for it and beg their forgiveness,

David's birthday card to Jan Cormack, 13 June 1993. JAN CORMACK, PRIVATE COLLECTION

saying he knew people were only trying to help. His remorse and sense of isolation were palpable. 'I really now only have John Fields to talk to and of course Anne [Simmons] on the Isle of Man. All the other people have fallen by the wayside … There is no work and no prospects.' He lived, he admitted, on the memories of Peter. Even the recollections of their rows had lost their sting.

The letter was sent to celebrate Jan's birthday, and it arrived inside a large card with a dainty illustration of a rose on the front. 'For your Birthday Jan with our greatest love,' David had scrawled in largish looped writing at the top, as if he were calling to her over the London traffic. At the bottom of the card in smaller capital letters, and a quieter register, is a postscript that reads: 'THIS IS THE LAST TIME PETER WROTE HIS NAME. I THOUGHT IT BETTER THAN I WRITING ON HIS BEHALF.'[2] Beside his words is Peter's signature, neatly cut out of a piece of lined pad paper and Sellotaped in place. The card was signed by both of them – by Peter posthumously. The letter reads as a kind of farewell, both heart-wrenching and disturbing. Clearly David had not moved on. But this was less of a cry for help than a bidding farewell.

*

David began to take his end into his own hands. Although he continued to flip-flop between plans for the future and organising his own death, the periods of blackness and despair were becoming established. He needed to know how much morphine to take, so he experimented: 'Have taken one 60mg morphine tablet to see what effect,' he wrote in his diary. It was enough to knock him out for a few days. When his sister Janet inquired where he had been and why she couldn't get hold of him, he said he had been sleeping and that he had taken some of Peter's pills and they really worked. This was alarming in itself, but if Janet had read the rest of David's diary entry of 28 June, the day of his experiment, she would have been profoundly distressed. It began: 'ANOTHER TORMENTING AWAKENING … I HAVE NO ONE CLOSE TO ME NOW. I HAVE NO DESIRE TO DO ANYTHING FOR THE FUTURE. I'M IN DEEP DEBT – NO PROSPECTS. I HOPE I CAN FIND THE COURAGE TO STOP MY OWN EXISTENCE.'[3] His diary entries now were all in capital letters, instead of his usual looping style, as if he were shouting out in grief.

David's diary was his confidant, a repository for his thoughts and a sounding board. He had the means to kill himself and the knowledge of how to go about it. His final preparations were for the way he would be found after his death. He was appalled by the idea of one of his family – Janet or his mother Hilda – discovering him, and instead built his plans around one of his oldest and dearest friends, John Fields, to whom he had given the keys to his apartment.

There was a final reckoning. Perhaps it was after the *Good Morning* show, which aired three weeks before his death. There was no new approach to his 'work life' in him, which the presenter had told him he would need, and no solution to his financial problems either. In desperation David wrote, 'NOTHING IS GOING TO GET BETTER FOR ME EXCEPT THAT I GO TO MEET PETER IN THE NEXT LIFE. I DO NOT MEAN TO HURT ANYONE – BUT THERE IS NEVER "THE RIGHT TIME".'[4] His last, brief note to Carleen Spencer was also written in capital letters. Undated, it reads: 'I AM TRYING TO COPE WITH EVERYTHING BUT I'M NOT HANDLING IT TOO WELL WITHOUT PETER – I LOVE HIM, AND STILL DO, ABOVE EVERYTHING ELSE.'[5]

His final diary entry was written on 17 November 1993. 'I AM REALLY DOWN. GOD GIVE ME COURAGE.' Lower down on the page he wrote, '6.30 ME', with the number 1 in a large circle, 'AT CAPRICE', the restaurant where he and Peter had loved to eat.[6] David ate there alone, sent off his correspondence, listed instructions for John, wrote a suicide note, and rang his mum and dad to tell them he was going away to the countryside for a few days. They were not to worry if they couldn't get hold of him.

Then he called and left a message on John Fields' answer phone, asking him to come over to the flat the next day. If John had been in that night and heard the message he would, he says, have known to go around and try to deflect David's plans. When he finally listened to the message and went over, a few days later, it was with a sense of trepidation. He let himself in through the huge heavy outside door on to Jermyn Street. Then he mounted the elegant internal staircase to David's first-floor flat. As soon as he was inside he saw the note. 'This has nothing to do with you,' he remembers it began. It was David's thoughtful exoneration of John's involvement in his death. He left instructions, and a list of people close to him that John must inform. There was also a note addressed to his sister Janet and her husband Alan, a man for whom he had a great respect.

He asked Alan to beg his mother, father and family to forgive him, and to pray for him 'THAT I WILL BE TAKEN INTO GOD'S HAND SWIFTLY AND THAT HE WILL ALSO FORGIVE ME AND LET ME BE IN PEACE WITH PETER FOR ALL ETERNITY'.[7] David was still worried about money, and wanted his friend Anne to be paid what she was owed.

[I] CANNOT SEE A FUTURE WITHOUT PETER. PRAY FOR MY SOUL AND SPIRIT AND [ASK] EVERYONE ALSO [TO] PRAY THAT I BE FORGIVEN. I'M SURE GOD WILL FIND IT IN HIS HEART TO FORGIVE.

DAVID HUDSON-HALLS.[8]

David was lying on the bed as if he were asleep, peaceful and holding a photograph of Peter.

John Fields rang the police, who were quick to contact David's niece Mandy. 'I think this is for you,' her sergeant said late that night, handing her a telexed sheet that had just come through. Immediately Mandy saw the name Hudson-Halls she knew it was her Uncle David, and when she read the words 'suspected suicide' she understood at once. However, she was still disbelieving: 'No, he wouldn't have done this,' she thought. 'Surely he would have done it last year if he was going to do it.'[9] The family had all desperately hoped that his mood had improved and that he was feeling more optimistic about the future.

Combining the roles of police officer and dutiful daughter, Mandy went around to her parents' place to tell them. Having to break the news that Uncle David had died was one of the hardest things she'd ever done. Between 11 and 12 o'clock that night, Janet went to tell her own parents, Hilda and George. They hadn't heard from David for a little longer than they expected, and there had been phone calls between

Janet and her mother. Janet had also tried to ring him. No answer. She had left a couple of messages on his answer phone. In some small way, their doubt helped prepare them. Janet's distressed face was enough.

'He's gone and done it?' she recalls her mother saying.

'I'm afraid he has, Mum.'[10]

Carleen Spencer was in New Zealand when the phone call came through from her husband Jerry in New York. She was staying in New Plymouth, looking after her mother who had been ill in hospital. David had been ringing her long distance 'every single day'. Just a short time before, they had hooted hilariously, like a couple of cackling crows on a wire. She was telling him a story about a country and western theatre production in which the white replica horse outside the paint shop in town had turned up on stage. 'I was cracking up about the way it was being carted around,' she remembers, 'and I told him, and we were both laughing.'[11] '"I don't know how to tell you this, but David's killed himself,"' she remembers Jerry saying. 'I mean, it was such a shock.' But it also made sense of the odd note she had received from David, which included the words, 'KEEP YOUR PECKER UP DARLING WHATEVER THE OUTCOME. REMEMBER WE WILL *ALL* BE TOGETHER IN THE NEXT LIFE.'[12]

She was so distraught that she put her mother in a wheelchair and went up to Brooklands Park, where they sat down on a bench among the lush semi-tropical vegetation. Carleen was conflicted. David was the friend she had wanted to grow old with. He was her companion and comfort, and he had stolen these things away from her. But she knew that death was what David had wanted and had been building towards. Holding on, for him, was a living hell. She was not sure there could have been another conclusion, but wished sincerely that there had been.

As they sat there, she and her mother noticed a flock of birds in a far corner of the park. 'One of them started walking towards us,' Carleen recalls, 'walking, walking, walking, and it comes right up to me and it's sitting at my feet staring up at me and my mother said, "That bird is really trying to tell you something," and it just stood there and stared and stared and stared, then it gradually backed off and went and joined the other birds.'[13] When she returned home and looked at the envelope that contained David's last disturbing note, there was the bird of peace on the stamp. She felt as if this was an echo of the bird that had approached her in the park. As if the bird was emblematic and David was at last at peace: and this is how it made any sense to her.

*

As executor of David's will, it was Alan's responsibility to ensure that his brother-in-law's wishes were carried out. 'It just said that he wanted their ashes together in the park,' remembers Janet. So she and Alan and their youngest son went to scatter them. It was springtime in London and the daffodils were all out. They went to David's flat in Jermyn Street first. Janet recalls that she 'suddenly realised they've got to be mixed up. I decided it was a good idea to put [the ashes] in a Harrods bag, and got very dusty mixing [David and Peter] up with the cats as well.'[14] They walked through Green Park, getting closer to the assigned place near Horse Guards Parade. The sun was low and it was early in the morning, but on a spring day in London there are always more people about than you expect, enjoying the crisp fresh air.

There were no signs in the park that said 'Please don't sprinkle ashes on the grass', but just being there made them realise this was probably prohibited. With David, Peter and the two Burmese cats, they had quite a pile. What's worse, the ash was very white. Making a hole in the bag and walking around releasing it in a stream could not be done casually. Instead Janet set herself down and recalls 'chucking' the ashes between the flowers. 'I was desperate to get rid of those ashes, bless 'em. I just mixed them around with the daffodils. They will probably come up twice the size,' she says, with an amused expression reminiscent of her brother's. 'I bet David was looking down, saying, "Silly buggers, they've gone and done it."'[15]

Janet and her family have never been back, though each spring they remember the daffodils at Horse Guards Parade and think of David and Peter, inseparable, together forever.

In the spring of 1994, David's sister Janet, her husband Alan and their youngest son spread the combined ashes of Peter, David and their two Burmese cats, disposing of the white ash discreetly between the stands of spring daffodils in London's Green Park.

JANET PUTTNAM, PRIVATE COLLECTION

Christmas Pudding

(FR JOHN & STUART)

Add and mix together:

4 oz currants
4 oz raisins
4 oz sultanas
4 oz figs
4 oz prunes
4 oz apricots
4 oz dates
8 oz Muscovy sugar
grated peel of ½ lemon
grated peel of ½ orange plus all the
    juice
1 large cooking apple, cored and
    chopped
4 oz shredded carrot

Soak overnight in ½–¾ pint of fine
rum. The following day, add the
following dried and mixed ingredients
to the soaked fruit.

8 oz self-raising flour
4 oz suet
1 level teaspoon mixed spices
½ level teaspoon ground cinnamon
½ level teaspoon grated nutmeg
2 oz ground almonds
2 oz candied peel
2 large eggs

Stir well together. Divide the mixture
into two 2-pint basins and cover with
greased paper and foil. Steam for 8
hours. Allow to cool, then re-cover
with greased paper and foil.

The puddings are best made
in August and left to stand until
Christmas or New Year. Steam for a
further 3 hours before serving.

12. Postscript: 2001–17

What makes you pick up a story and write about it? There are probably many reasons: fascination, dedication, evangelism, ego, ambition … maybe it's simply that compelling feeling that this is the next chapter in the book of stories you have to tell. Peter and David's story wasn't absolutely any of these for me. I remember seeing the documentary *Hudson & Halls: A love story* when it first aired on television in May 2001. I came into the lounge, slumped into my favourite easy chair and began watching when the programme was about two-thirds of the way through. Having missed so much, I wondered whether it was worthwhile sitting there. But I became engrossed. As the narrative narrowed its focus on David's suicide, I found myself crying. First, sly tears, the ones that slip quietly down from the outer corner of your eye, then the full-blown tale-telling handkerchief.

My emotion wasn't all about David, or his grief over the loss of Peter. The documentary was a catalyst for something personal. Like all great stories, theirs rose above the detail and spoke to me of my own same-sex union. Ours is a relationship that has survived in spite of a lack of social endorsement; has weathered intense condescension; and had been embattled for most of its 27 years by the fact that we were not fully franchised citizens of our own country. The losses are like bodies piled up in every corner of our lives: job prospects, financial security, family, friends and, most poignantly for me, a child. I knew how intense same-sex love was, and how exclusive and isolating it could become.

I remember thinking the production company was brave to call Peter Hudson and David Halls' relationship 'a love story'. Even in 2001 this would have jarred with many people. No one I knew would have called my relationship with Sue 'a love story'. Perhaps this was the trigger. The realisation that homophobia, including my own, had never given us permission to call the relationship what it was.

If the emotion – let's call it in this instance *self-pity* – dried up with my tears, then the details of Peter Hudson and David Halls' story did not. If anything, they grew in fascination, connecting to experiences of seeing the duo on television when I was a teen. Of watching their kitchen antics, and of Mum's cooking habits changing. Not that she ever wrote the recipes down, but suddenly there was a bottle exiled from the rest in the grog cabinet and labelled 'cooking sherry', and apricots began appearing with the roast chicken.

The more I talked about Hudson and Halls to people, the more they shared their memories. So I began to think I had a story *for me*. I wanted to know more.

My start was getting in touch with Greenstone Pictures and documentary producer Juliet Monaghan. I read in an online article about the diary in which David recorded events in his last year of life. The diary was a 'breakthrough in helping understand the man,' Juliet Monaghan told the interviewer for the *New Zealand Herald* in May 2001. It had captured some of David's work frustrations and his longing to be with Peter. She had a sense that the diary was not just personal, but a conscious act of communication. She reiterated this to me when I emailed her in May 2013, responding: 'I think David wrote [it] knowing [it] would be found and read by many.' The diary had been returned to the family after the documentary screened, she explained.

A gap of 12 years meant Greenstone Pictures could not locate its Hudson and Halls archive for me, and this was complicated by the fact that it had just been taken over by another company. Equally, Television New Zealand had got rid of all but a few of their *Hudson and Halls* programmes. In spite of the frustration, I needed to know more. I wanted to find David's diary and talk to his family.

In December–January 2014 Sue and I flew to London to research the pair. There was no book contract. This was purely speculative: a fishing trip. We stayed in basic student accommodation at the London School of Economics. A beautiful irony, I thought, as I navigated the narrow corridor to use the communal toilet. Nothing Sue and I had done was economic. Every spare cent we had was blown on my crazy expeditions in search of information.

In a claustrophobic viewing room at the British Film Institute, we watched the full collection of the BBC *Hudson and Halls* programmes. Next we went to the Reuben Library on the busy Thames Embankment and photocopied newspaper reviews of the shows.

It was Sue who tracked down the address of David's sister Janet, in Epping. Fresh faced and attractive like her brother, Janet proved to be a good-natured interviewee. In the two days we sat around her kitchen table, she generously shared her information and experiences. The subject of David's homosexuality was an uneasy one. His sexual orientation had been a challenge for his parents and wider family, and his suicide compounded things. She explained to me that David's letters, papers and final diary had been destroyed.

More frustration; another disappearing of the Hudson and Halls story. I knew that the diary, particularly, was an important document.

But David wasn't my brother, or part of my family, and I could see that the hurt went deep. There is something in the critic Janet Malcolm's assertion that a key territory of the biographer (or storyteller) is 'busybodyism'. I felt that discomfort and unease, and wondered by what framework I should judge this family's purging of the record. By the family's or the biographer's: by theirs or mine?

Longstanding family frictions and difficulties made it problematic to talk directly to Janet's siblings. Tensions and tenderness were still there, and very regrettably my investigations provoked more family strife.

*

The beginning of 2014 proved to be a tough time for me. In March I was among the nearly 50 staff in the Design Department at Auckland's Unitec who were restructured out of a job. After 14 years at Unitec and nearly 20 working in the tertiary sector, this was a colossal blow.

So was the initial reaction to my proposal for a book on Hudson and Halls. Even after the success of my previous book, a *New York Times* bestseller twice over, my editor at HarperCollins got back to me with the response that, 'given our margins and priorities' they just 'couldn't make it work'.[1] I confess: I was profoundly depressed. After more attempts to find funding and raise interest in the project, I packed up my notes, digital scans and voice recordings and shut them away. I considered destroying or even ritually burning them on a bonfire, but the hoarder in me won.

It was more than a year later, by which time I was teaching in the English Department at Avondale College, when my friends Mark Hangartner and Alan Masters insisted Sue and I go to the stage show *Hudson & Halls Live*. My hope was reignited. Auckland's Silo Theatre was packed. The audience, many of whom remembered David and Peter vividly, and many who didn't, *loved it*. Full houses, an extended season and a national tour: I felt certain there must be an audience for a book. With faltering faith in New Zealand publishers, I asked my agent Meg Davis to have another shot, and the answer came back immediately. Rachel Scott at Otago University Press would give me a contract.

Mark Hangartner introduced me to Jan Cormack. She and her ex-husband Gavin had been two of Peter and David's closest friends. Jan helped unravel their social world. She put me in touch with Michael Williams SC, Ross Palmer and John Fields. When she came to our home to talk about the couple, she shared memories, photographs and David's final farewell card and letter. 'I was so angry at David for doing what he did,' she told me, '[but] they worked together, they lived together, they did everything together.'[2]

Through 2016 I discovered and interviewed more people with connections to Peter and David, such as our own friend Abby and her ex-husband Geoffrey Collins. Through an exhibition at Webb's auction house I met Murdoch McLennan and later his ex-partner Richard Matthews, and I listened to their hilarious and heart-rending accounts. A breakthrough came from talking to the writer-director of *Hudson & Halls Live*, Kip Chapman, and his co-writer and real-life partner who played Peter, Todd Emerson. They recommended I contact a close associate of Hudson and Halls, Carleen Spencer, who lived in New York. I emailed Carleen and she agreed to speak to me. We Skyped, and ended our conversation with the understanding that we would meet in New York in January 2017.

Our London-based Kiwi friends Jocelyn Cuming and Celia Thompson had offered us their flat in Charleston Street, off Walworth Road in Elephant and Castle; and the local Anglican priest, Father John Walker, and his partner Stuart Bednall had invited us for Christmas dinner. This was too good an opportunity to miss. The plan was a trip to London, returning via New York to interview Carleen.

Then the most unexpected thing happened. For a second time this project moved me to tears, but not ones of self-pity. All year I had applied for funding assistance – a residency, time off to write … anything. My email inbox and office floor were littered with refusals. Rejection became a default and after a while the expectation. Sue urged me to apply to the Carey Institute in the US. I left it until the last minute. 'This fellowship is perfect and if you don't apply I'll never look for anything for you again.' Her threat steeled my resolve. I applied, and some months later, out of the blue, came an invitation to submit a full application, then to send more of my writing to assist them in making a decision. Finally, just two and a half weeks before we left for London, I was offered a Logan Fellowship to begin writing about Hudson and Halls at the Carey Institute for Global Good in Upstate New York. I had to urgently beg my boss, principal Brent Lewis, for time off work and change my airline ticket home. Sue and I left New Zealand for London on 14 December 2016.

*

Christmas dinner in London with Fr John and Stuart at the vicarage at St John's Church, Larcom Street, was like stepping into an Anthony Trollope novel. The church itself was completed in 1860, and directly across the lane from it was the equally old three-storey vicarage. The bottom level, lower than London's water table and partly underground, once contained the vicarage kitchen and live-in quarters for staff. Food to be served in the dining room on the floor above was transported up by an elaborate pulley system known as a dumb-waiter.

Almost opposite the tiny graveyard of mossy memorial stones was the vicarage gate with its heavy wrought-iron lock. Through the gateway and across a short path were the high concrete steps that led to the front door. At the top of the steps Fr John and Stuart loomed large in the entranceway to greet us with kisses and a glass each of French champagne. Their high-ceilinged front room was dressed for Christmas, with a tree, branches of holly, strings of lights, and presents wrapped and stacked. Our flutes were re-filled with foaming bubbles until everything shimmered with warmth and abundance. The dining room was a blaze of silver and crystal caught in soft flickering candlelight.

Seven courses was a tough line-up. Christmas turkey with stuffing, new potatoes, the first of the season's broad beans, and gravy to die for. But the brightest star of the Christmas table was the pudding, consumed by a burning blue flame of rum. Stuart had cooked it months earlier and it had hung in a cloth until the fruit had taken on a waxy black sheen. Its flavour was ancient – created before cookbooks and possibly even Christmas celebrations began. 'My grandmother was in service,' Fr John explained as he served slices onto our plates. 'Her recipes were written for enormous quantities.'

The experience of ritual and hierarchies, and of festive food and love, are the things that link lives across time and geographical distance. This was the background David Halls was escaping as a young man when he sailed to the Antipodes and met Peter, and it was the one to which they both returned before they died.

Later, we visited Essex. First to Epping to see the co-op where David sold shoes when he was straight out of school (it is now a Marks & Spencer's). Then to the fields around Theydon Bois where he picked spuds for sixpence a bag. Our aim was to see Theydon Hall and its lodge, where the Halls family lived for four formative years.

CLOCKWISE FROM TOP LEFT:
The author outside the gates of Theydon Hall, Theydon Bois, 2017; Theydon Lodge, where Hilda and George Halls lived with their young family, still stands in the grounds of Theydon Hall; Theydon Hall lies at the end of a long drive.

AUTHOR'S PRIVATE COLLECTION

In January, and on foot, it was a cold muddy trudge along the grassy shoulder of Abridge Road. Just over a mile out of town, the gates of the hall were revealed rather suddenly around a bend. The dramatic effect of the black and gold painted ironwork with its elaborate crests was jarring in this gently rolling rural landscape. We craned our necks to see the magnificent pale-yellow Georgian mansion set in its splendid grounds. The owners wouldn't let us in the gate and there was no one at home in the lodge, so we took away some photographs. We were voyeurs who, like David, had stolen a glimpse of an unobtainable life.

Before leaving, I grated the soles of my shoes across the concrete lip of the road to remove the thick sods of mud that had collected on them as I rubbernecked. We picked our way more cautiously back along Abridge Road towards the village, carefully leaping across dank puddles and slushes of dead leaves. On a rise about halfway to the train station is Theydon Bois graveyard, where Hilda and George Halls are at rest. Stopping in front of the sign at the gate, I remembered Janet saying to me, 'I often go up there and talk to them.' Sometimes she took her young grandson, Jack, and they would chat with Hilda and George. It was important for her to know her parents were close by. George would be pleased with the spot. 'It's a beautiful place,' she had told me, 'in the countryside surrounded by paddocks and horses' and vistas of the farmland where he had worked.[3]

*

We visited the British Library, which held copies of Peter and David's three cookbooks. And before we left for Heathrow Airport I posted a parcel of books I had been reading, on the history of television, back to New Zealand. Our plane to New York left so early in the morning that we stayed overnight in the terminal, dozing occasionally, but for the most part draped drowsily between café stool and upturned suitcase, waiting until we could check in.

Jane Croessmann, a buddy of mine from school days in the US in the late 1970s, met us at the airport and took us by taxi to her friend Martin's flat in Tudor City on 41st Street where we stayed for the week. We spent the first day sightseeing, then on Monday took the underground train to Harlem. I went to meet Carleen Spencer while Sue and Jane continued their exploration of New York, visiting the Hungarian Pastry Shop on 111th and Amsterdam and the Cathedral of St John the Divine.

Carleen's apartment was on the fourth floor of a redbrick building overlooking the Hudson River. I buzzed the intercom and the mechanical door clicked open to let me in. The lift looked difficult to operate so I took the stairs two at a time. Always a sense of anxiety precedes my meeting someone for the first time, especially when there is an interview involved. But I needn't have worried. As soon as I met Carleen I could see why David and Peter had been so captivated. She was gregariously welcoming, and still attractive, with her silver hair pulled stylishly back to reveal her fine bone structure. She was then in her late seventies.

She met me at the door holding Baxter, a roguish white terrier that could have come straight off a whisky bottle label. Her apartment was a white gallery space with splashes of colourful art, beautiful objects, books and music programmes. But the cream couches were comfortable, and the room felt lived in. Baxter lay along the back of one of the pale sofas in the late-morning sun and breathed heavily, sighing and snoring so there was no chance we would forget he was there. Carleen explained that her son Chris had found him shivering on the side of the road in a winter storm in Arkansas. Out there much longer and he would have died. They couldn't find the owner, so Baxter became Carleen's.

'You should talk to Chris,' she told me. 'He's got a great story about the boys. I'll ring him up. He lives close by and if he's home he might come over.'

Her son Chris's arrival at the door transformed Baxter. He leapt off the couch like an Olympic gymnast in a frenzy of excitement. Once he could be convinced to settle down, I began my voice recording. Even as I captured Chris and Carleen's words, I knew they were significant. We parted outside the apartment block, everyone in their winter coats except Baxter, who had refused to wear his. They went for a walk and I met Sue and Jane at McDonald's, our designated rendezvous point.

Carleen loaned me her archive of letters and photographs, and Sue and I scanned and returned them. We flew out on 21 January 2017, the day of the Women's March. It felt momentous as we walked along trailing our suitcases because no taxi could make it through the throng of people. I saw Sue back to Los Angeles and onto the plane home to New Zealand. I flew to Chicago and stayed with my friend Jane and her partner Mary Jo for a week before travelling to the tiny town of Rensselaerville in Upstate New York to begin my fellowship.

*

The snow was already thick on the ground when I arrived, and in the weeks since much more has fallen. The view from my window is across a carpet of whiteness punctuated by the dark twisted trunks of trees. Nothing survives here without the freezing cold or driving winds leaving their mark. The sun shines more often now it's

Carleen Spencer and her dog Baxter, New York, 2017. AUTHOR'S PRIVATE COLLECTION

almost spring and I have developed a reputation for writing while I walk the forest-fringed dirt roads around the lake.

Without this white winter space to write I would never have been able to tackle this project. Some days I organise material, read letters and newspaper clippings, look at photographs; and every day I speak to Sue about how things are going. There are still gaps in this story to be filled. A trip to Melbourne, yet, to investigate Peter's mysterious childhood, and more people to talk to in New Zealand. But the book has been born here in this wild and magnificent place where you can still hear the coyotes howl after a kill at dusk.

I was sitting at my desk with earphones on when I finally had a chance to listen to my New York voice recordings. The first voice was Carleen's, a flat New Zealand tone overlaid by a New York accent. She made me think about love and how it affects people differently. She had always wondered, she explained, how different things might have been if 'David … had died instead of Peter. Because I can remember [Peter] saying to me … "If the cooking show doesn't go well on BBC, I'm going to open the best fish and chip restaurant in London" ... so maybe [Peter] was a bit stronger in that way.'[4]

How we handle setbacks and sadness often determines how we end our stories, and it is with Chris's words that I want to end this story.

'Any review of [Peter and David] is going to deal with a lot of outrageousness and flamboyance, but it takes a great deal of courage in this day and age to be who you are and live that way, forget New Zealand in the ... 60s and the 70s ... When people talk about them they don't talk about courage ... The two things that stand out for me are *courage* ... and *love*. That was a real love story. Above and beyond anything else, despite all the fighting and the drinking ... they loved each other so much that when [one] died, the second [one] killed himself – *for love*.'[5]

Rensselaerville,
22 March 2017

Acknowledgements

Writing biography is a journey, or rather a series of journeys. There are plane flights, bus rides, car trips, phone calls, letters and emails that travel across land, sea and time zones, through wires and along waves of electrical impulse, moving a writer physically and digitally, communicating ideas and information, so that in the end there are words. A book is a matrix of all the memories it contains and the movements that made it. Robert Louis Stevenson once said, 'I travel not to go anywhere but to go. I travel for travel's sake. The great affair is to move.' For me, the great affair is not just travel but the people encountered along the way. These often unexpected meetings are enthralling. Some people stay with me on my journey, while others pass by like shimmering headlights across a watery windscreen.

I am indebted to Peter Hudson's and David Halls' families, friends and television fans. To people I have met and interviewed along the way who have shared their memories and memorabilia with me. I would like to thank for their insights and unstinting support: Carleen Spencer, Chris Spencer, Jan Cormack, Janet Puttnam, Mandy Puttnam, Michael Williams, John Fields, David Atkinson, Stephanie Hall, Murdoch McLennan, Richard Matthews, John Mains, Ross Palmer, Abby Collins, Geoffrey Collins, Lindsay Waugh, Roy Good, David Hartnell, Tony Astle, Karen Kay, Kip Chapman, Todd Emerson, Lois Neunz, Robyn Agnew, Kerry Stevens, Michelle Osborne and Sheila Mickleson.

My research has been assisted by the excellent scholarship of several academics and writers and I am immensely grateful to David Veart, Chris Brickell, Peter Wells, David Herkt, Robert Boyd-Bell and Rosabel Tan. I would also like to sincerely thank the archivists whose research assistance was crucial to this project, especially Geoff

Laurenson the archivist at Geelong Grammar (who was both gracious and helpful), as well as Graham Frankel, Steve Tollervey, Darren Sharp, Susan Todd Eady and Barbara Mackay.

I am profoundly indebted to Pamela Stirling and Lauren Buckeridge of the *New Zealand Listener* for their generous assistance with photographs. These images are a rare visual record and make a wonderful contribution to the book.

Many friends and special people have helped the project along the way. I would like to offer my heartfelt thanks especially to Mark Hangartner and Alan Masters (whose encouragement prompted me to keep believing in this book), Linda Tyler, Fr John Walker, Stuart Bednall, Jocelyn Cuming, Celia Thompson, Diane Refaie, Jane Croessmann, Mary Jo Arthur, Martin Murray, Tanya Aspel, Jan Browne, Harriet Allan, Kate Stone, Clare de Lore, Libby Sheehy, Rebecca Johns and Judi Tiller.

The great wonder of all the travels embedded in this book was my stay on a Logan Fellowship at the Carey Institute for Global Good in Upstate New York. Magical as well as motivating and inspirational, it was a rare opportunity to immerse myself uninterrupted in the writer's life. I am eternally grateful to Jon Logan for his generosity in making this opportunity possible, and to the staff at the Carey Institute, especially Tom Jennings, Carol Ash, Josh Friedman, Gareth Crawford, Sue Shufelt and John Murray, who worked tirelessly to make this such a profound experience for all the fellows. I am indebted to Mark Kramer for his extraordinary masterclass in long-form non-fiction that changed my words forever; to all the fellows at Carey, especially Rasha Elass, Katherine Reynolds Lewis, Kenneth Rosen, Michael Scott Moore, Simon Akam, Taran Khan and Raphael Minder (who lived with me in Ford) for their friendship and long walks; to Anastasia Taylor-Lind and MT Connolly for fantastic times in London and Washington; and to Patti Gurekian for braving the wild winter weather to visit me in Rensselaerville. I also value immensely my wonderful encounters with Molly O'Neill, food critic for the *New York Times*, and Suzannah Lessard, writer and journalist for the *New Yorker*, while I was living in Rensselaerville.

My time at the Carey Institute was possible only because of the support of the principal, Brent Lewis, and the board of Avondale College where I work. I would also like to thank my head of department Sharon Cope, and friends Rebecca Hayward, Claire Houliston, Rachel Lamont and Tanya Wood for Friday coffees and their endless good humour.

My warmest thanks to Rachel Scott for her vision in taking this project on, and also to editor Jane Parkin and all the team at OUP – thank you for your sure and steady support, and for your criticism, encouragement and inspiration. (See below for a photo of the wonderful OUP team.)

My very special thanks go to Meg Davis, my agent, who has been a guiding light over many years. Without the love and support of my family, this book would never have been written. Thank you for your patient acceptance of the sacrifices required. I would like to thank especially my mother, Pat Drayton, my brother Guy, and my partner Sue Marshall and our children.

For their Christmas party in 2017, the Otago University Press team got into the spirit for working on this book by catching the stage show **Hudson & Halls Live!** *at the Fortune Theatre in Dunedin. Flanked here by actors Chris Parker (left) and Kip Chapman are Glenis Thomas, Rachel Scott, Victor Billot, Imogen Coxhead and Fiona Moffat.*

Notes

1. PROLOGUE

1. Janet Puttnam interviews, Epping, 1 and 4 January 2014.
2. *Hudson & Halls: A love story*, Greenstone Pictures, 2001.
3. Ibid.
4. Ibid.
5. Jan Cormack interview, Auckland, 21 March 2016.
6. *Hudson & Halls: A love story*.
7. Jan Cormack interview.
8. Letter from David Halls to Jerry Podell and Carleen Spencer, c. 16 September 1992.
9. Carleen Spencer interviews, New York, 21 July 2016 and 16 January 2017.
10. Richard Matthews interview, Auckland, 17 September 2016.
11. Abby Collins interview, Auckland, 27 November 2016.
12. Geoffrey Collins interview, Chang Mai, Thailand, 12 December 2016.
13. Abby Collins interview.
14. Janet Puttnam interviews.
15. Letter from David Halls to Jan and Gavin Cormack, 13 June 1993.
16. Carleen Spencer interviews.
17. Geoffrey Collins interview.
18. Carleen Spencer interviews.

2. DAVID'S YOUTH: 1936–59

1. Janet Puttnam, family papers, Epping.
2. http://militaryhistorynow.com/2015/02/06/buzz-kill-15-amazing-facts-about-the-v-1-flying-bomb/
3. www.andersonshelters.org.uk
4. Janet Puttnam interviews, Epping, 1 and 4 January 2014.
5. http://militaryhistorynow.com/2015/02/06/buzz-kill-15-amazing-facts-about-the-v-1-flying-bomb/
6. www.bbc.co.uk/history/ww2peopleswar/stories/88/a1971588.shtml
7. www.bbc.co.uk/history/ww2peopleswar/stories/04/a3501604.shtml
8. Janet Puttnam, family papers.
9. Alison Light, *Mrs Woolf & the Servants* (London: Penguin, 2007), xv.
10. Ibid., 61.
11. www.churchill-society-london.org.uk/YrVictry.html
12. www.british-history.ac.uk/vch/essex/vol4/pp251–255
13. Light, *Mrs Woolf & the Servants*, 33.
14. Ibid., 106.
15. www.columbia.edu/~em36/MrBennettAndMrsBrown.pdf
16. Light, *Mrs Woolf & the Servants*, 82.
17. Ibid., 2.

18. Janet Puttnam interviews.
19. Ibid.
20. Ibid.
21. Ibid.
22. Steven Pewsey, *Epping and Ongar: A pictorial history* (Chichester: Phillimore & Co., 1997), xii.
23. Quoted in ibid., xcix.
24. Ibid.
25. Janet Puttnam interviews.
26. Ibid.
27. Ibid.
28. Les Wilson, *Sunday,* 18 November 1990, 6.
29. Janet Puttnam interviews.
30. John Timpson, *High Street Heroes: The story of British retail in 50 people* (London: Icon Books, 2015): https://books.google.co.nz/ books?id=raB8CAAAQBAJ&p-g=PT92&lpg =PT92&dq= John+Timp-son,+High+Street+Heroes
31. www.stratfordeast.com/about-us/the-theatre/
32. Janet Puttnam interviews.
33. Ibid.
34. 'The Kennedy interview: They're NZ's wackiest cooks – on and off TV!', 18 December 1976.
35. Ibid.
36. *Sunday,* 18 March 1990, 16.
37. Lois Neunz interview, Orewa, 11 June 2017.

3. PETER'S YOUTH & A VISIT TO NEW ZEALAND: 1931–62

1. *Argus*, 24 April 1926, 25.
2. Ibid.
3. *Weekly Times*, 1 May 1926, 6.
4. *Recorder*, 24 April 1926, 1.
5. *Argus*, 24 April 1926, 25.
6. Ibid.
7. *News*, 25 May 1926, 1.
8. *News*, 26 May 1926, 1.
9. *Daily Telegraph*, 20 April 1926, 4.
10. Quoted in Appendix A – History of Abortion Law Policy: Victorian law reform: www.lawreform.vic.gov.au/content/appendix-history-abortion-law-policy
11. Appendix A – History of Abortion Law Policy.
12. *Weekly Times*, 1 May 1926, 6.
13. Ibid.
14. *News*, 27 May 1926, 1; *Daily News*, 25 May 1926, 1.
15. *Sun*, 25 May 1926, 9.
16. *News*, 25 May 1926, 1.
17. *Weekly Times*, 1 May 1926, 6.
18. *Telegraph*, 24 April 1926, 2.
19. *Weekly Times*, 1 May 1926, 6.
20. Ibid.
21. *Weekly Times*, 29 May 1926, 7.
22. *Weekly Times*, 1 May 1926, 6.
23. *Weekly Times*, 29 May 1926, 7.
24. *News*, 26 May 1926, 1.
25. *Weekly Times*, 29 May 1926, 7.
26. *News*, 27 May 1926, 1.
27. Ibid.
28. *News*, 26 May 1926, 1.
29. *Argus*, 27 November 1920, 22.
30. *Argus*, 24 April 1926, 25.
31. *Sydney Morning Herald*, 26 January 1932, 7.
32. *Truth*, 20 February 1915, 5.
33. Email from Geoff Laurenson to author, 12 July 2017. Mary Ethel placed advertisements in newspapers offering babies for adoption before and after these dates. It is likely that she also advertised under other aliases, giving her Fitzroy, Northcote or Toorak addresses.
34. *Hudson & Halls: A love story*, Greenstone Pictures, 2001. There remains some doubt around the year that Peter Hudson was born. 1931 has been given as year of his birth, however, his death certificate (the only record publicly available), gives his birth date as 8 November 1930. But this was information supplied by David Halls at a time of considerable distress. Unfortunately, neither of these years can

be verified because Births, Deaths and Marriages Victoria has a 50-year embargo on its records after a person's death. The circumstances of Peter's birth, and ambiguity of his parentage, only add to the enigma.

35. Ibid.
36. Ibid.
37. Ibid.
38. *Argus*, 16 November 1940, 17.
39. Email from Geoff Laurenson to author.
40. *Christchurch Star*, 14 September 1976.
41. Ross Palmer interview, Auckland, 5 June 2016.
42. Abby Collins interview, Auckland, 27 November 2016.
43. Geoffrey Collins interview, 12 December 2016.
44. Les Wilson, *Sunday*, 18 March 1990, 16. Mary Ethel Hudson's mother's maiden name was Macley, her full name being Amelia Frances Macley. The spelling of Macley and Macleay is similar.
45. Toni McRae, 'Hilda's pie is missing', [no source information], Auckland Central Library Archive.
46. Heather Chapman and Judith Stillman, *Melbourne: Then and now* (London: Pavilion, 2016), 38.
47. Les Wilson, *Sunday*, 18 March 1990, 15–18.
48. *Hudson & Halls: A love story*.
49. Chris Brickell, *Mates & Lovers: A history of gay New Zealand* (Auckland: Godwit, 2008), 234.
50. Graham Willett and John Arnold (eds), 'Queen city of the south: Gay and lesbian Melbourne', *The La Trobe Journal*, no. 87, May 2011, 21.
51. Ibid.
52. Ibid., 23.
53. Ibid., 26.
54. William J. Mann, *Behind the Screen: How gays and lesbians shaped Hollywood: 1910–1969* (New York: Penguin, 2001), xiii–xiv.
55. 'The Kennedy interview: They're NZ's wackiest cooks – on and off TV!', 8 December 1976.
56. Brickell, *Mates & Lovers*, 73.
57. In 1895, German medical practitioner Richard von Krafft Ebbing published his globally influential treatise *Psychopathia Sexualis*. Just as religion was beginning to lose some of its powers of social control, the debate shifted to the new paradigm of pathology. Homosexuality was not just a sickness of the soul but also of the mind. Added to Krafft Ebbing's ideas were the writings of Sigmund Freud and Havelock Ellis who offered theories of transition around same-sex orientation. Both Freud and Ellis saw homoerotic crushes and passions as a necessary phase in the youthful development of a fully formed heterosexual. Most young people, they argued, went through these stages and came out of them.
58. Brickell, *Mates & Lovers*, 147.
59. Quoted in ibid., 176.
60. Ibid., 221–22.
61. Joanne Drayton, *The Search for Anne Perry* (Auckland: HarperCollins, 2012).
62. *Hudson & Halls: A love story*.
63. Ibid.

4. SHOES, SHIPS & STONEWALL: 1962–70

1. Michael Williams interview, Sydney, 11 March 2017.
2. Murdoch McLennan interview, Auckland, 6 September 2016.
3. Ibid.
4. Richard Matthews, *To Whom It May Concern: A romp through the life and times of Richard Matthews* (Auckland: Richard Matthews, 2009), 169.
5. Michael Williams interview, Sydney, 11 March 2017.
6. Murdoch McLennan interview.
7. Michael Williams interview.
8. Ibid.

9. Murdoch McLennan interview.

10. Michael Williams interview.

11. Quoted in William J. Mann, *Behind the Screen: How gays and lesbians shaped Hollywood 1910–1969* (New York: Penguin, 2001), 293–94.

12. Lois Neunz interview, Orewa, 11 June 2017.

13. Carleen Spencer interviews, New York, 21 July 2016 and 16 January 2017.

14. Murdoch McLennan interview.

15. Ross Palmer interview, Auckland, 5 June 2016.

16. Ibid.

17. John Mains interview, Auckland, 21 February 2018.

18. Quoted in Chris Brickell, *Mates & Lovers: A history of gay New Zealand* (Auckland: Godwit, 2008), 277–78.

19. Richard Matthews interview, Auckland, 17 September, 2016.

20. Murdoch McLennan interview.

21. www.noted.co.nz/archive/listener-nz-2013/editorial-incident-in-hagley-park/

22. Brickell, *Mates & Lovers*, 306.

23. Victoria Broakes and Geoffrey Marsh (eds), *You Say You Want a Revolution? Records and rebels 1966–1970* (London: V&A, 2016), 71.

24. Nicholas Edsall, *Toward Stonewall: Homosexuality and society in the modern western world* (Charlottesville: University of Virginia Press, 2003), 333.

25. Broakes and Marsh, (eds), *You Say You Want a Revolution?*, 12.

26. Ibid., 56.

27. Ibid., 284.

28. Ibid., 101.

29. Ibid., 103.

30. David Herkt, 'Throwback Thursday: Hudson & Halls and the history of homosexuality on New Zealand TV': https://thespinoff.co.nz/features/26-11-2015/throwback-thursday-hudson-halls-and-the-history-of-homosexuality-on-new-zealand-tv/

31. Richard Matthews interview, Auckland, 17 September 2016.

32. Ross Palmer interview.

33. Broakes and Marsh (eds), *You Say You Want a Revolution?*, 100.

34. Jan Cormack interview, Auckland, 21 March 2016.

35. Ibid.

36. Matthews, *To Whom It May Concern*, 104.

37. Ibid., 88–89.

38. Murdoch McLennan interview.

39. Ibid.

40. Ibid.

41. Matthews, *To Whom It May Concern*, 251.

42. Jan Cormack interview.

43. Murdoch McLennan interview.

44. Abby Collins interview, Auckland, 27 November 2016.

45. Carmel Friedlander and Bob Sell, *Full of Life: The Bob Sell story* (Auckland: Radio Pacific Network, 1998), 172.

46. Ibid., 173.

47. Murdoch McLennan interview.

5. JULIUS GARFINKEL & QUAGG'S: 1971–73

1. Janet Puttnam interviews, Epping, 1 and 4 January 2014.

2. Chris Brickell, *Mates & Lovers: A history of gay New Zealand* (Auckland: Godwit, 2008), 260.

3. 'The Kennedy interview: They're NZ's wackiest cooks – on and off TV!', 18 December 1976.

4. Les Wilson, *Sunday*, 18 March 1990, 16.

5. Email from Sue McBride to author, 4 April 2017.

6. *Hudson & Halls: A love story*, Greenstone Pictures, 2001.

7. John Fields interviews, Noosa, Australia, 12 and 13 July 2017.

8. Carleen Spencer interviews, New York, 21 July 2016 and 16 January 2017.

9. Brickell, *Mates & Lovers*, 323.

10. Ibid.
11. Ross Palmer interview, Auckland, 5 June 2016.
12. Ibid.
13. Robyn Agnew interview, Auckland, 29 August 2017.
14. There was Rush Monroe's in Hastings, operating from 1926 as an 'Ice Cream Garden', and milk bars from 1935 in Wellington, and later in Auckland, but nothing with such a specialised focus on ice-cream that was intended from inception to become a chain.
15. Quoted in David Veart, *First Catch Your Weka: A story of New Zealand cooking* (Auckland: Auckland University Press, 2008), 180.
16. Robyn Agnew interview.
17. https://en.wikipedia.org/wiki/Westfield_St_Lukes
18. Brickell, *Mates & Lovers*, 295.
19. William J. Mann, *Behind the Screen: How gays and lesbians shaped Hollywood 1910–1969* (New York: Penguin, 2001), 295.
20. David Herkt, 'Throwback Thursday: Hudson & Halls and the history of homosexuality on New Zealand TV', *The Spinoff*, 26 November 2015: https://thespinoff.co.nz/features/26-11-2015/throwback-thursday-hudson-halls-and-the-history-of-homosexuality-on-new-zealand-tv/
21. Christopher Biggins, *Biggins: My story* (London: John Blake, 2008), 100.
22. Jan Cormack interview, Auckland, 21 March 2016.
23. Ibid.
24. Ross Palmer interview.
25. Tom Doyle, *Captain Fantastic: Elton John's stellar trip through the 70s* (New York: Ballantine Books, 2017), 140.
26. Ibid., 140.
27. Jan Cormack interview.
28. Doyle, *Captain Fantastic*, 141.
29. Ibid.
30. Ibid.
31. Michael Williams interview, Sydney, 11 March 2017.
32. Ibid.
33. Doyle, *Captain Fantastic*, 142.
34. Michael Williams interview.
35. Carleen Spencer interviews.
36. Doyle, *Captain Fantastic*, 144.

6. SPEAKEASY & THE BIRTH OF *HUDSON AND HALLS*: 1973–76

1. Robert Boyd-Bell, *New Zealand Television: The first 25 years* (Auckland: Reed Methuen, 1985), 73.
2. Ibid., 81.
3. Ibid., 87.
4. Ibid., 20.
5. Ibid., 28.
6. Ibid., 38.
7. David Veart, *First Catch Your Weka: A story of New Zealand cooking* (Auckland: Auckland University Press, 2008), 236.
8. Quoted in Rosabel Tan, 'Hudson & Halls, histories intertwined', *The Pantograph Punch*, 11 November 1915: http://pantograph-punch.com/post/hudson-and-halls-histories
9. 'The Kennedy interview: They're NZ's wackiest cooks – on and off TV!', 18 December 1976.
10. Ngā Taonga Sound & Vision Archive, Avalon, Wellington.
11. *Hudson & Halls: A love story*, Greenstone Pictures, 2001.
12. Quoted in Tan, 'Hudson & Halls'.
13. Email from Tom Finlayson to Lindsay Waugh, 25 November 2015.
14. Lindsay Waugh interview, Auckland, 4 May 2017.
15. Tony Reid, 'Cutting capers', *New Zealand Listener*, 2 April 1977, 13.
16. Ibid.
17. Felicity Anderson, 'She's a 77-year-old good luck charm', *Auckland Star*, 14 December 1977.
18. Lindsay Waugh interview.
19. Reid, 'Cutting capers'.

20. Ibid.
21. Anderson, 'She's a 77-year-old good luck charm'.
22. Ibid.
23. Ibid.
24. *Hudson & Halls: A love story*.
25. Anderson, 'She's a 77-year-old good luck charm'.
26. Murdoch McLennan interview, Auckland, 6 September 2016.
27. Reid, 'Cutting capers', and 'The Kennedy interview: They're NZ's wackiest cooks – on and off TV!', 18 December 1976.
28. Boyd-Bell, *New Zealand Television*, 149.
29. Ibid.
30. Ibid., 156.
31. Ibid., 159.
32. Lindsay Waugh interview.
33. Anderson, 'She's a 77-year-old good luck charm'.
34. Reid, 'Cutting capers'.
35. Lindsay Waugh interview.
36. Chris Brickell, *Mates & Lovers: A history of gay New Zealand*, Auckland: Godwit, 2008, 335.
37. Reid, 'Cutting capers'.

7. HUDSON AND HALLS & AN OYSTER AND FISH RESTAURANT: 1976–79

1. 'TV's zany cooks are at it again', *8 o'clock*, 14 May 1977.
2. *Hudson & Halls Cookbook*, Auckland: Books for Pleasure, Paul Hamlyn, 1977, 7.
3. 'Cooking show tidied up', *Auckland Star*, 22 September 1977.
4. 'Australian telly dates for TV2 cooks', *Auckland Star*, 6 June 1977.
5. Graeme Kennedy, 'What's all the fuss, asks TV cook Halls', *8 o'clock*, 2 July 1977.
6. Ibid.
7. Ibid.
8. 'Australian telly dates for TV2 cooks'.
9. 'Punk Pinholes Pow!', *8 o'clock*, 13 August 1977.
10. Ibid.
11. 'H and H on their hols: An ice-cream cone: $1.20', *8 o'clock*, 6 August 1977.
12. 'Punk Pinholes Pow!'
13. Ibid.
14. 'H & H off on their "hols", *8 o'clock*, 21 May 1977.
15. 'Australian telly dates for TV2 cooks'.
16. 'The Kennedy interview: They're NZ's wackiest cooks – on and off TV!', 18 December 1976.
17. 'H and H show's new "recipe"', *Auckland Star*, 20 May 1978.
18. Ibid.
19. Ibid.
20. Ngā Taonga Sound & Vision Archive, Avalon, Wellington.
21. Tony Reid, 'Cutting capers', *New Zealand Listener*, 2 April 1977, 12.
22. 'Cooks "wanted too much"', *Auckland Star*, 27 July 1978.
23. Ibid.
24. 'Those jolly television cooks Peter Hudson and David Halls have quit their TV-2 television show after the first of four scheduled series, and they now intend to go into the restaurant business', *New Zealand Herald*, 28 June 1978.
25. www.nzonscreen.com/person/alison-holst/biography
26. Ibid.
27. David Veart, *First Catch Your Weka: A story of New Zealand cooking* (Auckland: Auckland University Press, 2008), 256.
28. Ibid., 126.
29. Quoted in ibid., 83.
30. Ibid., 180–82.
31. Lindsay Waugh interview, Auckland, 4 May 2017.
32. 'TV's loss will be Auckland gourmets' gain', *Sun News*, 2 July 1978.
33. Geoffrey Collins interview, Chang Mai, Thailand, 12 December 2016.
34. Abby Collins interview, Auckland, 27 November 2016.
35. Ibid.

36. Reid, 'Cutting capers', 13.
37. Geoffey Collins interview.
38. 'A corner of a foreign field', *Auckland Star*, 8 February 1989.
39. Geoffrey Collins interview.
40. 'Felicity Ferret', *Metro*, March 1982, 3.
41. Stephanie Hall interview, Auckland, 12 August 2017.
42. Ibid.
43. Richard Matthews interview, Auckland, 17 September 2016.
44. Geoffrey Collins interview.

8. COOKS, FARMERS & ENTERTAINERS: 1980–82

1. Felicity Anderson, 'H and H comeback', *Auckland Star*, 14 March 1980.
2. Roy Good interview, Auckland, 25 June 2017.
3. Anderson, 'H and H comeback'.
4. 'Navarin of lamb has new meaning for TV chefs', *Auckland Star*, 18 September 1981.
5. Anderson, 'H and H comeback'.
6. 'Navarin of lamb has new meaning for TV chefs'.
7. Anderson, 'H and H comeback'.
8. 'Navarin of lamb has new meaning for TV chefs'.
9. *Hudson & Halls Cookbook* (Auckland: Books for Pleasure, Paul Hamlyn, 1977), 7.
10. 'Telly cook gets own show', *Auckland Star*, 13 January 1981.
11. Ibid.
12. Ibid.
13. Stephanie Hall interview, Auckland, 12 August 2017.
14. Ibid.
15. Ibid.
16. Chris Spencer interview, New York, 16 January 2017.
17. Stephanie Hall interview.
18. 'Navarin of lamb has new meaning for TV chefs'.
19. Geoffrey Collins interview, Chang Mai, Thailand, 12 December 2016.
20. Abby Collins interview, Auckland, 27 November 2016.
21. Letter from David to Carleen Spencer and Jerry Podell, 18 February 1983.
22. Abby Collins interview.
23. Ibid.
24. Letter from David Halls to Stephanie Hall and Chris Spencer, 8 August 1981.
25. Ibid.
26. Letter from David Halls to Carleen Spencer, Jerry Podell and Chris Spencer, 4 October 1981.
27. Letter from David Halls to Chris Spencer and Stephanie Hall, 8 August 1981.
28. John Fields interviews, Noosa, Australia, 12–13 July 2017.
29. Geoffrey Collins interview.
30. Letter from David Halls to Carleen Spencer, Jerry Podell and Chris Spencer, 4 October 1981.
31. Letter from David Halls to Carleen Spencer and Jerry Podell, 12 May 1984.
32. Letter from David Halls to Carleen Spencer, Jerry Podell and Chris Spencer, 4 October 1981.
33. Letter from David Halls to Carleen Spencer and Jerry Podell, 22 June 1984.
34. Letter from David Halls to Carleen Spencer and Jerry Podell, 9 March 1983.
35. Letter from David Halls to Carleen Spencer, Jerry Podell and Chris Spencer, 4 October 1981.
36. Tony Reid, 'Cutting capers', *New Zealand Listener*, 2 April 1977, 13.
37. 'Kristy may be special guest', *Auckland Star*, 19 November 1981.
38. 'Cooks' producer mops up', *Auckland Star*, 13 February 1982.
39. Sheila Mickleson interview, Auckland, 29 April 2017.
40. Michelle Osborne interview, Auckland, 14 June 2017.
41. Ibid.
42. *Hudson & Halls Cookbook*, 112.
43. Ibid., 155.

44. David Veart, *First Catch Your Weka: A story of New Zealand cooking* (Auckland: Auckland University Press, 2008), 289.

45. Des Britten, *The Des Britten Cookbook* (Auckland: Woolworths, 1977), 26.

46. Ibid., 31.

47. Ibid., 8.

48. Ibid., 27.

49. Ibid., 14.

50. Ibid., 26.

51. Ibid., 32.

52. *Hudson & Halls Cookbook*, 46.

53. Veart, *First Catch Your Weka*, 291.

54. *Hudson & Halls Cookbook*, 103.

55. Britten, *The Des Britten Cookbook*, 52.

56. Veart, *First Catch Your Weka*, 284.

57. Reid, 'Cutting capers'.

58. Geoffrey Collins interview.

59. CPI – Consumers Price Index News, April 2013.

60. *Favourite Recipes from Hudson & Halls* (Christchurch: Whitcoulls, 1985), 18, 68.

61. Alison Holst, *Alison Holst's Microwave Book* (Wellington: Inprint, 1982), 5.

62. 'New TV show to be examined', *Auckland Star*, 9 July 1982.

63. Kristen Warner, 'Grandma watches out for her "boys"', *Auckland Star*, 5 March 1982.

64. Ibid.

65. Roy Good interview.

66. 'Chefs to interpret Singapore cuisine', *Auckland Star*, 9 July 1982.

67. Ibid.

68. Ibid.

9. RATINGS, REJECTIONS & THE BBC: 1983–87

1. 'Chef, chat duo cut to 30 mins', *Auckland Star*, 16 March 1983.

2. Ibid.

3. Letter from David Halls to Carleen Spencer, 9 March 1983.

4. Philip Matthews, 'Camp cooking', *New Zealand Listener*, 5 May 2001, 34–35.

5. Caroline Kidd, 'Kitchen also stars', *Auckland Star*, 11 July 1983.

6. Letter from David Halls to Carleen Spencer and Jerry Podell, 12 May 1984.

7. Kidd, 'Kitchen also stars'.

8. 'Chef, chat duo cut to 30 mins', *Auckland Star*, 16 March 1983.

9. 'Food for fun', *Auckland Star*, 8 September 1983.

10. *Auckland Star*, 20 August 1984.

11. *New Zealand Herald*, 10 May 1984.

12. *Auckland Star*, 17 October 1984.

13. Letter from David Halls to Carleen Spencer and Jerry Podell, 22 May [1984?].

14. Ibid., 22 June 1984 and 22 May [1984?].

15. Letter from David Halls to Carleen Spencer, 13 March 1984.

16. 'Clowns of the kitchen', *Auckland Star*, 27 December 1985.

17. Ibid.

18. Ibid.

19. Robert Boyd-Bell, *New Zealand Television: The first 25 years* (Auckland: Reed Methuen, 1985), 185.

20. Ibid., 186. Author's emphasis.

21. Ibid., 189.

22. David Emanuel, Barry Spicer and Michael Powell, *The Remaking of Television New Zealand 1984–1992* (Auckland: Auckland University Press in association with the Broadcasting History Trust, 1996), 1.

23. Ibid., 3.

24. 'Clowns of the kitchen'.

25. Abby Collins interview, Auckland, 27 November 2016.

26. Letter from David Halls to Carleen Spencer and Jerry Podell, 13 February 1983.

27. Letter from David Halls to Carleen Spencer and Jerry Podell, 14 September 1984.

28. 'Burglars clean out home of TV stars', *Auckland Star*, 30 November 1983.

29. 'Clowns of the kitchen'.

30. Letter from David Halls to Carleen Spencer and Jerry Podell, 14 September 1985.

31. 'Clowns of the kitchen'.
32. Ibid.
33. Ibid.
34. Letter from David Halls to Carleen Spencer and Jerry Podell, 16 April 1985.
35. Foreword, *Favourite Recipes from Hudson & Halls* (Christchurch: Whitcoulls, 1985), n.p.
36. Ibid.
37. *Favourite Recipes from Hudson & Halls*, 62.
38. Ibid., 100.
39. Ibid., 48.
40. Ibid., 104.
41. Ibid., 92.
42. Ibid., 175.
43. Chris Brickell, *Mates & Lovers: A history of gay New Zealand* (Auckland: Godwit, 2008), 347–49.
44. Ibid., 349.
45. Ibid., 352.
46. 'Memories of Hudson and Halls from gossip columnist David Hartnell', MNZM, author's private papers, n.p.
47. Ibid.
48. 'Hudson and Halls – who cares what they cooked?' *Nelson Mail*, 10 May 2001.
49. 'Memories of Hudson and Halls from gossip columnist David Hartnell'.
50. Toni McRae, 'TV dumping saddened', *Auckland Star*, 20 September 1992.
51. Ngā Taonga Sound & Vision Archive, Avalon, Wellington.
52. Lester Kydd, *Truth*, 18 March 1986.
53. Ibid.
54. *Sunday News*, 16 March 1986.
55. Les Wilson, *Sunday*, 18 March 1990, 18.
56. Frances Levy, 'Hudson & Halls: They're walking on air', *New Zealand Woman's Weekly*, 18 May 1987.
57. Lester Kydd, *Truth*, 18 March 1986.
58. Wilson, *Sunday*, 15.
59. *Sunday News*, 16 March 1986.
60. Letter from David Halls to Carleen Spencer, 17 October 1986.
61. Wilson, *Sunday*, 15.
62. Ibid., 18.
63. Ibid.
64. Brenda Pratt, 'Lawsuit for TV chefs', *Auckland Star*, 21 December 1986.
65. Wilson, *Sunday*, 15–18.
66. Tim Murphy, 'From Tim Murphy in London', [newspaper unnamed], 17 September 1987.
67. Letter from David Halls to Carleen Spencer and Jerry Podell, 28 April 1987.
68. Letter from David Halls to Carleen Spencer and Jerry Podell, 30 June 1987.
69. Levy, 'Hudson & Halls: They're walking on air'.
70. Letter from David Halls to Jerry Podell and Carleen Spencer, 30 June 1987.
71. Levy, 'Hudson & Halls: They're walking on air'.
72. Murphy, 'From Tim Murphy in London'.
73. Levy, 'Hudson & Halls: They're walking on air'.
74. Daryl Passmore, 'Panned, but Hudson and Halls get new series', *Auckland Sun*, 23 February 1988.
75. *Auckland Star*, 21 October 1987.
76. *Evening Post* [date illegible – no title].
77. *New Zealand Herald*, 3 February 1988.
78. Nancy Banks-Smith, *Guardian*, 13 October 1987, 11.
79. Anna Raeburn, 'Pantomime courses', *London Evening Standard*, 16 October 1987, 26.
80. Patrick Stoddart, *Sunday Times*, 18 October 1987, 72.
81. Passmore, 'Panned, but Hudson and Halls get new series'.

10. LONDON & *BEGINNINGS, MIDDLES AND ENDS*: 1988–92

1. Daryl Passmore, 'Panned, but Hudson and Halls get new series', *Auckland Sun*, 23 February 1988.
2. Ibid.
3. Donna Chisholm, 'H&H cookbook fans don't need the show', *Sunday Star*, 7 May 1989.

4. Foreword, *Hudson & Halls: Beginnings, middles and ends* (London: Sphere Books, 1988), n.p.

5. *Hudson & Halls: Beginnings, middles and ends*, 25.

6. David Veart, *First Catch Your Weka: A story of New Zealand cooking* (Auckland: Auckland University Press, 2008), 306–07.

7. J. Stephen, *London Evening Standard*, 6 September 1988, 34.

8. C. Tookey, *Sunday Telegraph*, 18 December 1988, 46.

9. 'Angry mums have told TV cooks Hudson and Halls to clean up their act', *Truth*, 1 December 1989.

10. Victor Lewis-Smith, *London Evening Standard*, 23 September 1992, 45.

11. Peter Waymark, 'Television choice', *The Times*, 4 September 1989, 19.

12. Efforts to de-stigmatise HIV and Aids were slow to effect change and not universally successful. 'During the 1980s and 1990s, the Australian authorities now say, gangs of teenagers in Sydney hunted gay men for sport, sometimes forcing them off the cliffs to their deaths. But the police, many of whom had a reputation for hostility toward gay men, often carried out perfunctory investigations … Now [New South Wales] police … are reviewing the deaths of 88 men between 1976 and 2000 to determine whether they should be classified as anti-gay hate crimes.' (Michelle Innis, 'When gangs killed gay men for sport: Australia reviews 88 deaths', *New York Times*, 30 January 2017).

13. J. Stephen, *London Evening Standard*, 19 September 1989, 36. Author's emphasis.

14. Les Wilson, *Sunday*, 18 March 1990, 15–18.

15. Ibid.

16. Toni McRae, 'TV dumping saddened', *Auckland Star*, 20 September 1992.

17. *Hudson & Halls: A love story*, Greenstone Pictures, 2001.

18. David Emanuel, Barry Spicer and Michael Powell, *The Remaking of Television New Zealand 1984–1992* (Auckland: Auckland University Press in association with the Broadcasting History Trust, 1996), 67.

19. Ibid., 141.

20. Letter from David Halls to Carleen Spencer, 5 October 1989.

21. Toni McRae, 'Kiwi chefs to take pots and patter to UK', *Sunday Star*, 18 March 1990.

22. Letter from David Halls to Carleen Spencer, 5 October 1989.

23. Ibid.

24. *Hudson & Halls: A love story*.

25. 'By gum', [newspaper title not given], 1 April 1990.

26. Carleen Spencer interviews, New York, 21 July 2016 and 16 January 2017.

27. *Hudson & Halls: A love story*.

28. David Atkinson interview, Noosa, Australia, 13 July 2017.

29. Sue Heal, 'Camp Kiwis run rings around baffled Bruno', *Today*, 6 October 1990, 30.

30. Ibid.

31. J. Stephen, *Sunday Correspondent*, 7 October 1990, 81. Author's emphasis.

32. Janet Puttnam interviews, Epping, 1 and 4 January 2014.

33. Ibid.

34. Mandy Puttnam interview, London, 11 January 2017.

35. John Fields interviews.

36. David Atkinson interview.

37. Richard Matthews interview, Auckland, 17 September 2016.

38. John Fields interviews.

39. Ibid.

40. Carleen Spencer interviews.

41. Abby Collins interview, Auckland, 27 November 2016.

42. John Fields interviews.

43. Michael Williams, interview, Sydney, 11 March 2017.

44. John Fields interviews.

45. Ibid.

46. Ibid.
47. Ibid.
48. Victor Lewis-Smith, *London Evening Standard*, 23 September 1992, 45.
49. John Fields interviews.
50. Ibid.

11. DENOUEMENT

1. *Hudson & Halls: A love story*, Greenstone Pictures, 2001.
2. Ibid.
3. Ibid.
4. Ibid.
5. Note from David Halls to Carleen Spencer, c. November 1993.
6. *Hudson & Halls: A love story*.
7. Ibid.
8. Ibid.
9. Mandy Puttnam interview, London, 11 January 2017.
10. Janet Puttnam interviews, Epping, 1 and 4 January 2014.
11. Carleen Spencer interviews, New York, 21 July 2016 and 16 January 2017.
12. Note from David to Carleen Spencer, c. November 1993.
13. Carleen Spencer interviews.
14. Janet Puttnam interviews.
15. Ibid.

12. POSTSCRIPT: 2001–17

1. Email from Finlay Macdonald to author, 23 July 2014.
2. Jan Cormack interview, Auckland, 21 March 2016.
3. Janet Puttnam interviews, Epping, 1 and 4 January 2014.
4. Carleen Spencer interviews, New York, 21 July 2016 and 16 January 2017.
5. Chris Spencer interview, New York, 16 January 2017.

Select Bibliography

BOOKS

Ask Aunt Daisy: Aunt Daisy's book of handy hints (Christchurch: Whitcombe & Tombs, c. 1950)

Biggins, Christopher, *Biggins: My story* (London: John Black, 2008)

Boyd-Bell, Robert, *New Zealand Television: The first 25 years* (Auckland: Reed Methuen, 1985)

Brickell, Chris, *Mates & Lovers: A history of gay New Zealand* (Auckland: Godwit, 2008)

Britten, Des, *The Des Britten Cookbook* (Auckland: Woolworths, 1977)

Broakes, Victoria & Geoffrey Marsh (eds), *You Say You Want a Revolution? Records and rebels 1966–1970* (London: V&A, 2016)

Brookes, Barbara, Charlotte Macdonald & Margaret Tennant, *Women in History: Essays on European women in New Zealand*, (Wellington: Allen & Unwin; Port Nicholson Press, 1986)

Chapman, Heather & Judith Stillman, *Melbourne: Then and now* (London: Pavilion, 2016)

Coney, Sandra, *Standing in the Sunshine: A history of New Zealand women since they won the vote* (Auckland: Viking, 1993)

Cooper, Emmanuel, *The Sexual Perspective: Homosexuality and art in the last 100 years in the West* (London & New York: Routledge & Kegan Paul, 1986)

Doyle, Tom, *Captain Fantastic: Elton John's stellar trip through the 70s* (New York: Ballantine Books, 2017)

Emanuel, David, Barry Spicer & Michael Powell, *The Remaking of Television New Zealand 1984–1992* (Auckland: Auckland University Press/Broadcasting History Trust, 1996)

Flower, Tui, *Self-Raising Flower* (Auckland: Viking, 1998)

Friedlander, Carmel & Bob Sell, *Full of Life: The Bob Sell story* (Auckland: Radio Pacific Network, 1998)

Holst, Alison, *Alison Holst's Microwave Book* (Wellington: Inprint, 1982)

———, (ed.), *The New Zealand Radio & Television Cookbook* (Auckland: Summit Books, 1974)

Kerr, Graham, *Selected Recipes Presented by Graham Kerr* (Wellington: 1963)

———, *The Graham Kerr Cookbook by The Galloping Gourmet* (London: Sphere Books, 1973)

Labrum, Bronwyn, *Real Modern: Everyday New Zealand in the 1950s and 1960s* (Wellington: Te Papa Press, 2015)

Lachkar, Joan, *The Narcissistic/Borderline Couple* (New York and Hove: Brunner-Routledge, 2004)

Leach, Helen, *Kitchens: The New Zealand kitchen in the 20th century* (Dunedin: Otago University Press, 2014)

Light, Alison, *Mrs Woolf & the Servants* (London: Penguin, 2007)

Mann, William J., *Behind the Screen: How gays and lesbians shaped Hollywood 1910–1969* (New York: Penguin, 2001)

McLeod, Aorewa, *Who Was That Woman Anyway?: Snapshots of a lesbian life* (Wellington: Victoria University Press, 2013)

Matthews, Richard, *To Whom it May Concern: A romp through the life and times of Richard Matthews* (Auckland: Richard Matthews, 2009)

Mooney, Carol Garhart, *Theories of Attachment: An introduction to Bowlby, Ainsworth, Gerber, Brazelton, Kennell, & Klaus* (St Paul: Redleaf Press, 2010)

Mrs Wolfe's Recipes (Westerham, Kent: Squerryes Court, 1980)

Penfold, Merimeri & Bridget Williams (eds), *The Book of New Zealand Women/Ko Kui Ma te Kaupapa* (Wellington: Bridget Williams Books, 1991)

Pewsey, Stephen, *Epping & Ongar: A pictorial history* (Chichester: Phillimore & Co., 1997)

Phillips, Hazel, *David Hartnell: Memoirs of a gossip columnist* (Auckland: Penguin, 2011)

Rowland, Perrin, *Dining Out: A history of the restaurant in New Zealand* (Auckland: Auckland University Press, 2010).

Veart, David, *First Catch Your Weka: A story of New Zealand cooking* (Auckland: Auckland University Press, 2008)

Wells, Peter, *Long Loop Home: A memoir* (Auckland: Vintage, 2011)

Wells, Peter & Rex Pilgrim (eds), *Best Mates: Gay writing in Aotearoa New Zealand* (Auckland: Reed, 1997)

HUDSON & HALLS COOKBOOKS

Hudson & Halls Cookbook (Auckland: Books for Pleasure, Paul Hamlyn, 1977)

Favourite Recipes from Hudson & Halls (Christchurch: Whitcoulls, 1985)

Favourite Recipes from the Bestselling Cookery Duo: Hudson & Halls (London, Melbourne and Auckland: Century, 1987).

Hudson & Halls: Beginnings, middles and ends (London: Sphere Books, 1988)

MAGAZINE ARTICLES

'Hudson & Halls: They're walking on air', *New Zealand Woman's Weekly*, 18 May 1987

Matthews, Philip, 'Camp cooking', *New Zealand Listener*, 5 May 2001

Reid, Tony, 'Cutting capers', *New Zealand Listener*, 2 April 1977, 12–13

'Smile and the world smiles with you …', *New Zealand Woman's Weekly*, 11 May 1981

Willett, Graham & John Arnold (eds), 'Queen city of the south: Gay and lesbian Melbourne', *La Trobe Journal*, no. 87, May 2011

INTERNET ARTICLES

Herkt, David, 'Throwback Thursday: Hudson & Halls and the history of homosexuality on New Zealand TV', *The Spinoff*, 26 November 2015: https://thespinoff.co.nz/features/26-11-2015/throwback-thursday-hudson-halls-and-the-history-of-homosexuality-on-new-zealand-tv/

Tan, Rosabel, 'Hudson & Halls, histories intertwined', *Pantograph Punch*, 11 November 2015: http://pantograph-punch.com/post/hudson-and-halls-histories

AUSTRALIAN NEWSPAPER ARTICLES

'Alleged abortion: Melbourne trial opine', *Recorder*, 26 May 1926, 1

'Babies to order: How husbands are hoaxed & hoodwinked. Remarkable revelations at Collingwood Court', *Truth*, 20 February 1915, 5

'Charge of murder: Doctor and nurse committed', *Telegraph*, 26 April 1926, 2

'Charges of murder: Doctor and nurse committed: Inquest on death of woman', *Telegraph*, 24 April 1926, 2

'Death of Mrs Law: Case adjourned', *Riverine Herald*, 26 May 1926, 2

'Death of Mrs Law: "Mystery" witness: Doctor and nurse on trial', *News*, 26 May 1926, 1

'Death of Mrs Law: Verdict of murder: Doctor and nurse sent for trial', *Argus*, 24 April 1926, 25

'Doctor and nurse sent for trial: Inquiry into the death of Mrs Law', *Weekly Times*, 1 May 1926, 6

'Doctor on trial: On murder charge: Girl gives interesting evidence', *National Advocate*, 27 May 1926, 2

'Married woman's death: Illegal operation suggested', *Argus*, 27 November 1920, 22

'"Met by police": Law murder case: Girl's evidence', *Newcastle Sun*, 26 May 1926, 5

'Mrs Hudson on trial', *Observer*, 10 April 1926, 44

'Mrs Law's death again probed: Doctor and nurse face murder trial', *Weekly Times*, 29 May 1926, 7

'Murder trial: Mrs Law's death: Doctor and nurse', *Sun*, 26 May 1926, 9

'Murder charge: Accused for trial: Body left on roadside', *Daily Telegraph*, 20 April 1926, 4

'Murder charge: Nurse on trial', *Advocate*, 6 April 1926, 5

'Murder charge: Oakleigh tragedy: Trial in Melbourne', *Daily Mail*, 26 May 1926, 6

'Murder charge: Woman's body found on road: Propped against tree: Doctor and nurse on trial', *Sun*, 25 May 1926, 9

'Murder of a woman: Doctor and nurse acquitted', *Barrier Miner*, 27 May 1926, 1

'Murder of Mrs Law: Doctor and nurse on trial', *Advocate*, 26 May 1926, 5

'Murder trial: Death of Elizabeth Law: Doctor and nurse charged', *News*, 25 May 1926, 1

'Not guilty: Doctor and nurse acquitted: Law murder trial', *News*, 27 May 1926, 1

'Oakleigh murder trial', *Gippsland*, 27 May 1926, 3

'Oakleigh mystery: Nurse Hudson remanded', *West Australian*, 7 April 1926, 8

'Oakleigh tragedy: Accused committed for trial', *Recorder*, 24 April 1926, 1

'Oakleigh tragedy accused on trial: Array of barristers', *Daily News*, 25 May 1926, 1

'Oakleigh tragedy: Mrs Hudson on trial', *Register*, 6 April 1926, 9

'"Real" wages show an increase: Despite fall in rates', *Sydney Morning Herald*, 26 January 1932, 7

'The Oakleigh murder: Doctor and woman on trial: Case for the Crown', *Advertiser*, 26 May 1926, 16

'The Oakleigh tragedy: Arrests made', *Observer*, 10 April 1926, 44

'The Oakleigh tragedy: Doctor and woman on trial', *Advertiser*, 27 May 1926, 17

'The Toorak murder: Charges against Dr MacGillicuddy: Withdrawn after committal by coroner', *Evening News*, 28 April 1926, 4

'Women's death: Charges of murder: Nurse and doctor for trial', *Examiner*, 24 April 1926, 14

NEW ZEALAND NEWSPAPER ARTICLES

'A corner of a foreign field', *Auckland Star*, 8 February 1989

Anderson, Felicity, 'Cooks "wanted too much"', *Auckland Star*, 27 June 1978

'An icecream cone: $1.20', *8 o'clock*, 6 August 1977

'Australian telly dates for TV2 cooks', *Auckland Star*, 6 June 1977

'BBC serves a treat for saucy cooks', *New Zealand Herald*, 21 March 1987

'Britain beckons TV cooks', *Auckland Star*, 26 April 1984

'Burglaries admitted', *Auckland Star*, 5 March 1984

'Burglars clean out home of TV stars', *Auckland Star*, 30 November 1983

'Burglars do it again', *Auckland Star*, 1 December 1983

'Chef, chat duo cut to 30 mins', *Auckland Star*, 16 March 1983

'Chefs to interpret Singapore cuisine', *Auckland Star*, 9 July 1982

'Clowns of the kitchen', *Auckland Star*, 27 December 1985

'Colleagues recall TV chef', *New Zealand Herald*, 27 November 1993

'Comic cooks', *Sunday Star*, [n.d.], Central Library Research Centre, Auckland

'Cook David Halls dies', *New Zealand Herald*, 26 November 1993

'Cooks panned', *Auckland Star*, 19 August 1988

'Cooks' producer mops up', *Auckland Star*, 13 February 1982

'Cooking show tidied up', *Auckland Star*, 22 September 1977

'Flamboyant cook dies, 61', *New Zealand Herald*, 15 September 1992

'Food for fun', *Auckland Star*, 8 September 1983

'Grandma watches out for her "boys"', *Auckland Star*, 5 March 1982

'H & H cookbook fans don't need the show', *Sunday Star*, 7 May 1989

'H & H off on their "hol"', *8 o'clock*, 21 May 1977

'Kitchen couple's capers', *Auckland Star*, 20 January 1976

'Halls abandons shoes for food', *Auckland Star*, 6 November 1985

'Halls planted Hudson!', *Truth*, 21 January 1994

'H and H comeback', *Auckland Star*, 14 March 1980

'H and H show's new "recipe"', *Auckland Star*, 20 May 1978

'Hudson and Halls burglary charge', *Auckland Star*, 7 January 1984

'Hudson and Halls to live on', *Dominion Post*, 16 September 1992

'Kaleidoscope duo', *Auckland Star*, 13 January 1982

'Kirsty may be special guest', *Auckland Star*, 19 November 1981

'Kitchen also stars', *Auckland Star*, 11 July 1983

'Kiwi chefs to take pots and patter to UK', *Sunday Star*, 18 March 1990

'Kiwi chocolate log makes prime time', *Evening Post*, 17 August 1988

'Lawsuit for TV chefs', *Auckland Star*, 21 December 1986

'Let others do the cooking …' *Auckland Star*, 21 December 1985

'Making a meal of it for 20 years', *Auckland Star*, 16 November 1985

McRae, Toni, 'Hilda's pie is missing', [no details], Central Library Research Centre, Auckland

——, 'TV dumping saddened', [no details], Central Library Research Centre, Auckland

'Memorial service', *New Zealand Herald*, 20 October 1992

'Punk Pinholes Pow!', *8 o'clock*, 13 August 1977

'Navarin of lamb has new meaning for TV chefs', *Auckland Star*, 18 September 1981

'New TV show to be examined', *Auckland Star*, 9 July 1982

'Panel roasts Kiwi cooks', *Auckland Star*, 2 February 1988

'Panned, but Hudson and Halls get new series', *Auckland Star*, 23 February 1988

'Patter among the platters', *Sunday*, 18 March 1990

'Police believe fugitives injured in car crash', *New Zealand Herald*, 1 December 1983

'Police find suspect car', *Auckland Star*, 2 December 1983

'Rainy time cooking', *Auckland Star*, 17 May 1982

'PM is H & H's special guest', *Auckland Star*, 13 December 1982

'Screen cooks sign for BBC', *New Zealand Herald*, 6 March 1987

Shaw, Barry, 'Comic chefs step into Dinah's spot', *Auckland Star*, 21 September 1976

'She's a 77-year-old good luck charm', *Auckland Star*, 14 December 1977

'Show stopped, rain started', *Auckland Star*, 7 November 1980

'Soccer boys sing for their supper', *Auckland Star*, 17 April 1982

'Telly cook gets own show', *Auckland Star*, 13 January 1981

'The Kennedy interview: They're NZ's wackiest cooks – on and off TV!', 18 December 1976,
    Central Library Research Centre, Auckland

'This trick cyclist is no last straw', *Auckland Star*, 2 April 1982

'Trail points to chefs' burglars', *Auckland Star*, 1 December 1983

'TV chef overdosed', *New Zealand Herald*, 7 January 1994

'TV chef's death "not suspicious"', *New Zealand Herald*, 29 November 1993

'TV chef on tour with stage farce', *8 o'clock*, 17 August 1985

'TV's zany cooks are at it again', *8 o'clock*, 14 May 1977

'KU critic roasts television cooks', *Auckland Star*, 13 October 1987

'Wackiest cooks', *8 o'clock*, 18 December 1976

'What's all the fuss, asks TV cook Halls', *8 o'clock*, 2 July 1977

Wigmore, Caryn, 'Cook', *New Zealand Herald*, 21 October 1992

US NEWSPAPER ARTICLES

Innis, Michelle, 'When gangs killed gay men for sport: Australia reviews 88 deaths', *New York Times*, 30 January 2017

INTERVIEWS

Robyn Agnew, Auckland, 29 August 2017

Tony Astle, Auckland, 7 February 2018

David Atkinson, Noosa, Australia, 13 July 2017

Kip Chapman, Todd Emerson, Auckland, 18 July 2016

Abby Collins, Auckland, 27 November 2016.

Geoffrey Collins, Chiang Mai, Thailand, 12 December 2016

Jan Cormack, Auckland, 21 March 2016

John Fields, Noosa, Australia, 12 and 13 July 2017

Roy Good, Auckland, 25 June 2017

Stephanie Hall, Auckland, 12 August 2017

John Mains, Auckland, 21 February 2018

Christine Mangin, 11 May 2017

Murdoch McLennan, Auckland, 6 September 2016

Richard Matthews, Auckland, 17 September 2016

Sheila Mickleson, Auckland, 29 April 2017

Lois Neunz, Orewa, 11 June 2017

Michelle Osborne, Auckland, 14 June 2017

Ross Palmer, Auckland, 5 June 2016

Janet Puttnam, Epping, 1 and 4 January 2014

Mandy Puttnam, London, 11 January 2017
Carleen Spencer, New York, 21 July 2016 and 16 January 2017
Chris Spencer, New York, 16 January 2017
Lindsay Waugh, Auckland, 4 May 2017
Michael Williams, Sydney, 11 March 2017

DOCUMENTARY
Hudson & Halls: A love story, Greenstone Pictures, 2001

ARCHIVES & LIBRARIES
BFI National Archive, London
BFI Reuben Library, London
British Library, London
Central Library Research Centre, Auckland
Ngā Taonga Sound & Vision Archive, Avalon, Wellington
State Library of Victoria, Melbourne

RECIPES
Chapter 2: SWEET AVOCADO PIE: *Hudson & Halls: Beginnings, middles and ends* (London: Sphere Books, 1988), 146
Chapter 3: STUFFED SQUID: *Hudson & Halls: Beginnings, middles and ends* (London: Sphere Books, 1988), 32
Chapter 4: FROSTED CHEESE MOULD: *Hudson & Halls Cookbook* (Auckland: Books for Pleasure, Paul Hamlyn, 1977), 140.
Chapter 5 ROLLED, STUFFED CHICKEN BREASTS: *Hudson & Halls Cookbook* (Auckland: Books for Pleasure, Paul Hamlyn, 1977), 97
Chapter 6: VENETIAN LIVER: *Hudson & Halls Cookbook* (Auckland: Books for Pleasure, Paul Hamlyn, 1977), 117
Chapter 7: CRISP FRIED FISH WITH LEMON SAUCE: H*udson & Halls: Beginnings, middles and ends* (London: Sphere Books, 1988), 41
Chapter 8: CREPE CAKE: *Hudson & Halls Cookbook* (Auckland: Books for Pleasure, Paul Hamlyn, 1977), 43
Chapter 9: FRUIT FLANS: *Hudson & Halls Cookbook* (Auckland: Books for Pleasure, Paul Hamlyn, 1977), 148
Chapter 10: DOUBLE CHOCOLATE CAKE: *Hudson & Halls Cookbook* (Auckland: Books for Pleasure, Paul Hamlyn, 1977), 144

Index

Page numbers in **bold** refer to illustrations.

Aberhart, Charles 81–83
abortion 50–58
Abrams, Mrs 32
Addey, John 137
Agnew, Robby 100, 102
Aids 14, 16, 20, 202, 224, 239
Alan, Ray 222
alcohol
    cause of rows 79, 162
    in cooking 129, 176–77, 180, 199, 213,
       218
    drinking on *Hudson and Halls* set 158,
       162, 193, 204, 213, 222
    Elton John and entourage 107, 109
    Hudson and Halls Oyster and Fish
       Restaurant 154–55, 161
    New Zealand drinking culture 74, 114,
       145–46, 176
    Peter and David's parties 74, 75, 88, 90,
       137, 164–65
    Peter and David's regular use 92, 162, 163,
       170, 233
    relationship with food 175–76
Alison Holst's Microwave Cookbook **182**
Asquith, Robin 196
Astle, Tony 215
Atkinson, David **167,** 235, 236, 237
Auckland 95–96
    see also Parnell, Auckland
    7 London Street, St Marys Bay 64, 120,
       149–50, 163, 164, 165

58 Roberta Avenue, Glendowie 206, **207,**
    208, 209, 211, 228–29
gay-aligned bars, clubs, haunts and pick-
    up places 99
Strand Arcade 96, 97–99, 102
Aunt Daisy (Maud Basham) 142–43
Avalon television studio 115

'Babies to Order' scandal, Melbourne 58–59,
    61
Baker, Cheryl 222
Balmforth, Evelyn 121, 122–23, 126, 139, 184,
    208
Banks-Smith, Nancy 212
Baragwanath, Judith 107
Baron, Lynda 236, **236**
Basham, Maud (Aunt Daisy) 142–43
Basil Brush 211
BBC
    Good Morning show 245–46, 248
    Hudson and Halls shows 205–06, 209–14,
       213, 217, 218, 220–22, **223,** 224–26,
       230, 232–33, **236, 237,** 256
    Noel's House Party 239–40, **240**
Bednall, Stuart 258, 259
Beginnings, Middles and Ends cookbook 218,
    219, 220
Bell, Vanessa 40
Bennet, Jeff 158, 173, 184, 185
Biggins, Christopher 105, 236
Black Cat nightclub, Los Angeles 83–84

Black, Cilla 227
Black, Kevin 142
Blankety Blank television show 159–61
Boyd-Bell, Robert 193
British Academy of Film and Television Arts
    (BAFTA) 211, 212
Britten, Des 116, 143, 173, 176, 178–79, **179**, 181
Broadcasting Act 1962 112
Broadcasting Corporation of New Zealand
    (BCNZ) 124–25
Brown, Faith 222
Bruno, Frank 222, 232
Buckhurst Hill County High School 38, 39
Burke, Neville 97, 119

Callil, Carmen 212
Calvert, Eddie 122
camp style and humour 47, 83, 88, 98, 99,
    104–05, 150, 197, 203, 211, 212, 220, 221,
    224, 232, 233
Carey Institute for Global Good, Logan
    Fellowship 258–59, 262–63
Carlaw, John 123, 138
Carry On movies 104
Cassidy, David 107
Caughey, Lady Mary 161
Chapman, Kip 258
Chisholm, Donna 218
Churchill, Winston 33, 34
Clarke & Coventry, Auckland 46–47, 77–78
Collins, Abby (née Smith) 19, 64, 92, 149, 150–
    51, **151**, 164, 195, 239–40, 258
Collins, Geoffrey 19, 20, 64, 149, 150–51, **151**,
    154, 164, 170, 181, 258
Columbus, Ray 112, 160, 172
Combine, Noel 71
cooking
    David Halls' early experience 38, 42
    David and Peter's home entertaining 75,
        88–89, 100, 164, 170, 195
    David and Peter's paid guests at home 170,
        206, **209**
    David and Peter's Sydney meal for
        friends 117
    Hilda Halls 35–36, 42
    Nellie Halls 30–32, 42
    New Zealand 143–45, 147, 176–81, 183,
        199–201, 218 (*see also* food, New
        Zealand)

Cooper, Chris 190
Corbett, John 66
Cordwainers College, London 46
Cormack, Danielle **231**
Cormack, Gavin (Gabby) 87, 105, **106**, 246, 258
Cormack, Jamie 87, **171**
Cormack, Jan 14–15, 87, 89, 101, **101**, 105, 107,
    231, 246–47, 258
    David's birthday card 247, **247**
Cornelius, Rod 194
'cottaging' 81, 82
counter culture groups 85, 103, 136
Coward, Noël 127
Craddock, Fanny 212–13
Crompton's Cafeteria, San Francisco 83
Cross, Ian 194
Cross, Tina 172, 173
Crowther, Leslie 222

Dallas, Lorna 222
D'Audney, Angela 160
De Paul, Lynsey 222
Des Britten Cookbook 178–79, **179**
Diana, Princess of Wales 224
domestic service, England 31–32, 35–36
Doncaster 28
Dorday, Debbie 160
Downes, Lorraine **188**
Drake, Gabrielle 135, 138
drug use, recreational 85, 107, 109

East, Dolly and Ken 105–06
Emerson, Todd 258
Epping 38, 39, 97, 137–38, 233, 259
Epping's Co-op 39, 40, 42, 259
Ewens, Michael 206, 208

Farnell, Billy 17
Favourite Recipes from Hudson & Halls 196,
    198, 199–201
Felicity Ferret, *Metro* magazine 150–51
Feltex Best Entertainers of the Year, 1981 172
feminist movement 84, 103, 116, 135
Fenton, Colin 47
Festival Records 107
Fields, John **18**, 98–99, **167**, **208**, 232, 235, 239,
    240, 258
    close friend of David and Peter 76, 137,
        236–38, 247, 248

David's suicide 241–42, 243, 248, 249
Finlay, John 69–70
Finlayson, Tom 119, 120
Floyd, Keith 224
food festivals 196
food, New Zealand 143–45, 147–48, 173, 177–79, 181, 199–201, 220
    see also restaurants, New Zealand
Freer, Warren 201
French, Brian and Harriet 34, 36–37, 38
French, Jonathan and Amanda 37

Gascoine, Jill 232
gay rights groups 84, 85, 102–03, 201–02
'gay,' use of term 83
Georges department store 64–65, **65**
glam rock 106–07
Good, Roy 157, 184, 193
The Great Wellington Show 196
Greenbie, Sydney 100–01
Greenstone Pictures 256
Grenville, Tina 160
Gubay, Albert 228

Hall, Brett 169
Hall, Carole 169
Hall, Stephanie 152, 161, 162–63, 166, **166,** 169
Halls, Ann 23, 24, 28, 29, 30, 32, 33, **33,** 39, 44
    wedding 44–45, **45**
Halls, David
    see also Hudson–Halls relationship
    ashes scattered in Green Park, London 251, **253**
    finances 16, 20, 89, 98, 163, 170, 172, 195, 228, 229, 232, 238, 248, 249
    grief after Peter's death 15–17, 19–21, 241–43, 245–46, 248
    homosexuality 38, 40, 42, 43, 73, 75, 81, 86–87, 126–27, 128, 174, 203, 224, 235, 241, 257
    and Peter's prostate cancer 13–15, 215, 217, 239, 240–41
    suicide 241–42, 243, 246–50, 255
    in New Zealand
        see also Auckland – 7 London Street, St Marys Bay; Auckland – 58 Roberta Ave, Glendowie; Hudson and Halls Oyster and Fish Restaurant, Auckland; *Hudson and Halls*

television shows; Parnell, Auckland – 103 Brighton Road; Ti Point, Leigh, The Farm
        arrival and 1960s 44, 45–47, 71, 73–81, 86–93, 111
        Bentley S3 1962 car 150, 163, 164, 228
        Blankety Blank television show presenter 159–61
        commercials, advertising and endorsements 183, 192, 208
        dogs, Bullet and Nero 165, 166, **167,** 170, 195, 199, 205, **207,** 210, 228
        Julius Garfinkel business 96–99, 102, 119
        leaving New Zealand, 1990 225, 226, 228–29
        part in play *Run for Your Wife* 196, 227
        Quagg's ice-cream parlour 100–02
        radio shows 142, 148, 208, 225
        Telethon, 1977 135, 136
        travel within New Zealand to maintain celebrity profile 195–96, **197**
    in the UK
        see also London – Jermyn Street flat
        BBC production of *Hudson and Halls* shows 209–14, **213,** 220–22, **223,** 224–26, 232–33, **236, 237,** 238, 242
        BBC show, *Noel's House Party* 239–40, **240**
        birth, childhood and family 23, 24, **25,** 25–33, **26, 31, 33,** 34, 37–39
        family visits 210, 211, 233, **234,** 235
        friends and acquaintances 235–26, **236**
        Good Morning show 245–46, 248
        move to London, 1990 226–30, **227, 231**
        theatre interests 43, **44**
        youth and early employment 39–40, **41,** 42–43, 259
    international travel
        Australia 105, 117, 135
        book promotion tour, 1977 136–38, **137**
        Cook's Tour hosting plan 196
        Miami 117
        UK trips, 1970s 96–97, 105
Halls, George (David's father) **25,** 43–44, 45, 261
    David's suicide 241, 242, 248, 249–50, 257

Theydon Bois 39, 40, 211
Theydon Hall 34, 35, 37, 38
visits from David 96, 137–38, **234**
World War II 23–30
Halls, George (David's grandfather) 24, 25, 29, 32, **32**, 37, 38
Halls, Hilda (née Manley) 23, 24–27, **25**, 39–40, 44, **45**, 45–46, 210, **234**, 257, 261
David's suicide 21, 241, 242, 248, 249–50, 257
Theydon Bois 38, 39–40, 211
Theydon Hall 34, 35–38, 42
visits from David 96, 137–38, **234**
World War II 23, 27–30
Halls, Nellie 24, 29–33, **32**, 37, 38, 42, 122
Halls, Tony 37, 44, 45
Hamill, Mark 162
Harris, Rebecca 173
Hartnell, David 203, 204
Heal, Sue 232
Hemmings, David 158
Herkt, David 85
Hildred, Stafford 220
Hill, Vince 122
hippies 85, 89, 98
Holcroft, Monte 82–83
Holst, Alison 143–44, 173, 183, **188,** 189–90
Alison Holst's Microwave Cookbook **182**
The New Zealand Radio & Television Cookbook 181, **182**
homophobia 40, 46, 67, 68–71, 81–83, 103–04, 105, 201–02, 203, 224, 256
Homosexual Law Reform Act 1986 202–03
homosexuality 33
see also camp style and humour; gay rights groups
camp 104–05
classified as a psychiatric illness 69, 81, 103
'coming out,' impact on family bonds 235
David 38, 40, 42, 43, 73, 75, 81, 86–87, 126–27, 128, 174, 203, 224, 235, 241, 257
'gay,' use of term 83
impact on *Hudson and Halls* television shows 127, 174, 224, 233
language 83
law reform, New Zealand 201–03
literature and cultural influences 103–05
Melbourne 66–67

New Zealand 68–71, 73, 80, 81–83, 85–87, 128, 174
organised protest 83–84
Peter 66–67, 73, 75, 81, 86–87, 126–27, 203, 224, 235, 241
police entrapment 67, 69, 84
United Kingdom 84, 88
United States 83–83
Hudson, Arthur 56, 59, 61, 62
Hudson, Mark 226–27, 228, 238
Hudson, Mary Ethel (Keast) 50–59, **51,** 61, 62, 64, 65, 66
Hudson, Peter
see also Hudson–Halls relationship
ashes scattered in Green Park, London 251, **253**
birth, childhood and family 59, 61–64, **63**
finances 16, 20, 79, 89, 163, 170, 172, 195, 227, 228, 232, 238–39
homosexuality 66–67, 73, 75, 81, 86–87, 126–27, 203, 224, 235, 241
lunch held as a tribute to his memory 16, **17, 18**
memorial service, Auckland 16–17
prostate cancer, terminal illness and death 13–15, 16, 214–15, 217, 237–38, 239, 240–41, 246
youth and early employment 64–66
in New Zealand
see also Auckland – 7 London Street, St Marys Bay; Auckland – 58 Roberta Ave, Glendowie; Hudson and Halls Oyster and Fish Restaurant; *Hudson and Halls* television shows; Parnell, Auckland – 103 Brighton Road; Ti Point, Leigh, The Farm
arrival and 1960s 68, 71, 73–76, 78–81, 86–93
Bentley S3 1962 car 150, 163, 164, 228
commercials, advertising and endorsements 183, 192, 208
dogs, Bullet and Nero 165, 166, **167,** 170, 195, 199, 205, **207,** 210, 228
drug overdose 92
Julius Garfinkel business 96–99, 102, 119
leaving New Zealand, 1990 225, 226, 228–29
Quagg's ice-cream parlour 100–02

radio shows 142, 148, 208, 225
travel within New Zealand to maintain
    celebrity profile 195–96, **197**
in the UK
    see also London – Jermyn Street flat
    BBC production of *Hudson and Halls*
        shows 209–14, **213**, 220–22, **223**,
        224–26, 230, 232–33, **236**, **237**, 238
    BBC show, *Noel's House Party* 239–40,
        240
    friends and acquaintances 235–26, **236**
    move to London, 1990 226–30, **227**,
        231
    refused entry to the UK without
        visa 230, 232, 233, 238
    visits to David's family 211, 233, **234**,
        235, **238**
international travel
    Australia 105, 117, 135
    book promotion tour, 1977 136–38,
        137
    Cook's Tour hosting plan 196
    Miami 117
    New York **91, 108**
    UK trip, 1950s 66, 67–68
    UK trips, 1970s 97, 105
Hudson & Halls: A love story
    (documentary) 255, 256
Hudson and Halls cookbooks
    Beginnings, Middles and Ends 218, **219**, 220
    Favourite Recipes from Hudson & Halls 196,
        198, 199–201
    Hudson & Halls Cookbook 129, **130, 131,
        132, 133, 134**, 135, 137, 159, 174–78,
        180
Hudson and Halls Food Fests 196
Hudson & Halls Live (stage show) 257–58
Hudson and Halls Oyster and Fish Restaurant,
    Auckland 148–49, 151–55, **153**, 159, 161–
    62, 163, 166, 169, 184
    sale of restaurant 206, 208
Hudson and Halls television shows 87, 256
    BBC purchase and production of
        shows 205–06, 209–14, **213**, 217, 218,
        220–22, **223**, 224–26, 230, 232–33, **236**,
        237, 238, 242, 256
    Feltex Best Entertainers of the Year,
        1981 172
    final New Zealand show 204

impact of David and Peter's
    homosexuality 127, 174, 224, 233
negotiations for sale of show overseas 192,
    196
salad days (summer) series 190–91
Singapore programmes 184–85
South Pacific Television, afternoon
    show 120–24, **123**
South Pacific Television, evening show 124,
    125, 126, 129, 135, 136, 138–39, **139**,
    141–42, 157, 159, 172
South Pacific Television, *Speakeasy*
    programme 117, 119, 120, 121, 122
Television New Zealand one-hour
    show 157–59, 161, 163, 172–74, **175**,
    176–77, 183–85, 187
Television New Zealand 30-minute
    show 187, **188**, 189–93
termination of show 203–04
Hudson-Halls relationship
    documentary, *Hudson & Halls: A love
        story* 255, 256
    jealousy 75–76
    love story 9, 11, 14, 87, 246, 255, 264
    meeting in Auckland, 1962 47, 71
    public image 92–93
    rows 75, 78–79, 88–89, 99, 120, 158, 162,
        169–70, 204
    separation while Peter waited for UK
        visa 230, 232
    use to sell themselves as food presenters
        116, 119, 120
Hume, Juliet 70–71
Hunt, Thomas 54–55, 56

Jackson, Gordon 222, **223**
James, Billy T. 125, 126, 172, 173
Jenkins, Peter 73, 75
John, Elton 105, 106–07, 109
Julius Garfinkel shop, Strand Arcade,
    Auckland 96–99, 102, 119
Julius gay bar, New York 97

Kaleidoscope television programme 193
Kaye, Gordon 235–36
Keast, Percy George 55
Kemp, Malcolm 203–04
Kennedy, Ludovic 212
Kerr, Graham 112, **113**, 115–16, 143, 173

Kidd, Lester 205
Kirkcaldie & Stains, Wellington 78
Kitt, Suzi 89, 148, 205, 210

La Rue, Danny 236
Law, Annie Isabel 55
Law, Elizabeth 50, 51–57, 58, 62
Law, William Dunlop 55
Lawrence, Bruno 189–90
Laws, John 105
Leary, Timothy 85
Lee, Dinah 112
Levy, Frances 210
Lewis, Brent 259
Lewis, Wally 160
Lewisham, Richard 76
Lewis-Smith, Victor 222, 242
Linklater, Eric 144
Littlewood, Chic 160
Littlewood, Joan 43
London
    107 Prospect Rd 24
    air raids, World War II 23–24, 27–28
    Gainsborough Rd, Woodford 23, 25, 26,
        27–28, 29
    Jermyn Street flat 13, 19, 228, 229, **230,
        231,** 232, 235–36, 243, 246, 249, 251
    Langan's Brasserie 16, **17, 18**
    Peter and David's visits 136–37, **137**

MacGillicuddy, Daniel Florance 51–54, **52,**
    56–58
Macleay, Alexander 64
Mains, John 80
Manley, Annie 25, 40
Manley, Henry 25
Mann, William J. 67
marijuana 85, 89–92
Marshall, Sue 255–56, 257, 258, 259, 261, 262,
    263
Martin, Allan 183, 194
Masters, Alan 257
Mattachine Society, New York 83
Matthews, Richard 16, 74, 86, 88, 89, 90, 154,
    205, 231, 258
Maxwell, G.A. 54, 56
Mazengarb Report 70
McBride, Sue 98
McCarthyism 103

McLennan, Murdoch 74, 75, 76, 79, 81, 88, 89,
    90, 91, 92, 123, 258
McLeod, Edward (Emerald) 14, 16, **18,** 19, 20,
    239, 242, 246
McNichol, Kristy 173
McPhail and Gadsby 172
McRae, Toni 225
Meades, Jonathan 212
Melbourne 49–58, 64–68, 71
    Iona Avenue, Toorak 50, 51, 55, 56, 58, 59,
        60, 61, 62, 63, 197
Melrose, Bridget (Biddy) (Keast) 61, **61,** 62,
    64, 66, **68**
Metzger, Derek 184
Mickelson, Sheila 173–74
Milligan, Spike 212
Monaghan, Juliet 256
Moore, Kevan 159–60
Mounter, Julian 225–26
Moyle, Colin 126–27
Muldoon, Robert 125, 127
Murphy, Tim 210
music industry, 1970s 105–07, 109

Neunz, Lois 47, 77
New Zealand Broadcasting Corporation 112,
    117, 143, 194
*The New Zealand Radio & Television
    Cookbook* 181, **182**

O'Brien, Barry 135, 142, 157
Offences Against the Person Act 1867 68–69
O'Keefe, Detective 50, 56, 57, 58
Osborne, Michelle 174
O'Sullivan, Richard 184

Pacific Rim cuisine 181
Palmer, Ross 63, 79, 86, 100, 105, 258
Palmerston North trade fair 196
Parker, Honorah 70
Parker, Pauline 70–71
Parkinson, Tom 157–59, 184, 187, 189, 191
Parnell, Auckland 80
    103 Brighton Road 74, 75, 76, 78, 88–92,
        101, 105, 109, **118,** 149
    Peter's art supplies business 80, 88
    Rose Garden 107
    St Stephens Avenue 71, 74
Payne, Jeremy 117, 122

P&O shipping company 66, 67, 68, 71, 79–80
Podell, Jerry 15, 16, **18,** 20, 91, 108, 164, 169, 190, 192, 195, 196, 210, 215, 239, 250
Powell, Jonathan 242
protest movement 83–85, 102–03, 177
Pryme, Lew 183–84
Puttnam, Alan 233, 249, 251
Puttnam, Janet (née Halls) 13, 15, 19, 20, 21, 37, 38, 39–40, 42, 44, 45, 96, 233, **234,** 238, 248, 257
    David's suicide 249–50
    scattering of David and Peter's ashes in Green Park, London 251, 253
Puttnam, Mandy 233, 235, 249

Quagg's ice-cream parlours, Auckland 100–02

Racey, British pop group on *Hudson and Halls* 158
radio cooking shows 142–44, 148
Radio Hauraki 142
Radio Pacific 208, 225
Radio Times variety show 125
Raeburn, Anna 213
Ray, Johnny 75–76
Reid, John 105, 107, 109
restaurants, New Zealand 146–47
    Antoine's, Auckland 152–53
    Auckland 74–75, 79, 100
    Bistro 260, Auckland 152
    Britannia, Auckland 152
    The Bronze Goat, Auckland 152
    The Coachman, Wellington 116
    Hudson and Halls Oyster and Fish Restaurant, Auckland 148–49, 151–55, **153,** 159, 161–62, 166, 169, 184
    La Boheme, Auckland 100
    Melba, Auckland 149
    Oblio's, Auckland 148, 152
    Papillon, Auckland 206, 208
Richard, Wendy 232
Righetti, Brenda 61, 63
Rothwell, Derek 217
Royal Variety performance, Auckland, 1981 172
Run for Your Wife (play) 196, 227
Russell & Bromley's shoe store, Stratford 42–43, 46–47, 96
Russell, Marcia 117, 119, 120

Sell, Bob 92, 100
Sell, Jean 100
sexual segregation, New Zealand 80, 116
Shone, Kerry 190
Silcock, Richard, *The New Zealand Radio & Television Cookbook* 181, **182**
Simmons, Anne (previously Gubay) 228, 238, 240, 247, 249
South Pacific Television 115, 117, 126, 135
    Hudson and Halls 120–24, **123,** 125, 126, 129, 135, 136, 138–39, **139, 140, 141,** 141–42, 157, 159, 172
    Speakeasy 117, 120, 121, 122
    A Week of It 125, 126, 139, 142
Special Committee on Moral Delinquency in Children and Adolescents 70
Spencer, Carleen **18,** 78, **79,** 99, 109, **118,** 158–59, 162, **168, 208**
    David's suicide 250
    letters from David 15–16, 164, 169, 187, 189, 192, 195, 196, 206, 210, 215, 226, 228, 229, 248
    in New York 20, 91, **108, 166,** 239, **263**
    time spent with David after Peter's death 20–21
Spencer, Chris 162–63, 166, **166,** 262, 264
Spicer, Barry 226
St Mary's Church, Parnell, memorial service for Peter 16–17
State Owned Enterprises Act 1986 194
Stephen Jaci 220, 224, 233
Stoddart, Patrick 214
Stonewall Inn, Greenwich Village, New York 83, 84, 103
Strachey, Lytton 40
Strand Arcade, Auckland 96, 97–99, 102
Stratful, Ricky 192

Taylor, Alice 24, 27, 29
Taylor, George 24
Telethon 135, 136
television, Australia 135
television, New Zealand 111–15, 183, 225–26
    cooking shows 112, **113,** 115–16, 143–44, 173, 176, 181, 183 (*see also Hudson and Halls* television shows)
    local productions 112, 114, 115–16, 125–26, 193
    1980s 193–94

television channels 115, 124–25, 193–94, 226

Television New Zealand (TVNZ) 157, 193, 194, 197, 203–04, 208, 225, 226, 256

Television One 115, 124

Theatre Royal Stratford East 43

Theatre Workshop Company 43

Theydon Bois 29–33, 38, 39, 45, 97, 211, 233, 259

Theydon Hall 34–37, **35**, 38, 42, 74, 197, **260,** 261

Theydon Bois primary school 33, 37

Thompson, Sue 208

Ti Point, Leigh, The Farm 164–65, **165**, 166, **167, 168**, 169–70, **171**, 190, 194–95

David's release of Peter's doves 169

dogs, Bullet and Nero 165, 166, **167**, 170, 195, 199, 205

sale of property 205, 206

Tookey, Christopher 220

Trenwith Brothers 77–78

Uncle Albert's Orgasmic Orchestra 184

V-1 and V-2 buzz bombs 23–24, 27–28

Veart, David 116, 144, 220

Vietnam War protest 84–85

Walker, Father John 258, 259

Walsh, Alan 211

Waugh, Lindsay 120, 121, 126

Waymark, Peter 224

A Week of It television show 125, 126, 139, 142

Weirn, Joan **168**

Wertham, Frederic 70

Wheeler, David 107, 109

Whittaker, Roger 122, 211, 214

Whittle, Annie 160

Wilde, Fran 202

Wilde, Oscar 69

Williams, Basil 129, 131, 174–75

Williams, Billy Dee 162

Williams, Kenneth 104

Williams, Kevin 107

Williams, Michael 73, 75, 109, 241, 258

Wilson, Les 206, 225

Windsor, Barbara 222, 227, **237**

Winters, Bernie 232

Wise, Ernie **223**

Wolfe, Henrietta 10

women's liberation movement 84, 103, 116, 135

Woolf, Ray 172

Woolf, Virginia 36, 103

World War Two 23–24, 25–34, 36

Yeats, Eddie 196

Young, Venn 201

yuppies (Young Urban Professionals) 180